ATARI
PROGRAMMING
WITH 55 PROGRAMS

ATARI
PROGRAMMING
WITH 55 PROGRAMS

BY LINDA M. SCHREIBER

TAB BOOKS Inc.

BLUE RIDGE SUMMIT, PA. 17214

This book is dedicated to my husband Allen, who introduced me to computers; to my son Stephen, who helped test the programs in this book; and to my daughters Karen and Jacquelyn for their support.

FIRST EDITION

FIRST PRINTING

Copyright © 1982 by TAB BOOKS Inc.

Printed in the United States of America

Library of Congress Cataloging in Publication Data

Schreiber, Linda M.
    ATARI programming—with 55 programs.

    Includes index.
    1. Atari computer—Programming. 2. Basic (Computer
program language) I. Title. II. Title: ATARI program-
ming—with fifty-five programs.
QA76.8.A82S37 1982   001.64′2   82-5856
ISBN 0-8306-1385-4   AACR2
ISBN 0-8306-1485-0 (pbk.)

Contents

Program Listings

Introduction

This book is designed to give you a hands-on experience with your ATARI computer. It assumes you have access to an ATARI computer complete with BASIC cartridge CXL4002. You do not need any previous knowledge of computers. If you can turn your system on, you are ready to begin.

The first chapters will acquaint you with your computer and the different accessories that can be attached to it. You will be introduced to new terms gradually. After you are thoroughly acquainted with your system, you will begin to program.

Each chapter introduces a few related commands. An explanation of each command is followed by an example of the way to use the command. The programs included with the chapter further illustrate the use of the new command. Each program is accompanied by a detailed explanation.

Sound, color, and graphics are included in several programs. The different graphics modes are explained along with a program that moves and rearranges the character base. A complete explanation of the error codes is also included. Chapter 15 shows you how to make your programs crash-proof, as well as how to find and correct errors in an existing program.

Once you have mastered the skills presented here, you will find that this book will serve as a handy reference guide.

Note: Because many of the listings in this book use graphics characters and/or reverse video, the following codes have been used in the listings:

● [clear] Press the escape key and the shift/clear key. This clears the screen.
● [characters or letters] Press the control key and the letter indicated between the brackets. *All* characters or letters between the brackets [ ] are graphic characters.
● Underlined characters or letters are in reverse video.

Chapter 1

What Is a Program?

Computers . . . the information age . . . a new and fascinating experience for anyone and everyone. Using computers can be fun, but exploring what can be done with them is pure delight!

Programming a computer requires only logical thinking and the spirit of adventure. You have been programmed and reprogrammed throughout your life. When you teacher gave you instructions, she was programming you. Your parents, bosses, and friends have all programmed you in some way. Think about the last time you went to the store. Did you count your change immediately after the clerk handed it to you? Why or why not? Habit—or preprogramming? You probably program your children, too: change your clothes, brush your teeth, say your prayers, then get into bed. Carrying out a task in a logical sequence is an important element of good programming.

Computers need programs (*software*) to operate properly. A *program* is a set of instructions the computer follows. It is written in a language the computer understands. We will be writing programs in BASIC for the ATARI computer throughout this book.

Programs can be very simple or very complex depending on their purpose.

```
10 REM A DEMONSTRATION OF A PROGRAM
20 PRINT "HELLO, I AM AN ATARI PERSONAL COMPUTER",
30 GOTO 20
```

This is a very simple program that will display

HELLO, I AM AN ATARI PERSONAL COMPUTER

over and over again on your television screen or video screen. Your computer will continue forever if you let it. It will also follow any instructions in the order they were given. It will not correct your spelling (unless it is programmed to), or tell you that your formula is incorrect.

The accuracy of a program depends upon the programmer. Errors occurring within a program are a result of human errors and are referred to as *bugs*. It is the programmer's responsibility to make the programs as bug free as possible. This book will show you where bugs are most likely to appear, how to test for them, and how to correct them.

PROGRAM POSSIBILITIES

Games are a large portion of the software market. Arcade games are very popular; these programs offer the same thrills and challenges without the cost of a real arcade. The ATARI computer is capable of duplicating most current arcade games because its special built-in features allow smooth continuous movement of objects. You can program your computer so you may play pinball, space games, or a shooting arcade on it.

Your computer can also be programmed for traditional family games. The graphics on your ATARI allow you to duplicate card games, board games, or games of skill and strategy easily.

The paddles and joysticks that are available for this computer help improve hand-eye coordination.

Educational

Educational computer programs are steadily becoming more popular. In the home or classroom, the computer can be a powerful and valuable instructor. It can be programmed to provide drill exercises in repetitive subjects such as math tables, states and capitals, or spelling. Your computer can also be used as a tutor for self-paced instruction.

Another effective method of learning with a computer is through simulation. A good simulation program can train a person in weeks to do what would normally take a lifetime to learn, providing the experience of normal and extreme situations. Games can stimulate the mind as well as the imagination.

Your computer can be programmed to compose tests, store grades on a cassette or disk, and average the grades later, generating report cards.

Home Applications

Your ATARI computer can be used effectively throughout your home. It can store information or help plan and organize your activities. It can be your secretary or security guard, librarian, or accountant.

A program could act as a dietician and select menus for the week or month, generating a shopping list for the meals you will prepare. While you're at it, you may want to program the computer to recall your coupons and refunds.

Your computer is an ideal librarian. It can keep track of all your books, records, and tapes. Your program can store valuable information about anything you own.

If you have been trying to decide whether it's better to save for an item or take out a loan, write a program to show you the amount of interest your savings account would earn versus the interest on a loan over the same period of time. Take into consideration the inflation rate and the price of the item once you have saved enough for it.

If you are buying a house, your program can show you what your mortgage payments would be over different lengths of time with varying down-payments.

And, of course, you will want to program your computer to balance your checking account. Your program can also store your deductions for income tax records while it is balancing your checkbook.

2

In the area of health and safety, a program can help you learn first aid. With its graphics capabilities, it can teach you where the pressure points are for bleeding or how to splint a broken bone.

You can write a program for your flower or vegetable garden to help you plan your garden, estimate the yield of your crops, compare it to your family's needs, and show you a layout for your garden.

Darkroom enthusiasts can use a computer program to time the development of their films or store processing information.

With a special device called a *modem* and your telephone, you can call and connect your computer into large message centers called *networks*. Some of these networks serve as electronic mail boxes where you can leave a message for another person who also belongs to this network. Others are giant data banks that offer UPI news, stock market reports, airline schedules, and other information.

These are some of the programs possible for your computer. Sample programs are included throughout this book. As you become more familiar with your ATARI, you will continue to discover more ideas and uses for it.

PROGRAM SOURCES

Programs for your ATARI are available from a wide variety of sources. Several software firms produce well-written programs for many different applications. These programs are *usually* available on a cassette or disk and come with some instructions (*documentation*) on how to use the program. Your local computer store should be able to demonstrate these programs for you. Others are available only through mail-order firms. Most software firms offer a catalog describing their programs and the amount of memory necessary to use them.

Another source of programs are books. Programs in books give you the opportunity to read through a program before you type it in. The best way to learn to program is by studying the programs others have written. The disadvantage of programs published in books is the time you need to type the programs into the computer. If you make a typographical error, you will have to find and correct your mistake before the program will work correctly.

Magazines are a third source of programs. There are many good articles containing programs or routines that explain the inner workings of a computer. However, unless the magazine is written strictly for the ATARI, you may find some programs won't work on the ATARI unless you rewrite them.

PROGRAM DIFFERENCES

Even though most popular computers on the market today are programmed in BASIC, each manufacturer chooses a slightly different dialect of BASIC. If you find a program written for another computer and the program is fairly simple, you should have no problem rewriting it for the ATARI. You must also take into account the graphics the program uses. Color generation, plotting points, and animation differ from one computer to another. Once you are familiar with your ATARI and how the BASIC language works, you should be able to translate many programs written for other computers.

Most computers can also accept programs written in many other languages, such as PASCAL, LISP, PILOT, and assembly language. Each language varies from one computer to another. Each language is designed differently and has its own advantages. For most applications, the programs you will want to write can be written very efficiently in BASIC. When timing becomes important, as with arcade games, you will want to learn assembly language.

Whether you purchase programs from a software firm or copy them from a magazine or book, you may find the program almost fits your needs. By learning how to program, you will be able to change the program to suit yourself.

Chapter 2
The Making
of a Computer

The most vital part of a computer is its *central processing unit* (CPU). Often no bigger than a dime, it controls and maintains the computer and many devices attached to it.

The CPU can be thought of as the brain of the computer. All instructions are read and interpreted by it. It sends the correct commands to different parts of the computer and ensures the program is followed. If you own a microwave oven, programmable video recorder, or programmable calculator, you have already worked with a CPU. The difference between the one in your computer and those in your appliances is its internal design. Your computer can be programmed for multiple uses; your microwave can only be programmed to start and stop and cook at the correct temperature.

Every computer contains at least one CPU. The type of CPU used by each manufacturer differs. This means that the manner in which the CPU follows instructions and the way that instructions are written are different.

The ATARI, Apple, Kim, and Pet microcomputers all use the same CPU, the 6502. The 6502 has some advantages over other CPUs.

The language the computer uses is called *machine language*. We understand it as groupings of numbers the CPU can translate into executeable instructions. When we write a program in *assembly language*, the *assembler*, the part of the computer that reads and assembles the program into a form the machine can use, translates our program into machine language. One advantage of programs written in machine language is that if a routine is written for a particular CPU, it will work (within certain limitations) on all computers containing that CPU. Most people don't try to program in assembly language until they have mastered BASIC.

MEMORY TYPES

Memory is used to store programs. Programs consist of instructions and useful information (*data*). The amount of memory your computer has is measured in *bytes*. Some instructions use one byte of memory, others occupy more. Each letter or number of data occupies one byte of memory. The longer your programs are, the more memory you need. Memory capacity is measured per thousand (K) bytes. Thus, a 32K machine contains 32768 bytes of RAM.

There are two types of memory in your ATARI, *RAM* and *ROM*. RAM means random-access

5

memory. It is sometimes called read/write memory. Program data can be placed anywhere in RAM (writing to RAM) or your program can get information from any byte in RAM (reading from RAM). RAM should never be used for permanent storage since it can't retain information once the power is shut off. It is needed for programming because it can be changed by the user or through a program.

Static RAM is used in some computers. This type of RAM is stable. Once an instruction is placed into it, it will retain the instruction until it is changed or the power is shut off.

Dynamic RAM is used in most computers, including the ATARI. After an instruction is placed in this type of memory, the CPU must constantly refresh (remind) the memory of the information placed there. This makes the CPU run slower than it would with static memory, but for most applications, this is not crucial. Some devices cannot run properly with dynamic memory, but they are few. Dynamic RAM is much less expensive than static RAM.

Memory from different manufacturers may have different *access times*, the amount of time the CPU has to retrieve an instruction from memory. Space becomes an important factor if your program must do many different calculations before arriving at the answer. In most programs, you will not notice the difference in speed.

ROM means read-only memory. Your ATARI also contains a 10K ROM cartridge. The program on this cartridge (the ATARI operating system) has been permanently fixed on the memory chips and will remain there whether the unit is turned on or off. The ATARI operating system contains the routines used by BASIC, Editor/Assembler, and other ROM program cartridges. The operating system also uses some RAM to store information. As you use this book, you will become more familiar with their locations and uses.

Your ATARI uses a BASIC ROM cartridge that plugs into the left slot on your ATARI 800. The ROM in this cartridge is very similar to the ROM in the operating system. The BASIC cartridge is permanently programmed. Once you plug the cartridge in, you do not have to wait for the computer to *load* (read into memory) BASIC from a cassette or disk. Turn on your computer and BASIC is ready for use. All ATARI ROM cartridges have the program permanently fixed onto the ROM in the cartridge. Each will also use some RAM for values that change during the program.

If you remove the cover from your ATARI 800, you will see four slots. This section is called the *mother board*. When you want to add more memory to your system, you will plug in the memory boards here. The ATARI 800 memory may be expanded to 48K of RAM. It is possible to expand it further if you purchase memory cards from other manufacturers with compatible memory systems. For most applications, 24K RAM is adequate. If you plan to add a disk to your system, you will need 32K to 40K of RAM.

MASS STORAGE

Once you have written a program, you will want to save it for future use. Cassette recorders are an inexpensive and easy-to-use way to store programs or data. Once a program is placed on the cassette it will stay there until it is erased or recorded over. The computer records the program on the tape by generating two tones. These tones represent the instructions in the program. This can be done because the most basic instructions used by the computer, called *machine code*, is a binary code consisting of combinations of 1's and 0's. The computer loads a program from the cassette by listening to the tones and translating them into the corresponding binary digits.

Cassettes are inexpensive, easy to use, and, because they are in a plastic case, easily handled by children. They can be shipped or stored with minimum precautions.

Cassettes save and load programs very slowly, and you cannot access the information on them easily. If you purchase inferior tapes, or tapes that are too thin, you run the risk of having your program destroyed by the recorder. If you do not wish to purchase tape designed for computer use, you may use recording tape, but don't use the long-playing (45 to 120 minutes) tape which is too thin.

A more efficient way of storing programs is with a disk drive. There are two different disk drives available for the ATARI—the single ATARI 810 and the double density ATARI 815 Dual Disk Drive. A double density drive stores twice as much information on a disk as a single density drive.

A *floppy disk* (sometimes called diskette) is a thin Mylar circular medium similar to a record, covered with a thin jacket. There is a slot cut out on both sides of the jacket exposing the surface of the disk (Fig. 2-1). Touching this surface could damage the disk. Programs are stored on disks by electrical impulses that magnatize the surface. Because the disk spins rapidly inside the drive, the computer can save or load a program much faster on it than with a cassette. Also, the disk has tracks much like a record has grooves, so any part of the disk can be accessed at any time.

Disks are very vulnerable to static charges. An electrical charge, even a mild one produced by walking across the carpet, can destroy the programs on the disk. The jacket on the disk is for

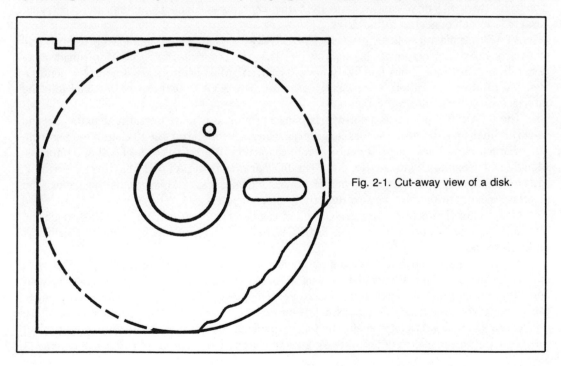

Fig. 2-1. Cut-away view of a disk.

protection against dust and dirt. If the disk is bent, it will not spin properly, and the computer will not be able to read a program or data stored on it.

Since both disks and cassettes store information magnetically, you should not place them near a magnetic field such as the top of a speaker, a motor, or a television. A strong magnetic field could destroy your program.

In addition, Corvus Systems Inc. has introduced a system for the ATARI. The main difference between a floppy disk and a hard disk is speed and storage capacity. The ATARI 810 disk drive can store 88K bytes of data, the ATARI 815 dual disk drive can store 178K bytes of data on each disk. The average hard disk can store 5, 10, or 20 megabytes of data. That is 5 to 20 million bytes of data.

ACCESSORIES

Many other accessories, or *peripherals*, are available for and compatible with the ATARI.

Although available cassette, disk drive, or certain printers can be connected directly to the ATARI, you would have to change the connections to use each unit. A simpler solution is the ATARI 850 Interface Module. The interface acts as a go-between for the computer and peripherals. Several peripherals can be attached to the interface at the same time. There are four outlets, or *ports*, on one side of the interface, one on the front, and two on the third side. The four ports are RS-232C compatible. One is designed for a modem and one for a 20 milliamp current loop. They are programmable for easy output to any serial device. The single port is a parallel port for use with the ATARI 825 printer. The ATARI computer connects to one of the ports in the set of two. Your cassette or disk drive can be connected to the other. If you connect your disk drive to it, your cassette can be connected to the drive.

ATARI manufactures three printers. The ATARI 820 is a 40-column impact printer. It will print a copy of your program 40 characters wide. The print is *dot matrix*; each letter is made up of dots rather than a continuous line like typewriter letters. Most printers are dot matrix; continuous line printers are called letter-quality printers. The ATARI 820 can be plugged into the interface or directly into the computer.

The ATARI 825 printer is a dot-matrix impact printer. It is more versatile than the 820 and can print lines that are 80 characters long. It can also space the letters at 10 characters per inch, 16.7 characters per inch, or print double-width characters. It requires the ATARI 850 Interface Module and uses the single parallel port. The third printer is the ATARI 822 Thermal Printer. This printer is also a 40-column dot matrix printer and uses a special heat-sensitive paper. The printer connects to the interface or directly to the computer.

Many other fine printers are available that can be connected to your ATARI through the interface. Terminals, such as a Teletype or DECWriter, can be connected by using the fourth port on the interface.

The ATARI 830 Acoustical Modem can connect your ATARI to the outside world. The word *modem* means modulator-demodulator. That is, it can change the signals you send from your computer into signals that can be transmitted over telephone lines. Demodulate means it changes the signals it receives from the telephone line into signals your computer can understand. There are several *network* services available that can provide you with up-to-the-minute stock market reports, UPI transmissions, or software for your computer. The modem will allow you to connect with these message centers that serve as electronic mailboxes in certain areas of the country. Often a computer club will host such a message center.

Your computer can speak through an electronic speech synthesizer such as the Type-'n-Talk from Votrax. This device connects to the RS-232C port on the interface. It translates text (words) sent to it into electronic speech.

Your ATARI can be connected to your color television or a color monitor. A *monitor* is essentially the same as a television without a receiver. A color monitor will provide you with a clearer, crisper picture than a television set, but for most applications, a television screen will do fine.

Using the keyboard to play arcade games just doesn't feel quite right. These games need a quick response from the player who shouldn't be fumbling with a keyboard. Along the front edge of your ATARI are four more outlets or ports. You can add up to four joysticks or eight paddles to these ports. You can even use joysticks and paddles together for the same game (use a different port for each). The *joystick* is a rectangular box with one stick and a button on it. This stick sends signals to the computer. Your program can determine if you are moving the stick in any of eight directions, or pressing the red button.

The *paddle* has a dial you can turn and a button on its side. The numerical signal the computer reads from it increases or decreases depending on which way the dial is being turned. It is readily adaptable for games that would be speed controlled, such as a road race. The computer can also be programmed to check if the red button on the paddle's side has been pressed.

You can also attach a light pen to the ports on the front edge of your ATARI. By bringing the tip of a light pen to the television screen, the computer can determine the location of the information you are pointing to. You can use it as an electronic paint brush, a menu selector, or to indicate the correct answer in a multiple-choice test.

Chapter 20 has programs that use these controllers.

Chapter 3

The
Keyboard

The best way to learn about your ATARI is to use it. Remove the BASIC cartridge (or any other cartridge in your ATARI), turn on your television or monitor, and turn on your computer. The screen should say   ATARI MEMO PAD   in the upper left corner. The white square on the left of your screen is a *cursor*. It marks the position that the next character will occupy.

The keyboard is laid out in standard typewriter fashion. Your ATARI supports both upper- and lowercase letters. The lowercase does not have true descenders, the parts of letters that normally appear below the line, so a p or q would appear p or q on your screen.

The large key on the right of the keyboard labeled return acts as a carriage return. It moves the cursor down one line and to the left side of the screen. Beneath the return key is a key labeled caps/lowr. This is your shift-lock key. By pressing the shift key and the caps/lowr key, you will lock the computer into using capital letters. Press the caps/lowr key to unlock the shift/caps, letting you type in upper- and lowercase. The number and symbol keys do not work like a typewriter; you must press the shift key for the symbols above the numbers, the comma or period, or the other character keys. Most programmers use capital letters exclusively (BASIC doesn't recognize lowercase commands) so the shift/caps key is usually set. It would be cumbersome to have to unlock the shift key for the numbers.

GRAPHICS

Your ATARI comes with a set of built-in graphic characters (Fig. 3-1). You display these by pressing the left-hand key marked *control* and any letter. Try this on your ATARI while it is in the Memo Pad mode:

Press the return key five times,
Press the space bar 10 times, control N, control N, space, control N, control N, return;
Press 11 spaces, control V, space, control B, return;
Press 11 spaces, press the inverse video key (the key with the ATARI logo on it), shift, space, shift, inverse video key, return;
Press 11 spaces, inverse key, control K, space, control L, inverse key, return;
Press 11 spaces, inverse key, space, control M, space, inverse key, return;
Press 12 spaces, inverse key, space, inverse key, return;

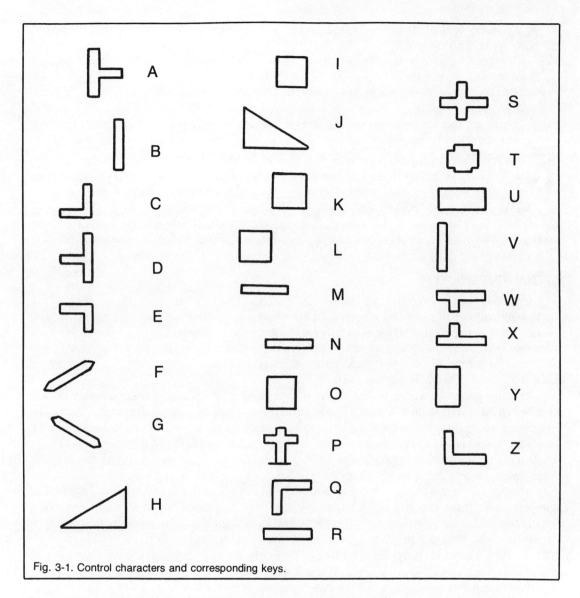

Fig. 3-1. Control characters and corresponding keys.

Press 9 spaces, control H, inverse key, five spaces, inverse key, control J, return;

Press 9 spaces, inverse key, space, inverse key, control B, inverse key, space, control T, space, inverse key, control V, inverse key, space, inverse key, return;

Press 9 spaces, inverse key, space, inverse key, control B, inverse key, space, control T, space, inverse key, control T, space, inverse key, control V, inverse, space, inverse key, return;

Press 9 spaces, inverse key, space, inverse key, control B, inverse key, three control G's, inverse key, control V, inverse key, space, inverse key, return;

Press 9 spaces, control comma, control B, inverse key, three spaces, inverse key, control V, control comma, return;

Press 10 spaces, control B, inverse key, space, inverse key, space, inverse key, space, inverse key, control V, return;

Press 10 spaces, control B, inverse key, space, inverse key, space, inverse key, space, inverse key, control V, return;

Press 10 spaces, inverse key, two spaces, inverse key, space, inverse key, two spaces, inverse key, return;

Press 10 spaces, control Z, control X, space, control X, control X, control C, return.

You should have a drawing similar to the one in Fig. 3-2 on your screen. You can design your own characters with any combination of graphic keys and the letters, numbers, and symbols.

You can also control your cursor with the arrow keys. By pressing the control key and one of the arrow keys, you can move your cursor up, down, left, or right. Try to redraw the character on your screen by using the cursor and control keys rather than the return key and spaces.

SPECIAL FUNCTION KEYS

The upper left key on your keyboard is marked ESC. This key will allow you to "escape" the normal function of the key and give you additional control. Press the escape key twice. The second time you press it, a strange character will appear on the screen. Pressing the escape key, then the control key with the clear, insert, delete, or any arrow key will make the computer print different characters. These keys and functions will be very useful when you edit your program or have messages printed on the screen.

Like any good typewriter, your ATARI can set and clear tabs. The key in the second row, left side has clr, set, and tab on it. Pressing the key will move the cursor across the screen. There are five preset tab positions. To clear the tab position, simply press the tab key until it stops at the character you want to remove, then press the control key and the tab key at the same time. To set a tab position, move the cursor to the correct location, press the shift key and the tab key simultaneously and the new tab will be set.

The key to the right of the shift key has the ATARI symbol on it. When you press this key, the computer will print the letters, numbers, symbols, or graphics characters in *reverse video* (characters and screen switch color). This feature lets you highlight important words in messages or instructions. Pressing this key again returns you to normal type.

The break key lets you interrupt a BASIC program. When you interrupt your program, you can usually continue it from the place where it stopped.

To erase the contents of the screen, simply press the clear key with the shift key. Since it erases the screen quickly, you will use it often during a program requiring a clear screen.

Along the far right of the keyboard are four yellow keys. These keys are in this location so they will not be confused with the keyboard. The top key is marked System Reset. It is shielded by plastic strips so it can't be pressed accidentally. If it is pressed, you will have to rerun the program, which may destroy some values you set. The three keys under it are used by cartridge games. They can also be used in any BASIC program and their use depends on the programmer.

There are four accessory ports along the front of your keyboard. The joysticks, paddles, and

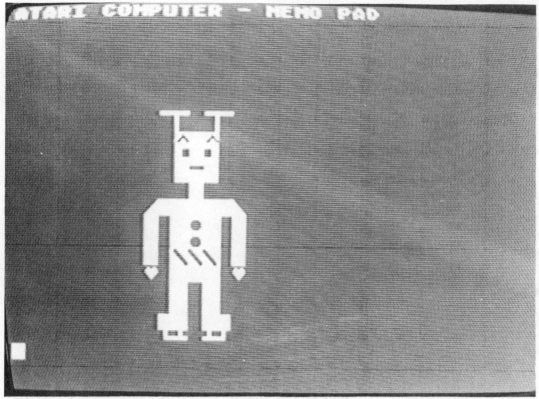

Fig. 3-2. Screen display using control characters with ATARI memo pad.

light pens can be connected to your ATARI in any of these location. Each port is independent of the other three, so you can use all four in any program.

Along the right hand side of the computer is the peripheral jack to which the cassette recorder, disk drive, interface, or serial printer can be connected. Just before that jack is the monitor jack. You can connect a color monitor or video tape player to this jack. These can be used in addition to the color television, so you can display your program on two monitors—great for the classroom—or record a program while you are using it. The tape can be played back later to analyze your moves in a chess game or to record a student's progress.

13

Chapter 4

Organizing Your Program

No matter how creative a program appears, the rudiments of programming are the same. Very few programmers can conceive an idea, sit down at the keyboard, and enter the program without a plan or guideline. Good programs are carefully thought out and developed. Consideration is given to the parts of the program the computer will perform, the information the user will provide, and the information stored in the program.

Let's say you would like to write a program that will determine the cost of the floor covering for a room, complete with a cost comparison of the different floor treatments possible. This program would consist of several small programs, or *routines*. This chapter develops a portion of that program. The program computes the area of the floor in square feet and square yards.

PARTS OF A PROGRAM

The computer will compute the area of the floor, the amount of floor covering needed, the price of the floor covering, and the cost per year, determined by the average life of the floor covering. To do this, the computer must be given the essential facts: the measurements of the room, the price of the floor covering, and what flooring is being considered. This information is provided by you, the user. The computer also needs information about the expected life of floor coverings, the conversion from square feet to square yards, and the pricing formula. All these figures remain constant and can be stored in the program.

The set of instructions the computer will follow regardless of the information entered is called the *algorithm*. The answers to the questions the program asks are user *input* and will change from person to person depending on the questions and the circumstances. Many errors (or *bugs*) are generated if the user enters incorrect information. The information stored in a program and used to perform calculations is the *data base*. If the data is incorrect, the outcome of the program will also be in error.

FLOWCHARTS

A *flowchart* is an outline of a program that the programmer uses to develop the program. It serves as a guide, showing the parts of the program that must be included for it to function correctly. To program without a flowchart would be like trying to take a trip to an unknown region without a map. It can be done, but it can also be a waste of time and energy.

Every programmer develops a personal style of flowcharting. There are several well-known types, including Warner-Orr diagramming, data-flow diagrams, structure charts, and structured pseudocode. Throughout this book, the standard symbols, shown in Fig. 4-1, are used.

The terminal symbol is used to indicate the beginning and ending of the program. Input/output indicates where the user must provide information, the program will "read" its own data base, or information will be printed to the screen or printer. The decision symbol indicates where the computer will have to determine which set of instructions to follow. Predefined process is the sequence of program statements (*instructions*) the computer will follow regardless of what has been entered by the user. The connector is used to show that the flowchart continues on another part of the page, or even to another page. The connecting connectors will be the same number.

When you flowchart a large program, you may find it helpful to divide it into several small modules before you draw a detailed flowchart.

Figure 4-2 is a block diagram of the different parts of the program. The first block indicates the routine that determines the size of the room. The next three modules determine the different treatments being considered, the price (in cost per yard), and the user's preference. The program computes the cost of the treatments in terms of the overall price and price per year over the expected life. The program would show the user the most expensive treatment, the least expensive treatment, and the cost of the treatment the user prefers. A good program would give the user the option of changing some of the treatments or adding new ones. The end result would be the amount of material needed to cover the floor and the approximate cost. Each of these modules can be flowcharted with a very detailed flowchart. Figure 4-3 is a flowchart containing the routine for the first module of the program.

PUTTING THE PROGRAM ON PAPER

Jot down your program idea after you've thought it out, using the block diagram. Now think . . . what is the best way to handle the details of the program? Look again at Fig. 4-3. The first thing

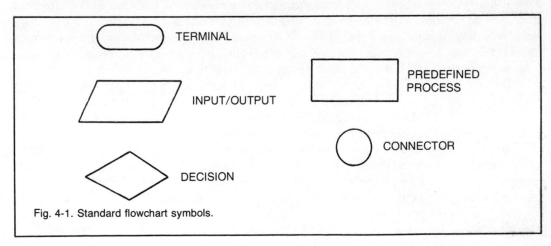

Fig. 4-1. Standard flowchart symbols.

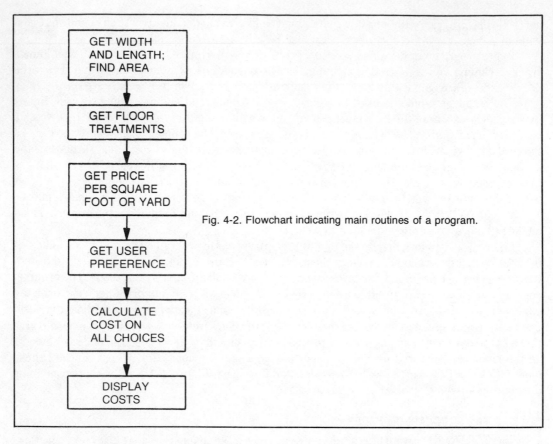

Fig. 4-2. Flowchart indicating main routines of a program.

the program does is ask the user for the dimensions of the room. The program needs this information. Provide it first, not after information about whether the user will tile or carpet the floor. Any information vital to the program should be provided as soon as possible. The message written on the side of the flowchart is a *remark*, a reminder to the programmer why this command should be included in the program, or an explanation of how this part of the program should work. The more remarks you make, the clearer your program will be.

The next part of the flowchart requests the type of flooring and the cost per square foot. The diamond reading "any more" indicates a decision the computer will make. If the user says there are more types of floorings to be entered, the program will go back to the step asking for the type of flooring. If there are no more entries, the program will continue.

The computer will determine if more than one entry was made. If so, it requests the user's preference, then computes the cost of each type of flooring and determines the initial cost and the cost per year. The last part of the program shows the user the cost of the preferred treatment, the most expansive treatment, and the least expensive treatment. It also indicates the best way based on the average cost per year.

The size of the room, the types of flooring, and their cost are data the user inputs. The

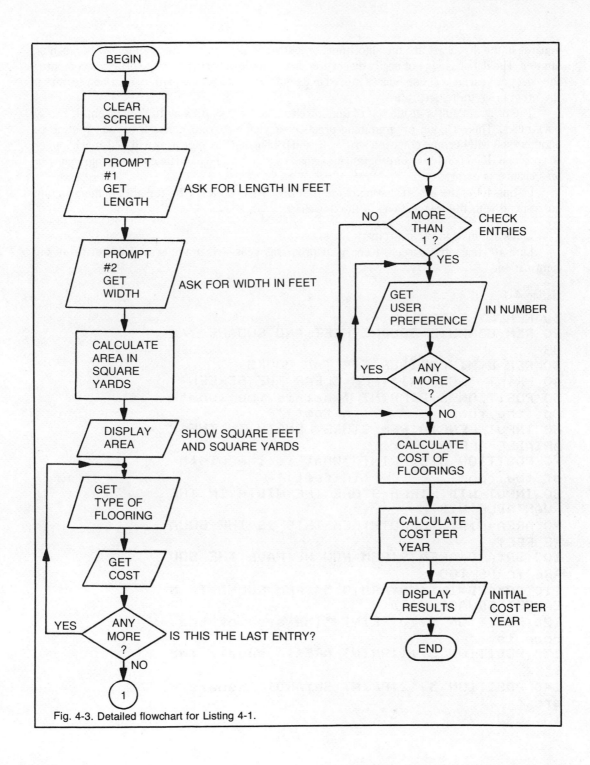

Fig. 4-3. Detailed flowchart for Listing 4-1.

squares in the flowchart are the algorithms or instructions the computer will follow to reach an answer. The data base is not easily discovered from the flowchart. When the program computes the cost per year, it will use figures stored in its data base. This information must be accurate if the program is to be accurate.

The program starts at the top of the flowchart, and works its way to the bottom. It rarely backtracks. This is good programming practice; if your program jumps from one routine to another, you will become confused writing it, and if a bug should appear, it will take much longer to correct it. If you divide your program into small routines, you will write cleaner programs with less chance of errors.

Listing 4-1 is the BASIC listing of the first flowchart routine. The remarks in the program correspond with the instructions in the flowchart.

Lines 10 through 30 are remark lines.

Line 40 clears the screen. Keep your programs neat—clear the screen to get rid of old information.

Listing 4-1

```
10 REM LISTING IV-1
20 REM COMPUTE SQUARE FEET AND SQUARE YAR
DS
30 REM L.M.SCREIBER FOR TAB BOOKS
40 PRINT ")CLEAR)":REM CLEAR THE SCREEN
50 POSITION 5,2:PRINT "What is the length
 of the room       (in feet)";
60 INPUT LENGTH:REM STORE LENGTH IN THE V
ARIABLE 'LENGTH'
70 POSITION 5,5:PRINT "What is the width
of the room        (in feet)";
80 INPUT WIDTH:REM STORE THE WIDTH IN THE
 VARIABLE WIDTH
90 AREA=WIDTH*LENGTH:REM THIS IS THE SQUA
RE FEET
100 SQYARD=AREA/9:REM NOW WE HAVE THE SQU
ARE YARDS TOO
110 SQYARD=INT(SQYARD+0.5):REM ROUND TO N
EAREST SQUARE YARD
120 POSITION 5,10:PRINT "The area of the
room is -"
130 POSITION 5,11:PRINT AREA;" square fee
t"
140 POSITION 5,12:PRINT SQYARD;" square y
ards"
150 END
```

Line 50 prints a question on the screen. The program would like the length of the room in feet.

Line 60 waits for the user to enter the length. The amount entered will be stored in the length variable.

Line 70 prints the next question; the program would like the width of the room in feet.

Line 80 waits until the width is entered. The program stores this number in the width variable.

(The numbers entered in lines 60 and 80 will change with each person using the program.)

Line 90 computes the area of the room in square feet.
Line 100 changes the square feet into square yards.

(These two algorithms, Lines 90 and 100, remain the same no matter what size the room is.)

Line 110 rounds the square yards to the nearest square yard.
Line 120 prints a message on the screen.
Line 130 prints the area of the room in square feet.
Line 140 prints the area of the room in square yards.
Line 150 tells the computer the program has ended.

Chapter 5

Commands
and Statements

There are two ways you can communicate with your ATARI. You can type an instruction, press the return key, and the computer will execute it, or you can enter a series of commands in a program. In the first example, the instruction you are giving the computer is a *direct command*. In the second example, the lines of a program contain the instructions. These are *indirect commands* or *program statements*.

DIRECT COMMANDS

Most commands can be used as direct commands. Many direct commands can be used in a program. When you type   RUN   to start a program, you are giving the computer a direct command. An entire line of a program can be entered as a direct command. Try this:

Type: FOR X=1 TO 10:PRINT X:NEXT X
Press the return key

Your screen should display the numbers from 1 to 10 along the left side. You could also type:
10 FOR X=1 TO 10:PRINT X:NEXT X (return)
Type: RUN (return)

The results should be the same.

New

One direct command that should be used sparingly is   NEW   which removes the program in the computer's memory. It can be used as part of a program, but it is best used when and *only* when you have finished a program, saved it, and want to enter another program. If you get into the habit of using this command, you may find that you have just wiped out two or more hours of hard work.

The New command does have its advantages, however. Since it clears a program out of memory, you can begin typing another program and not have lines leftover from the last program. You do not have to enter the New command before loading a program from a cassette or disk because this will be done automatically by the computer.

Bye

Another direct command is   BYE   . Type this when you want to use the ATARI Memo Pad. The Memo Pad is the ideal place to leave messages or try out an idea using the graphics characters. Pressing the system reset key returns you to BASIC with your program intact.

PROGRAM STATEMENTS

The instructions in the lines of a program are *program statements*. They are entered when you type in a program or load a program from cassette or disk. The computer stores these statements in its RAM. It will follow these instructions when the program is run.

Each program statement must begin with a line number. Most programmers start with 10 and number the lines with multiples of ten. This lets you easily add lines to your program without reorganizing the entire routine.

Program statements can be any length. Your ATARI will let you enter a line three video screen lines long or of 114 characters (including the line number). This is not a good programming practice; lengthy lines can confuse the programmer and are sometimes impossible to debug.

There are times, however, when you will need to put two program statements on the same line, for example, when you want the program to make a decision. Place a colon between the end of the first statement and the beginning of the second; the colon tells the computer not to go on to the next line, but to look at the rest of this line. The line you typed at the beginning of this chapter is an example of a line with multiple statements.

There is one program statement the computer will always ignore, but it is very useful to the programmer. That is the REM (remark) statement. Use the REM as a reminder to yourself about what the routine does, why you did it, when it will be used, etc. Often a good routine without remark statements is extremely confusing after any time has elapsed.

EDITING

Editing program lines is something that all programmers learn to do sooner or later (usually sooner). Typing errors, the need to change values, errors in the program, commands, or errors in the operation, the need to delete unnecessary instructions or to add instructions use the editing features. The ATARI has very good editing features.

A unique feature of the ATARI computer is that it checks each line as it is typed in for *syntax* or usage errors. If you use a command incorrectly, spell it wrong, or use a non-existent command, the ATARI will not accept that line. It will print the line with,   ERROR   , immediately following the line number. It will also display the first character of the portion it can't understand in reverse video. On the other hand, if you tell the computer to print a word wrong on the screen, the program will do so.

Programs are easily edited with one of seven keys plus the control or shift keys. To move the cursor up, press the control key and the up arrow key simultaneously. To move it down, press the control key and the down arrow key. Once the cursor is over the row needing editing, press the control key and left arrow until the cursor is over the area needing editing. If you are correcting the spelling of a word and do not need to insert or delete spaces, simply type the correct letters over the wrong letters and press return.

To add letters to a line, move the cursor over the place you want to add spaces and press the control key and the insert key at the same time. The letters to the right of the cursor will move to the right each time this combination of keys are pressed. To delete letters or characters from a line, press the control key and the delete key at the same time. The letters to the right of the cursor will be removed from the line. Always press the return key after editing a line; this tells the computer to store the corrected version.

Using the shift key with the insert or delete key will move entire lines on the screen. Shift-insert will move the line the cursor is on and all the lines below it down one line. Pressing the shift with the delete key will remove the line the cursor is over and the lines below that line will move up one line. Pressing shift with clear will erase the screen and place the cursor in the top left corner of the screen. Pressing Shift-clear while editing a line will not alter the line; you will have to list and edit the line again. Only the return key will correct the line in memory.

LINE NUMBERS

Change the line numbers in the same way you edited other lines. Place the cursor over the numbers, type the new numbers and press return. If you list your program, you will see the old lines are there also. Changing the numbers did not remove the lines; to delete them, simply type the line number and press return. The line will be removed from the program. *A note of caution:* sometimes if you delete too many lines, the ATARI will lock up and the only way for a BASIC programmer to unlock it is to turn off the computer, turn it back on, and reload the program. To avoid this delete a few lines, list a few lines, delete a few more lines, etc. This will usually keep the computer from locking up.

ERROR MESSAGES

Unfortunately, ATARI BASIC gives its error messages as numbers. Often you will find yourself staring at strange numbers on the screen and an aborted program. The following is an explanation of the error numbers and what steps to take to correct the error.

Error	Message and Correction
2	**Memory insufficient.** There is not enough RAM to run the program. If you are writing the program, check your dimension statement. You may be setting aside more memory than you need to. The program may be too long for the amount of memory in your system. Try to chain parts of the program together. If it is a purchased program and you have the amount of memory the package calls for, turn off your disk drive and/or interface and turn the computer on again. Many software firms do not take a drive or interface into consideration when they arrive at the amount of memory needed to run a program.
3	**Value error.** The computer cannot use the value the program has given it to perform the instruction. This is a common problem in

graphics mode when the character is being moved on the screen and the routine calculating where the character should be displayed produces a negative number. Check the routine carefully to find out why it is generating negative numbers or set a trap for the routine.

4   **Too Many Variables.** The ATARI limits the number of variables a program can use to 128. If you get this error number, go over the program and delete variables.

5   **String Length Error.** You are trying to place information in a string that hasn't been dimensioned, or you are trying to place information beyond the point the string was dimensioned to. Redimension the string length and run the program again, or correct the instruction to store or access the string correctly.

6   **Out of Data.** The lines of the program that contain data don't have enough data for the program, or, you want to access the same data and didn't restore the data pointer.

7   **Number Greater Than 32767.** The value of an integer cannot be greater than 32676. Go over the statement and see why your program is generating such a large number.

8   **Input Statement Error.** The program needs a number but a letter or character was entered. If a letter or character is supposed to be entered, change the variable to a string variable. Catch wrong inputs for variables with a trap.

9   **Array or String DIM Error.** A string or array cannot be dimensioned to a size larger than 32676. The program is trying to access information beyond the area that has been dimensioned, or the program is trying to access a string or array that has not been dimensioned, or the program is trying to dimension an array that has already been dimensioned. Check the size of the array and the value of the variables trying to access it. Correct the routine(s) that determine the area of the string or array to be accessed, or enlarge the string or array to store the additional information. A string or array can only be dimensioned once in a program. Remove any lines that try to redimension an array or string.

Error	Message and Correction
10	**Argument Stack Overflow.** The program contains too many GOSUB commands without any corresponding return commands. Consolidate subroutines as much as possible.
11	**Floating Point Overflow/Underflow Error.** The program attempted to divide by 0 or the number it is trying to store is too large or small. Check and correct routines for correct computations.
12	**Line Not Found.** A GOSUB, GOTO, or Then command referred to a line not in the program. Correct the line by adding the correct line number or add the missing line to the program.
13	**No Matching FOR Statement.** The Next part of a For . . . Next loop could not find the matching For. Check for incorrect variables after Next, and for incorrectly nested loops.
14	**Line Too Long Error.** The line is too long for BASIC to understand. Shorten the lines.
15	**GOSUB or FOR Line Deleted.** The correct line for a return or the Next command has been deleted since the program was run. This deletion occurred during the actual running of the program. Check your program to make sure that you are not POKEing values where they do not belong.
16	**Return Error.** A return command cannot find the matching GOSUB. If you place your subroutines at the end of your program, be sure there is an end statement before the first subroutine. Make sure the program is not using a GOTO where there should be a GOSUB.
17	**Garbage Error.** The instructions that the computer tried to execute could not be understood. This could be caused by POKE statements, or it could be a hardware problem. Type, **NEW** ,or shut off the computer, then turn it back on. Try the program without POKE statements.
18	**Invalid String Character.** A string does not contain a number, yet the program is trying to get the value of the string. Check the string contents.

Error	Message and Correction
129	**IOCB Already Opened.** The program is using the same block of memory for two different functions. Use a different IOCB or file number.
130	**Nonexistent Device Specified.** The program is trying to access a device not attached to the computer. Check to make sure the interface is on or the device the program is trying to access is connected. If your are using the disk drive, make sure it was turned on before the interface and the DOS contains the routines to initialize the interface. Turning on the devices in the wrong sequence can cause the computer to ignore them.
141	**Cursor Out of Range.** The program is trying to plot or draw to an area out of range for the mode the computer is in. Check the routine(s) that determine the points to be plotted, or change the graphics mode.
147	**Insufficient RAM.** The program is trying to use a graphics mode that uses more memory than the computer has. Use a lower graphics mode.

These are the most common errors you can get from a BASIC program. There are other errors related to the use of the disk drives, printers, and other accessories.

Chapter 6
Storing
the Program

Programs can be stored on cassettes or floppy disks. This chapter discusses ways to store and load programs from the cassette recorder.

CLOAD/LOAD

To get a program from a cassette tape into the computer, place the cassette into the recorder, make sure it is properly positioned, type   CLOAD   and press return. One tone will sound. Press the play button on the recorder and press the return key again. The computer will listen to the tape and convert the tones that it hears into instructions. If the tape loads successfully, the screen will display   READY   . Type   RUN   and begin the program.

If the load was not successful, an error message will be displayed. Sometimes this means the tape has a defect in it. Other times you may have placed the wrong or blank tape in the recorder, or did not position it correctly. Most often, it will mean the heads on the tape recorder are dirty and should be cleaned.

Some tapes may have instructions to use the LOAD "C:" command. This command is usually used for loading a program from disk, but can be used with the cassette. The C in quotation marks tells the computer to load the program from the cassette.

Both the LOAD"C:" and CLOAD command, erase the old program from the computer's memory and replace it with the new program. If an error occurs during a load, the computer will reset all its pointers and erase whatever it loaded.

CSAVE/SAVE

Once you have typed a program into the computer, you will want to store it before shutting off the machine. The CSAVE command will place the program in RAM onto a cassette. First type   LP   and press return. Sometimes, when the system reset key has been pressed while the program is running, the computer will not reset the buffers correctly. This will not affect running the program, but it can cause the computer to transfer garbage or nothing at all to the cassette. Use the LP command before saving a program to cassette whether you pressed the system reset key or not.

Another way to save a program is to type SAVE "C:" and press return. This command is used when you want to chain programs or parts of programs together.

The program is saved the same way for both commands—the computer converts the instructions into tones and sends these tones to the recorder. The tones represent binary numbers the computer converts into instructions. If you listen to the program as it is being saved, you will hear longer gaps between the sets of tones when you use SAVE "C:".

For most purposes you will use CSAVE when you want to save your programs to cassette.

ENTER "C:"/LIST "C:"

There may be times when you will want to add or change lines in a program but keep the main part of the program intact. There may also be parts of the program you will want to save without saving the entire program. Since the CSAVE and CLOAD commands save or load entire programs, and CLOAD or LOAD will also erase the old program, you'll need a command that will merge two or more programs. The ENTER "C:" and LIST "C:" commands can be used for this purpose.

Let's say you have just finished this routine and expect to use it in several other programs. You can save only the lines of the routine by typing LIST "C:", (line number), (line number). Be sure both keys are pressed on the recorder. Press the return key after you hear two tones. Now the lines of your routine are being stored on the tape; you can retrieve them any time and merge them with an existing program. You can also LIST "C:" an entire program to tape if you like.

The list command does not save the instructions of the program in a numeric or tokenized form. It sends the information to the tape in the same form it would send it to the screen or printer when you tell it to list a program. It is slower than a CSAVE or save command and uses more tape.

When you want to load a program that has been listed to the cassette, you will type ENTER "C:" and press return. When you hear one tone, press the play button on the recorder and press return again. When the computer listens to the tape, it will take the instructions from the tape and place it in the computer as if the program were being typed in from the keyboard. If there is a program in memory at the time you are entering a program from the cassette, the computer will replace the lines in the old program with the lines being entered if they have the same line numbers. The rest of the program will remain intact. This merges the two programs into one program.

This is a good feature to use in a program that uses lots of data. A spelling program could have a master program with interchangeable spelling words. The words could be stored on a separate cassette and entered into the program as needed.

RUN "C:"

What if the program uses more memory than you have and you can't or don't want to get more memory for your computer? Divide the program into two or more parts and *chain* the parts together.

The ATARI BASIC has a command—RUN "C:"—that can be used as a direct command or as a statement in a program. If you use it as a direct command, it will load and run the program from the cassette. As a program statement, it will do the same thing under program control.

A lengthy program can be divided into several smaller routines. The first part should do the computation. When it is finished, the program will load the second part of the program and continue. The only drawback is, like CLOAD, the RUN "C:" command destroys the old program before it loads the new one. If you want to return the old program, you will have to reload it.

To use the RUN "C:" command, you must save the program with the SAVE "C:" command. Use the following procedure when writing a program in two or more parts.

1. Be sure the last line to be executed in the first part of the program is RUN "C:".
2. Save the first part of the program on a cassette. Use either the CSAVE or SAVE "C:" command.
3. Do not rewind the cassette.
4. Enter the second part of the program into the computer.
5. If there is another part of the program following this routine, be sure this part ends with RUN "C:" also.
6. Use the SAVE "C:" command to store this part of the program on tape.
7. Repeat steps 3-6 until the entire program has been stored on tape.

To load a chained program, simply load the first part of the program with CLOAD or RUN "C:", depending on how you saved it. Be sure the play button on the recorder is pressed down. *Do not* press the stop button after the first part of the program is loaded. When the second part of the program is ready to be loaded, the computer will signal you, with one beep, to press the return key. The computer will load and run each additional part of the program this way.

Chapter 7

Understanding the Screen

When you are writing a program not requiring graphics or large letters, you will use *mode 0*, or the text mode. This is the mode the computer uses automatically when it displays READY . You can print 40 letters or characters across the screen and 24 lines of text on the screen. Because some screens cannot show all 40 characters, the BASIC cartridge changes the left margin and gives you 38 characters across the screen. You can still place information in any of the 40 positions across the screen, but you will have to specify this in the program.

Since you have an area of 40 characters by 24 lines, the resolution of the screen in mode 0 is 40 × 24 and requires 960 bytes of memory. Figure 7-1 shows the memory requirements and resolution of all the graphics modes.

When you are writing and editing a program, you will use mode 0.

DISPLAYING THE PROGRAM

Once you load a program into memory, you may want to look at it to see what commands are used, or to change instructions in the program. You can look at the program by typing LIST and pressing return. The entire program will be printed on the screen. If the program is longer than 20 lines, the first lines will scroll off the top of the screen. Unless you can speed read, stop the program listing at any time by pressing the control key and the numeral 1 key at the same time. Press the control key and number 1 again to continue the listing.

You may also tell the computer to list only the lines you would like to read LIST 10,50 tells the computer to start with line 10 and list the program statements up to and including line 50. If there are more lines than can fit on the screen, the first lines will scroll off.

To tell the computer to execute the program in memory, type RUN and press return. The computer will start with the first line of the program and complete the instructions in that line, proceed to the next line and follow those instructions. Should you want to stop a program, you can press either the break key, or the system reset key. The system reset key will clear the screen when it stops the program, the screen will not clear when you press the break key. The break key is the last key in the top row of the keyboard.

If, after you press the break key, you want to continue the program, type

	Graphics Mode	Memory Required (RAM)
	0	993
	1	513
	2	261
	3	273
	4	537
	5	1017
	6	2025
	7	3945
	8	7900

Fig. 7-1. RAM requirements for the graphics modes.

CONT and press return. The computer will start with the line it was on when it was interrupted and continue with the program. Sometimes, however, if the program uses different graphics modes, the CONT command will produce an error it would not have encountered if the program had not been interrupted. Even so, the break key with the CONT command are very useful when testing and debugging a program.

FRE(X)

Ever wonder how much memory a program uses, or how much room (free RAM) you have left? Type PRINT FRE(X) and press return to find out how much memory (RAM) is left. To find out how much memory a program uses, type PRINT FRE(X) before you load a program. This will tell you how much memory the computer can use for a program. Figure 7-2 is a listing of the free RAM for the RAM the computer contains. The BASIC cartridge uses about 4000 bytes. After you load and run the program, type PRINT FRE(X) and subtract this number from the first number to arrive at the amount of memory the program uses.

Amount of RAM	Available Memory (no disk or interface)
16K	13323 bytes
24K	21515 bytes
32K	29707 bytes
40K	37899 bytes

Fig. 7-2. Amount of RAM available when using the BASIC cartridge and graphics 0.

Always run the program to get the true amount of free RAM because the program may set aside some of the memory for storage, not evident until you run the program.

PRINTING TO THE SCREEN

The video screen is the primary visual display for your program. Even though you can use a printer, voice synthesizer, or other accessories with your ATARI, you will present most programs on the video screen. You should try to keep unrelated information off the screen when you are running your program. After your remark lines, clear the screen. The format for clearing the screen during a program is:

PRINT "(escape key) (control key & clear key)"
50 PRINT CHR$"125"

This will remove any garbage on the screen. Directions can be printed on the screen for the user to read while the computer is setting up the program.

In mode 0, displaying words or characters to the screen is accomplished with the print command.

PRINT "ANYTHING YOU WANT"
60 PRINT "ANYTHING YOU WANT"

The computer places whatever is between the quotation marks on the screen. There must be quotation marks before and after the words you want printed on the screen. If there are several lines in a program to be printed, each new line will be displayed under the previous one.

There may be times you will want several different items printed on the same line with or without spaces between them, for example, columns with headings above each column. Two characters will hold the cursor in the same line—the comma and the semicolon. The semicolon will not advance the cursor after the last character of a print statement has been printed. The first character of the next print statement will occupy the next position on the screen.

60 PRINT "THIS IS THE FIRST SENTENCE";
70 PRINT "THIS IS THE SECOND SENTENCE!"

If you run this two-line program your screen should display:

THIS IS THE FIRST SENTENCETHIS IS THE SECOND SENTENCE!

There is no space between the last E in "sentence" and the T in "this." Now try these lines:

60 PRINT "DATE",
70 PRINT "PLACE",
80 PRINT "TIME"

Run these lines; the display should read:

DATE   PLACE   TIME

There are three distinct columns on the screen (Fig. 7-3). You do not need a comma on line 80 if it is the last word you want printed on that line. The next print statement would place the

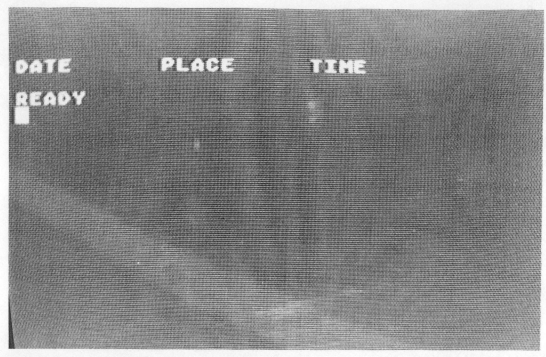

Fig. 7-3. Screen display using commas to separate words.

information under the heading date unless the program instructed it to print elsewhere. You can also use the tab feature with a print statement; you can set the tab and place it in a print statement. Use the tab key with the escape key when you use it in a print statement.

If you are using the other graphics modes, the print statement needs an additional piece of information. Print, by itself, tells the computer to place information in the *text window*. In mode 0, the text window is the entire screen. In the other modes, the text window is the last four rows on your screen. If you want information placed in the graphics window, you must tell the computer by placing   6;   after the print command. Using the semicolon will place the information in the next position after the cursor. Using a comma will shift the information to about the middle of the screen.

60 GRAPHICS 2
70 PRINT #6; "THIS IS PLACED HERE"
80 PRINT #6, "THIS IS MOVED OVER"

Add these lines to your program and run it. You should see a small text window at the bottom of the screen and the two statements near the top of the screen.

Now change line 60 to a different graphics mode:

60 GRAPHICS 5

32

Run the program and the letters will no longer appear. A line of colored squares will replace them. The different modes are discussed in detail in Chapter 16.

The computer also recognizes a symbol for the print command. A question mark (?) can be used interchangeably with the print command. The computer will print anything that appears after the question mark as if it had received the print command.

THE POSITION COMMAND

With the position command, you can specify which row and column your print statement should begin at. Change your program to this:

70 POSITION 4,8: PRINT "4th column - 8th row"
80 POSITION 10,15: PRINT "10th column - 15th row"

Before you run this version, be sure line 60 has been deleted. You should see both lines on your screen, each in its correct position, indicated by the two numbers following the word position. The first number indicates vertical placement, the second, horizontal placement (the screen prints 40 characters across and 24 lines down, remember). If you tell the computer to print something in an out-of-range position, for example, position 80,4, you will get a 141 error: cursor out of range.

The following programs will give you some ideas on how to use the print and position commands. The commands not yet introduced will be covered later in this book.

Listing 7-1 (see Fig. 7-4) prints a message on the screen. The entire program consists of print commands. You can use upper- and lowercase as well as reverse video and graphics in your print statements.

Listing 7-1. Print Command Demonstration

```
10 REM LISTING VII-1
20 REM PRINT POSSIBILITIES
30 REM L.M.SCHREIBER FOR TAB BOOKS
40 PRINT "}clear}":REM CLEAR SCREEN
50 POSITION 2,6:PRINT "}WWWWWWWWWWWWWWWW
WWWWWWWWWWWWWWWWWWWW}":REM 36 CONTROL W's
60 POSITION 14,8:PRINT "INSTRUCTIONS"
70 POSITION 6,10:PRINT "I CAN BE IN CAPIT
AL LETTERS"
80 POSITION 10,12:PRINT "or in small lett
ers."
90 POSITION 7,14:PRINT "I CAN BE IN REVER
SE VIDEO."
100 POSITION 2,16:PRINT "}XXXXXXXXXXXXXXX
XXXXXXXXXXXXXXXXXXXXX}":REM 36 CONTROL X'
s
110 END
```

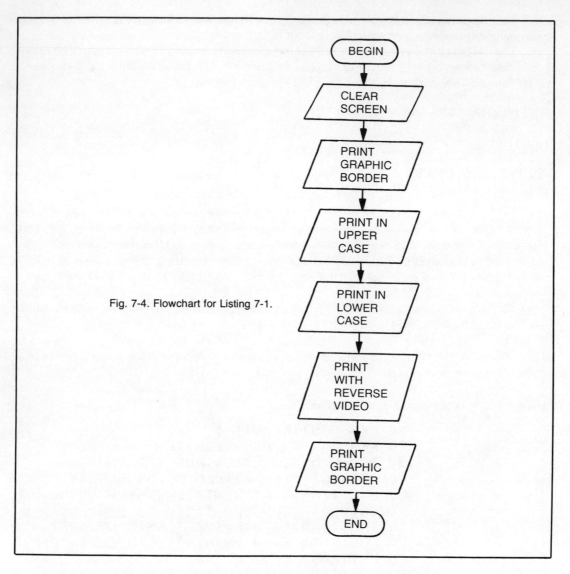

Fig. 7-4. Flowchart for Listing 7-1.

Lines 10-30 are the remark statements that name this program. Always include some remarks at the beginning of your programs.

Line 40 clears the screen. We don't want any distractions on the screen.

Line 50 starts printing at the second column in the sixth row. This character ends just before the end of the screen.

Line 60 sets the position of this print statement at the fourteenth column and the eighth row. The words in this statement are in capital letters.

Line 70 shows another print statement that uses capital letters.

34

Line 80 prints the message in lowercase letters after it sets the print position at the 10th column and the twelfth row.

Line 90 prints its message in capital letters, but this time the letters are in reverse video.

Line 100 prints another row of graphics characters.

The program ends with line 110. If there were program statements after line 110, the computer would not execute them unless it was told to.

Listing 7-2 (see Fig. 7-5) displays the Love graphic (Fig. 7-6). This is created by erasing characters from the screen rather than printing them. After the remarks in lines 10-30 the computer does the following:

Line 40 clears the screen and removes the cursor. If you type   POKE 752,1   as a program statement, the computer will make the cursor invisible.

Lines 50 through 290 print a continuous   LOVE   across the screen. Each line begins with the next letter in the word love. (There is an easier way to fill the screen. See if you can figure it out when you have finished this book.)

Lines 310-410 erases the letters that form the final letter L. The position command tells the computer where to place the cursor. There are spaces between the quotation marks to erase the letters on the screen.

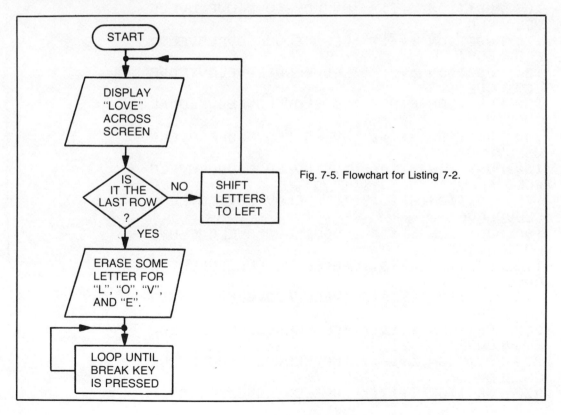

Fig. 7-5. Flowchart for Listing 7-2.

Listing 7-2. Love Program

```
10 REM LISTING VII-2
20 REM LOVE
30 REM L.M.SCHREIBER FOR TAB BOOKS
40 PRINT ")clear)":POKE 752,1:REM CLEAR S
CREEN-REMOVE CURSOR
50 POSITION 6,0:? "LOVELOVELOVELOVELOVELO
VELOVEL"
60 POSITION 6,1:? "OVELOVELOVELOVELOVELOV
ELOVELO"
70 POSITION 6,2:? "VELOVELOVELOVELOVELOVE
LOVELOV"
80 POSITION 6,3:? "ELOVELOVELOVELOVELOVEL
OVELOVE"
90 POSITION 6,4:? "LOVELOVELOVELOVELOVELO
VELOVEL"
100 POSITION 6,5:? "OVELOVELOVELOVELOVELO
VELOVELO"
110 POSITION 6,6:? "VELOVELOVELOVELOVELOV
ELOVELOV"
120 POSITION 6,7:? "ELOVELOVELOVELOVELOVE
LOVELOVE"
130 POSITION 6,8:? "LOVELOVELOVELOVELOVEL
OVELOVEL"
140 POSITION 6,9:? "OVELOVELOVELOVELOVELO
VELOVELO"
150 POSITION 6,10:? "VELOVELOVELOVELOVELO
VELOVELOV"
170 POSITION 6,11:? "ELOVELOVELOVELOVELOV
ELOVELOVE"
180 POSITION 6,12:? "LOVELOVELOVELOVELOVE
LOVELOVEL"
190 POSITION 6,13:? "OVELOVELOVELOVELOVEL
OVELOVELO"
200 POSITION 6,14:? "VELOVELOVELOVELOVELO
VELOVELOV"
210 POSITION 6,15:? "ELOVELOVELOVELOVELOV
ELOVELOVE"
220 POSITION 6,16:? "LOVELOVELOVELOVELOVE
LOVELOVEL"
230 POSITION 6,17:? "OVELOVELOVELOVELOVEL
```

```
OVELOVELO"
240 POSITION 6,18:? "VELOVELOVELOVELOVELO
VELOVELOV"
250 POSITION 6,19:? "ELOVELOVELOVELOVELOV
ELOVELOVE"
260 POSITION 6,20:? "LOVELOVELOVELOVELOVE
LOVELOVEL"
270 POSITION 6,21:? "OVELOVELOVELOVELOVEL
OVELOVELO"
280 POSITION 6,22:? "VELOVELOVELOVELOVELO
VELOVELOV"
290 POSITION 6,23:? "ELOVELOVELOVELOVELOV
ELOVELOVE";
300 REM MAKE AN 'L'
310 POSITION 10,1:? "    ":REM 4 SPACES
320 POSITION 10,2:? "    ":REM 4 SPACES
330 POSITION 11,3:? "  ":REM 2 SPACES
340 POSITION 11,4:? "  ":REM 2 SPACES
350 POSITION 11,5:? "  ":REM 2 SPACES
360 POSITION 11,6:? "  ":REM 2 SPACES
370 POSITION 11,7:? "  ":REM 2 SPACES
380 POSITION 11,8:? "  ":REM 2 SPACES
390 POSITION 11,9:? "  ":REM 2 SPACES
400 POSITION 11,10:? "       ":REM 7 SPAC
ES
410 POSITION 11,11:? "       ":REM 7 SPAC
ES
420 REM MAKE AN 'O'
430 POSITION 23,1:? "        ":REM 8 SPAC
ES
440 POSITION 23,2:? "        ":REM 8 SPAC
ES
450 POSITION 21,3:? "    ":POSITION 29,3:
? "    ":REM REM 2 SETS OF 4 SPACES
460 POSITION 21,4:? "    ":POSITION 29,4:
? "    ":REM REM 2 SETS OF 4 SPACES
470 POSITION 21,5:? "    ":POSITION 29,5:
? "    ":REM REM 2 SETS OF 4 SPACES
480 POSITION 21,6:? "    ":POSITION 29,6:
? "    ":REM REM 2 SETS OF 4 SPACES
490 POSITION 21,7:? "    ":POSITION 29,7:
? "    ":REM REM 2 SETS OF 4 SPACES
```

Listing 7-2. Love Program (Continued from page 37).

```
500 POSITION 21,8:? "    ":POSITION 29,8:
? "    ":REM REM 2 SETS OF 4 SPACES
510 POSITION 21,9:? "    ":POSITION 29,9:
? "    ":REM REM 2 SETS OF 4 SPACES
520 POSITION 23,10:? "       ":REM 7 SPAC
ES"
530 POSITION 23,11:? "       ":REM 7 SPAC
ES"
540 REM MAKE A 'V'
550 POSITION 8,13:? "  ":POSITION 19,13:?
 "  ":REM 2 SETS OF 2 SPACES
560 POSITION 8,14:? "   ":POSITION 18,14:
? "   ":REM 2 SETS OF 3 SPACES
570 POSITION 9,15:? "  ":POSITION 18,15:?
 "  ":REM 2 SETS OF 2 SPACES
580 POSITION 10,16:? "  ":POSITION 17,16:
? "  ":REM 2 SETS OF 2 SPACES
590 POSITION 10,17:? "  ":POSITION 17,17:
? "  ":REM 2 SETS OF 2 SPACES
600 POSITION 11,18:? "  ":POSITION 16,18:
? "  ":REM 2 SETS OF 2 SPACES
610 POSITION 11,19:? "  ":POSITION 16,19:
? "  ":REM 2 SETS OF 2 SPACES
620 POSITION 12,20:? "  ":POSITION 15,20:
? "  ":REM 2 SETS OF 2 SPACES
630 POSITION 12,21:? "  ":POSITION 15,21:
? "  ":REM 2 SETS OF 2 SPACES
640 POSITION 13,22:? "   ":REM 3 SPACES
650 POSITION 13,23:? "   ";:REM 3 SPACES
660 REM MAKE AN 'E'
670 POSITION 22,13:? "           ":REM 11
 SPACES
680 POSITION 22,14:? "           ":REM 11
 SPACES
690 POSITION 24,15:? "   ":POSITION 31,15
:? "  ":REM 3 SPACES & 2 SPACES
700 POSITION 24,16:? "   ":POSITION 31,16
:? "  ":REM 3 SPACES & 2 SPACES
710 POSITION 24,17:? "   ":REM 3 SPACES
720 POSITION 24,18:? "     ":REM 5 SPACES
```

```
730 POSITION 24,19:? "     ":REM 5 SPACES

740 POSITION 24,20:? "   ":POSITION 31,20:
? "   ":REM 2 SETS OF 3 SPACES
750 POSITION 24,21:? "   ":POSITION 31,21:
? "   ":REM 2 SETS OF 3 SPACES
760 POSITION 24,22:? "         ":REM 9 SP
ACES
770 POSITION 24,23:? "         ";:REM 9 S
PACES
780 GOTO 780:REM DON'T END THE PROGRAM ST
AY HERE UNTILL BREAK IS PRESSED
```

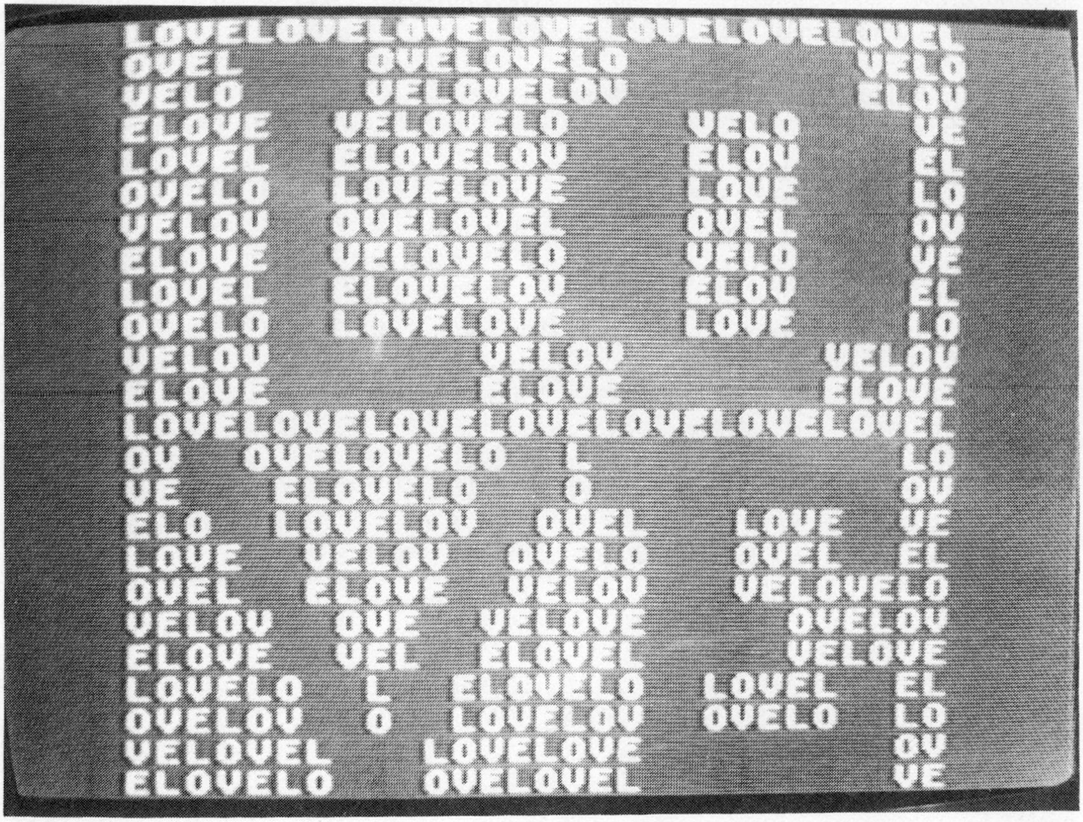

Fig. 7-6. Screen display for LOVE program.

Lines 430-530 form the letter O. Since there are two sides to an O, there are two position commands in several of the lines. There is no need for a comma or semicolon after the print command since the position command places the cursor in the proper place before each print command.

Lines 550-650 erase letters to form a V.

Lines 670-770 erase letters to form an E.

Lines 650 and 770 end with a semicolon. Without a semicolon at the end of these print statements, the computer would move the cursor one row down. Line 23 is the 24th line on the screen (the first line is line 0), so the entire screen would scroll up and we'd lose the first lines of the program.

Line 780 does not end the program with   END   which would tell the computer to display   READY   on the screen and we would lose part of the display. Instead, we give the computer a GOTO command, returning it to the beginning of this line. This is the only command on this line, so the computer continues to go to line 780 until you press the system reset or break key.

Listing 7-3 demonstrates the position command. The letters are printed in a specific location, erased, and reprinted in a new position (see flowchart, Fig. 7-7). Entire words can be moved across the screen this way.

Listing 7-3. Position Command Demonstration

```
10 REM LISTING VII-3
20 REM SIMPLE ANIMATION
30 REM L.M.SCHREIBER FOR TAB BOOKS
40 ? ")clear)":POKE 752,1:REM CLEAR SCREE
N-REMOVE CURSOR
50 FOR X=0 TO 10:REM THIS COMMAND SAVES M
EMORY & TYPING
60 POSITION X,5:REM CHANGE THE COLUMN BUT
 NOT THE ROW
65 ? " M"
70 NEXT X:REM DO IT 10 TIMES
80 FOR X=0 TO 11
90 POSITION X,6:REM NOW DO IT ONE ROW LOW
ER
100 ? " O"
110 NEXT X
120 POSITION 12,6:? " ":REM ERASE IT
130 POSITION 12,5:? "O":REM MOVE IT UP
140 FOR X=0 TO 12
150 POSITION X,4
160 ? " V"
```

```
170 NEXT X
180 POSITION 13,4:? " "
190 POSITION 13,5:? "V"
200 FOR X=0 TO 13
210 POSITION X,6
220 ? " I"
230 NEXT X
240 POSITION 14,6:? " "
250 POSITION 14,5:? "I"
260 FOR X=0 TO 14
270 POSITION X,4
280 ? " N"
290 NEXT X
300 POSITION 15,4:? " "
310 POSITION 15,5:? "N"
320 FOR X=0 TO 15
330 POSITION X,6
340 ? " G"
350 NEXT X
360 POSITION 16,6:? " "
370 POSITION 16,5:? "G"
380 FOR X=1 TO 20:REM MOVE IT ACROSS
390 POSITION X,2
400 ? " WORDS"
410 NEXT X
420 POSITION 21,2:? "      ":REM BRING IT
DOWN
430 POSITION 21,3:? "WORDS"
440 POSITION 21,3:? "     "
450 POSITION 21,4:? "WORDS"
460 POSITION 21,4:? "     "
470 POSITION 21,5:? "WORDS"
480 POKE 752,0:REM TURN CURSOR BACK ON
490 END
```

Lines 10-30 remarks about the program.

Line 40 clears the screen and removes the cursor. A cursor in this program would distract from the letters moving on the screen.

Line 50 is the beginning of a For . . . Next loop. This command saves memory and typing. The X will refer to the column in which the computer will be printing.

Line 60 is the position at which we want a letter printed. The X is after position and before 5. Each time the computer comes to this line the value of X will be different.

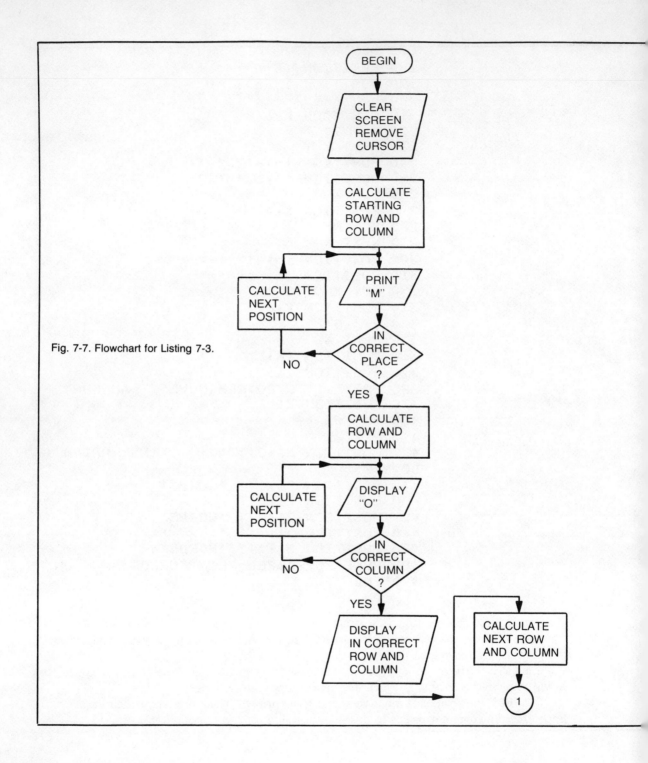

Fig. 7-7. Flowchart for Listing 7-3.

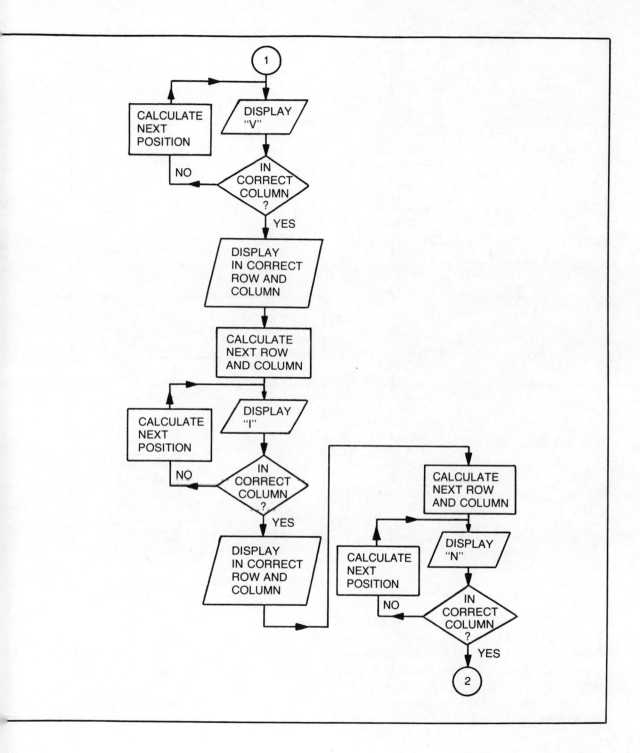

43

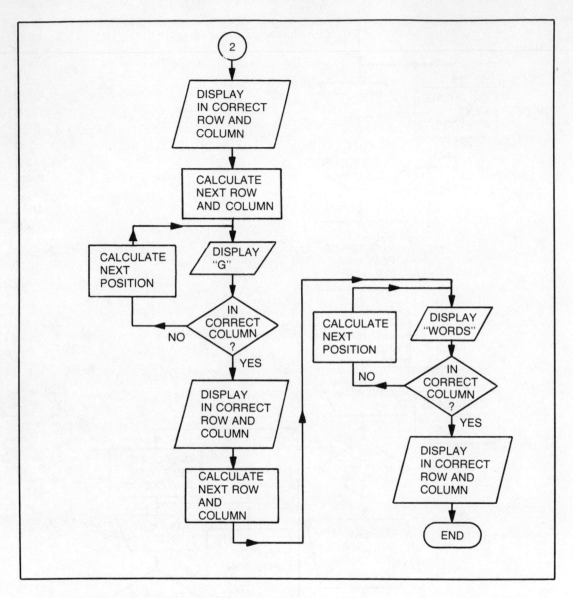

Line 65 prints a space and the letter M on the screen. This line works in conjunction with the last line. In the last line, the value of X increases by one each time the computer comes to it. This moves the cursor over one column. Before the computer prints an M in this line, it will print a space. This space will erase the M that was printed in the position. The two lines working together give the illusion of an M moving across the screen.

Line 70 finishes the loop. The computer will do lines 50 to 70 eleven times before it goes on to the next line.

The computer will do lines 80 to 110 in the same manner. This time it will repeat the loop 12 times.

Line 90 tells the computer to print the letter O one line below the M.

Line 120 erases the O from position 12,6.

Line 130 prints the O in the twelfth column of the fifth row. This places it immediately after the M.

Lines 140-170 make the letter V appear to move across the top of the letters MO.

Line 180 erases the letter from the thirteenth column of the fifth row.

Line 190 prints the V after the MO.

Lines 200-370 follow the same pattern of printing a letter on the left side of the screen, erasing it, and printing it one column over.

Lines 380-410 move an entire word across the screen. Again, the first position of the letters between the quotation marks is a space. This space erases the letter w in the word previously printed. If there were no space, a line of w's would be printed across the screen.

Lines 420-470 erases the entire word, then reprints it one row lower.

Line 480 turns the cursor back on.

Line 490 ends the program. The message **MOVING WORDS** should be on the screen, along with the ready prompt.

Although this program only moved letters across the screen, using this technique of printing and erasing you can make graphics created with graphics characters move across the screen.

Chapter 8

Getting the Answers

At times a value the program needs will change each time the program is run. Sometimes a new value will be entered by the computer user, other times the programmer wants the computer to use a different value that the computer arrives at from prior computation The computer needs to be able to keep track of the value by storing it in a place in memory so the computer can *recall* the value when it needs to. To accomplish this, the program would store the value as a *variable*. A variable is a letter, group of letters, or word that represents a value. If you were to enter

20 A=10

the computer would substitute the value 10 each time it encounters the variable A in a program. If the program contained

30 B=A+5

it would add 10 to 5. The variable B would become 15. If you have a program in your computer, type   NEW   and then type in Listing 8-1 (see flowchart in Fig. 8-1).

Line 50 makes the variable A equal to 10.
Line 60 makes the variable B equal to 15.
Line 70 makes the variable C equal to 20.
Line 80 prints all three variables on the same line.

As you can see, when the computer is told to print a variable, it will print the value stored in that variable. Your screen should display:

10   15   20

The value of a variable can be changed and reused throughout the program. A variable can also be used instead of a number for an arithmetic operation. Type   NEW   and enter the program shown in Listing 8-2 (see flowchart Fig. 8-2).

Line 50 assigns the length variable the value of 30 and width variable the value of 7. Names can also be used as variables.

Line 60 prints a message on the screen. Since the value of the variable will be used on the same line, a semicolon is placed after the quotation mark. A space is placed before the quotation

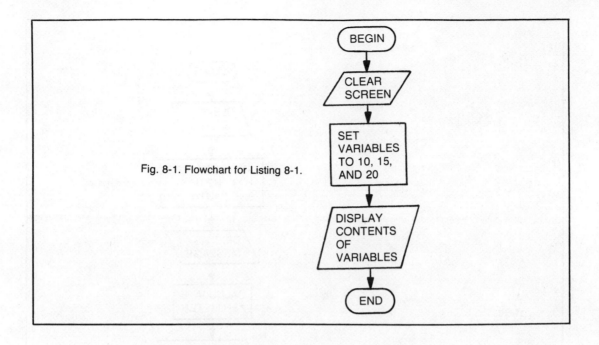

Fig. 8-1. Flowchart for Listing 8-1.

Listing 8-1. Assigning Values to Variables

```
10 REM LISTING VIII-1
20 REM ASSIGN VARIABLES VALUES
30 REM BY L.M.SCHREIBER FOR TAB BOOKS
40 ? "}clear}":REM CLEAR SCREEN
50 A=10:REM THE VARIABLE 'A' WILL BE 10
60 B=15:REM THE VARIABLE 'B' WILL BE 15
70 C=20:REM THE VARIABLE 'C' WILL BE 20
80 ? A,B,C:REM THE COMMAS WILL KEEP THE V
ALUES ON THE SAME LINE
90 END
```

mark so a space will show between the word length and the value stored in length. We want the computer to continue with the message in the next print statement, so place a semicolon after the length variable.

Line 65 finishes the message started in the preceding line. There is a space after the quotation mark so the word and will be one space from the value of the length variable.

Line 70 performs the formula that determines the perimeter of the room. The answer is stored in the variable perimeter.

Line 80 contains two print statements. The first is not followed by a message; brings the cursor down one line so the message printed in the second part of the line will be one row below

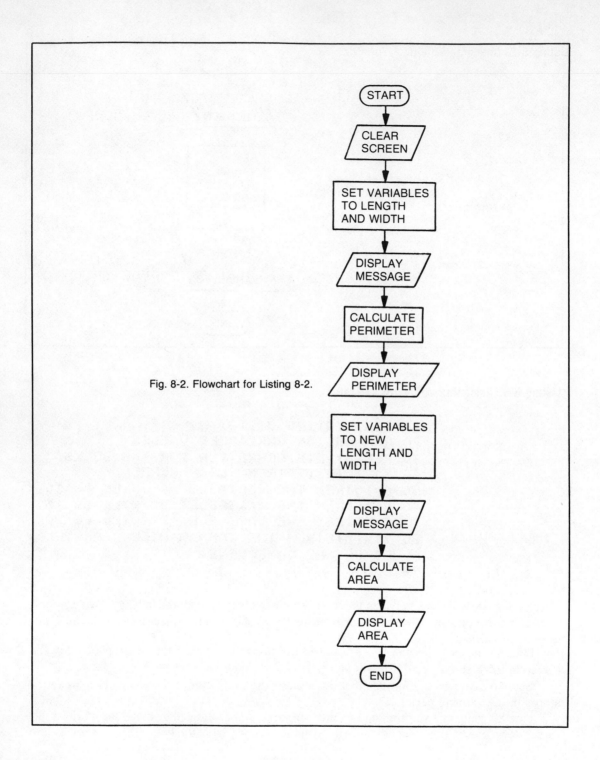

Fig. 8-2. Flowchart for Listing 8-2.

Listing 8-2. Changing Values of Variables

```
10 REM LISTING VIII-2
20 REM CHANGE VARIABLES VALUES
30 REM BY L.M.SCHREIBER FOR TAB BOOKS
40 ? "}clear}":REM CLEAR SCREEN
50 LENGTH=30:WIDTH=7:REM NAMES CAN BE VAR
IABLES
60 ? "I will now compute the perimeter of
 a room that has a length ";LENGTH;" and
a width of ";WIDTH
70 PERIMETER=2*WIDTH+2*LENGTH:REM FORMULA
 FOR PERIMETER
80 ? :? "THE PERIMETER IS ";PERIMETER
90 LENGTH=27:WIDTH=14:REM CHANGE THE VALU
ES OF THE VARIABLE
100 ? :? "Now I will calculate the area o
f a    room whose width is ";WIDTH;" and
whose        length is ";LENGTH
110 AREA=WIDTH*LENGTH:REM FORMULA FOR ARE
A
120 ? :? "THE AREA IS ";AREA
130 END
```

the last message. A print statement by itself skips a line on the screen. The message will be printed on the next line of the screen.

Line 90 changes the values of the variables length and width. Whenever possible, the same variables should be reused in a program. This saves memory and is time efficient. Each time a variable is assigned a new value, it forgets the old value.

Line 100 skips a line, then prints another message on the screen. The extra spaces between a and room allow for the wrap-around of the message. The semicolons keep the variable on the same line as the message.

Line 105 continues the message.

Line 110 calculates the area of the room and stores its answer in the area variable.

Line 120 skips a line on the screen, then prints the message containing the area of the room.

It is important to note there *must* be a semicolon or comma between the message and the variable in the print statements. Without semicolons, BASIC will not accept the line. To print the value of the variable on the next screen line, use a colon and another print in the line.

STRING VARIABLES

Numeric variables store numbers; *string variables* can store numbers, letters, or characters. String variables can't do any computation. Before you can use a string variable, you must let the computer set aside memory for it by using a *dimension statement:*

40 DIM VARIABLE$(##)

Listing 8-3. String Variables

```
10 REM LISTING VIII-3
20 REM STRING VARIABLES VALUES
30 REM BY L.M.SCHREIBER FOR TAB BOOKS
40 ? "}clear}":REM CLEAR SCREEN
50 DIM NAME$(20),ADDRESS$(15),CITY$(6),ST
ATE$(2),ZIP$(9)
60 NAME$="J.Q.PUBLIC":REM STORE NAME IN S
TRING
70 ADDRESS$="123 MAIN STREET":REM STORE A
DDRESS
80 CITY$="NEWTON":REM THIS IS THE CITY
90 STATE$="MI":REM USE THE TWO LETTER ABB
REVIATION
100 ZIP$="43201":REM ZIP CODE
110 POSITION 5,2:? "THE ADDRESS INFORMATI
ON IS:":REM SHOW WHAT IS STORED IN THE ST
RINGS
120 POSITION 7,4:? NAME$
130 POSITION 7,6:? ADDRESS$
140 POSITION 7,8:? CITY$
150 POSITION 17,8:? STATE$
160 POSITION 17,10:? ZIP$
170 END
```

By placing a $ at the end of a variable name, you are telling the computer this is a string variable. The number in the parenthesis indicates the number of characters to be stored in this string. You can store less than you allow for, but never more.

20 DIM NAME$(10)

This statement sets aside 10 bytes of memory for the name string, and can contain up to 10 letters or numbers.

Listing 8-3 (see flowchart, Fig. 8-3) demonstrates how strings can be used in a program. It uses five strings to store information.

Line 50 sets aside memory for each string. NAME$ sets aside 20 bytes, ADDRESS$ 15 bytes, CITY$ 6, STATE$ 2, and ZIP$ 9. By assigning a name indicative of the information the string will contain helps you keep track of what you are doing in the program.

Line 60-100 store information in each string. The letters, numbers, or characters that are placed in each string variable must be enclosed in quotation marks.

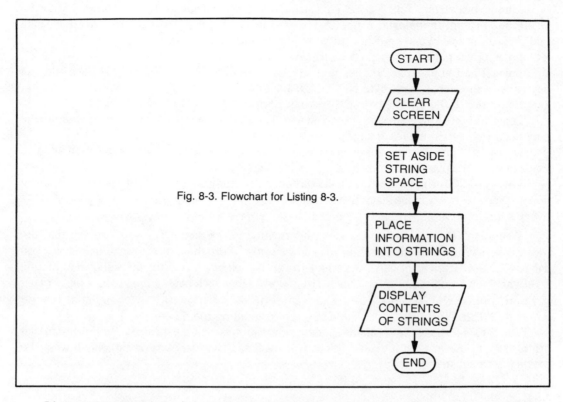

Fig. 8-3. Flowchart for Listing 8-3.

Lines 110-160 print the information in each string on the screen. There are no commas or semicolons after the strings, so each is printed on a separate line. If any of the string variables were assigned information exceeding the number of bytes set aside for that string, the computer would store and print only the amount of information it had room set aside for.

Like numeric variables, string variables hold the contents until they are changed by the program.

ATARI BASIC stores a string as a long line of characters, each with its own identifiable location. Figure 8-4 shows you how the computer sees a string. NAME$ is 20 characters long. The numbers under each letter indicate the location of that letter. If you want to print only part of the string, type PRINT NAME$ (starting location, ending location). PRINT NAME$ (1,3) would result in J.Q. The computer prints the contents of NAME$ beginning with the first character and ending with the third. If you want to print only one character from the string, both numbers must be the same: NAME$(6,6)

The string can be dimensioned to any length you need for the proper operation of your program. Listing 8-4 increases the amount of space reserved for NAME$ and adds three strings. Notice that numbers can be used with letters as a variable name.

Line 50 dimensions five string variables. Several strings can be dimensioned on the same line if you place a comma between their names.

Line 55 is a string of 52 spaces. This string (S$) will be used to clear the other variables.

Line 57 clears every string in line 50. If we did not clear every string before using it, we may find garbage in the bytes we didn't fill with information from the program.

Lines 60-90 place names in each string.

Lines 100-130 place an address in each   NAME$. Notice that each address begins with the twenty-first byte of   NAME$.

Lines 140-170 place a city in each string. Each city begins in location 36.

Lines 180-210 store the state in each string. The state is the two-letter abbreviation, so we only need two bytes in each string for the state.

Lines 220-250 store the zip code for each address. The zip code ends in location 48. The extra bytes were placed in the program for nine-digit zip codes.

Lines 270-300 print each string on the screen. If you study the contents of each printed string you will see that every name starts in location 1, every address location 21, every city location 36, every state location 42, and every zip code location 44.

When each string contains the same information in the same locations, we say that the strings are *fielded*. By fielding a string you know exactly where the information is stored, and you can have the program print only the parts of the string you need. Add the lines shown in Listing 8-5. When you rerun the program, lines 310-350 will label each part of the string as it is being printed. Since the strings have the same fields, you could just as easily have   NAME2$ or   NAME3$ printed on the screen.

The part of a string that contains specific information is called a *substring*. In a program that prints address labels, a routine can check each string for a particular state or zip code. It would be looking for a substring.

LEN

There are times you need to know the length of a string, for example, if the title of your new program to be centered on the screen with the instructions printed under it. Your program would look like Listing 8-6.

Line 50 sets aside the string space needed for the title of the program.

Line 60 places the title of the program in the string.

Line 70 uses the command   LEN   to find the length of the string. It places this information in the variable L.

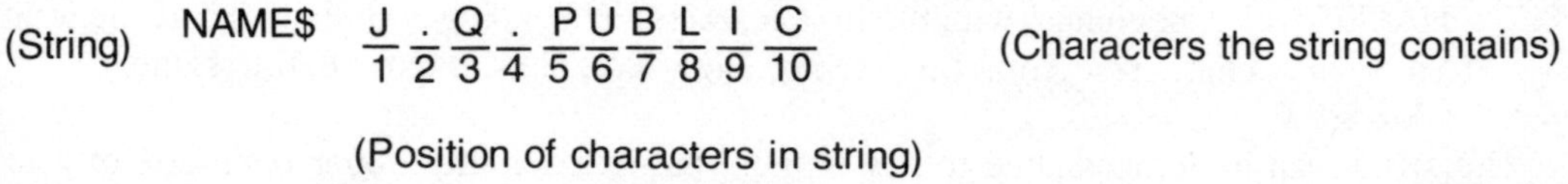

(String)   NAME$ $\underline{J}$. $\underline{Q}$. $\underline{P} \underline{U} \underline{B} \underline{L} \underline{I} \underline{C}$ (Characters the string contains)
                   1 2 3 4 5 6 7 8 9 10

(Position of characters in string)

Fig. 8-4. Position of characters in a string.

Listing 8-4. Fielding String Variables

```
10 REM LISTING VIII-4
20 REM FIELDING A STRING
30 REM BY L.M.SCHREIBER FOR TAB BOOKS
40 ? "}clear}"
50 DIM NAME1$(52),NAME2$(52),NAME3$(52),N
AME4$(52),S$(52):REM SET UP FOUR STRINGS
FOR FIELDING
55 S$(1)=" ":S$(52)=" ":S$(2)=S$:REM SET
THE STRING TO BLANKS
57 NAME1$=S$:NAME2$=S$:NAME3$=S$:NAME4$=S
$:REM CLEAR THE GARBAGE FROM THE STRINGS
60 NAME1$(1,10)="J.B. SMITH"
70 NAME2$(1,12)="MS. ROWLINGS"
80 NAME3$(1,10)="R.J. JONES"
90 NAME4$(1,11)="MARY GREENE"
100 NAME1$(21,37)="1731 CHEROKEE RD."
110 NAME2$(21,42)="11542 MAIN ST. APT. 25
"
120 NAME3$(21,35)="7 ROTUNDA DRIVE"
130 NAME4$(21,33)="1654 W. ADAMS"
140 NAME1$(36,41)="BROOKS"
150 NAME2$(36,39)="N.Y."
160 NAME3$(36,41)="CANTON"
170 NAME4$(36,39)="WEST"
180 NAME1$(42,43)="NJ"
190 NAME2$(42,43)="NY"
200 NAME3$(42,43)="MI"
210 NAME4$(42,43)="TX"
220 NAME1$(44,48)="12094"
230 NAME2$(44,48)="10021"
240 NAME3$(44,48)="48034"
250 NAME4$(44,48)="76043"
260 REM PRINT THE STRINGS
270 ? :? NAME1$
280 ? :? NAME2$
290 ? :? NAME3$
300 ? :? NAME4$
310 END
```

Line 80 divides the length of the title in half. Since the program is in mode 0, we know the center of the screen is location 20. If we subtract half the length from 20, we will know where we should start to print the title.

Listing 8-5. Fielding Strings, Version 2

```
10 REM LISTING VIII-5
20 REM FIELDING A STRING
30 REM BY L.M.SCHREIBER FOR TAB BOOKS
40 ? ">clear>"
50 DIM NAME1$(52),NAME2$(52),NAME3$(52),N
AME4$(52),S$(52):REM SET UP FOUR STRINGS
FOR FIELDING
55 S$(1)=" ":S$(52)=" ":S$(2)=S$:REM SET
THE STRING TO BLANKS
57 NAME1$=S$:NAME2$=S$:NAME3$=S$:NAME4$=S
$:REM CLEAR THE GARBAGE FROM THE STRINGS
60 NAME1$(1,10)="J.B. SMITH"
70 NAME2$(1,12)="MS. ROWLINGS"
80 NAME3$(1,10)="R.J. JONES"
90 NAME4$(1,11)="MARY GREENE"
100 NAME1$(21,37)="1731 CHEROKEE RD."
110 NAME2$(21,42)="11542 MAIN ST. APT.25"
120 NAME3$(21,35)="7 ROTUNDA DRIVE"
130 NAME4$(21,33)="1654 W. ADAMS"
140 NAME1$(36,41)="BROOKS"
150 NAME2$(36,39)="N.Y."
160 NAME3$(36,41)="CANTON"
162 NAME4$(36,39)="WEST"
180 NAME1$(42,43)="NJ"
190 NAME2$(42,43)="NY"
200 NAME3$(42,43)="MI"
210 NAME4$(42,43)="TX"
220 NAME1$(44,48)="12094"
230 NAME2$(44,48)="10021"
240 NAME3$(44,48)="48034"
250 NAME4$(44,48)="76043"
260 REM PRINT THE STRINGS
270 ? :? NAME1$
280 ? :? NAME2$
290 ? :? NAME3$
300 ? :? NAME4$
310 POSITION 5,14:? NAME1$(1,20)
320 POSITION 5,15:? NAME1$(21,35)
330 POSITION 5,16:? NAME1$(36,41)
340 POSITION 24,16:? NAME1$(42,43)
350 POSITION 24,17:? NAME1$(44,48)
```

Listing 8-6. Finding the Middle

```
10 REM LISTING VIII-6
20 REM FINDING THE MIDDLE
30 REM BY L.M.SCHREIBER FOR TAB BOOKS
40 ? ")clear}"
50 DIM TITLE$(20)
60 TITLE$="MORE SPACE WARS":REM GIVE THE
PROGRAM A TITLE
70 L=LEN(TITLE$):REM FIND OUT HOW LONG TH
E STRING IS
80 P=20-L/2:REM GET HALF OF THE LENGTH AN
D SUBTRACT IT FROM THE MIDDLE OF THE SCRE
EN
90 POSITION P,4:? TITLE$:REM 'P' IS THE S
TARTING POSITION OF THE STRING
100 ? :? "     This game requires good ha
nd eye coordination.  You are the comman
der of a space ship.     It is ";
110 ? "being drawn toward another planet.
"
120 GOTO 120:REM STAY HERE UNTIL BREAK OR
    SYSTEM RESET IS PRESSED
```

Line 90 sets the cursor in position P,4. P is the position we arrived at in line 80. The four places the title in the fifth row on the screen.

Lines 100-110 begin the instruction for this program.

Line 120 is a loop that makes the computer wait until the break key or system reset key has been pressed.

If a program repeats itself, and you do not want to use the old information, clear the previous information from the string by setting it equal to   "" (two quotation marks with nothing between them). This, in effect, is setting the length of the string to 0. However, if you place a character within the string, the old character, up to the location of the new character, will appear. Try the program in Listing 8-7.

Line 50 sets aside 20 bytes for S$.

Line 60 places the message in S$.

Line 70 gets the length of S$.

Lines 80-90 print the contents of S$ and its length.

Line 100 sets S$ equal to two quotation marks. If a string contains no spaces, is it empty?

Line 110 gets the new length of S$.

Lines 120-130 print the contents of S$ and its length. We can see on the screen that nothing has been printed and the length of S$ is 0.

Line 140 places the letter p in the fourth byte of S$.

Line 150 gets the length of S$ now a letter has been placed in it.

Lines 160-170 print the contents of S$ and its length. Since the letter p was placed in the fourth byte of S$, the length of S$ is now four. Also, the letters that were originally stored in S$ reappear, up to the new letter.

The word hello has been printed as help. Remember, S$ was dimensioned to 20, so you can place a letter or character in any location up to and including the twentieth. The computer will print all characters in the string up to the last position that had a character stored in it. If you change the letter in the fourth position and a letter in the second position, the computer will still print all four characters. Place a character in the string after the fourth position and it will become the last position in the string to be printed. Add the lines in Listing 8-8 (see flowchart, Fig. 8-5).

Line 190 changes the h in the first location of the string from a lowercase h to a capital H.

Line 200 gets the length of S$.

Lines 210-220 print the new contents of S$. We can see the length of S$ has not changed by changing the contents of the first byte.

Line 230 changes three bytes of S$ to a space and me.

Listing 8-7. Reappear

```
10 REM LISTING VIII.7
20 REM REAPPEAR
30 REM BY L.M.SCHREIBER FOR TAB BOOKS
40 ? "}clear}"
50 DIM S$(20):REM SPACE HAS BEEN SET ASID
E
60 S$="HELLO THERE":REM PLACE LETTERS IN
THE STRING
70 L=LEN(S$):REM FIND THE LENGTH OF THE S
TRING
80 ? :? "STRING CONTAINS -";S$
90 ? :? "ITS LENGTH IS -";L
100 S$="":REM NO SPACES - CLEARS A STRING
?
110 L=LEN(S$):REM GET ITS LENGTH - PROVE
IT IS EMPTY
120 ? :? :? "STRING CONTAINS-";S$
130 ? :? "ITS LENGTH IS -";L
140 S$(4,4)="P":REM PLACE A 'P' IN THE 4T
H POSITION OF THE STRING
150 L=LEN(S$):REM NOW GET ITS LENGTH
160 ? :? :? "STRING CONTAINS -";S$
170 ? :? "ITS LENGTH IS-";L
180 REM ALL THE CHARACTERS UP TO THE NEW
ONE REAPPEAR
```

Listing 8-8. Reappear, Version 2

```
10 REM LISTING VIII.8
20 REM REAPPEAR
30 REM BY L.M.SCHREIBER FOR TAB BOOKS
40 ? "}clear}"
50 DIM S$(20):REM SPACE HAS BEEN SET ASID
E
60 S$="hello there":REM PLACE LETTERS IN
THE STRING
70 L=LEN(S$):REM FIND THE LENGTH OF THE S
TRING
80 ? :? "STRING CONTAINS -";S$
90 ? :? "ITS LENGTH IS -";L
100 S$="":REM NO SPACES - CLEARS A STRING
?
110 L=LEN(S$):REM GET ITS LENGTH - PROVE
IT IS EMPTY
120 ? :? :? "STRING CONTAINS-";S$
130 ? :? "ITS LENGTH IS -";L
140 S$(4,4)="P":REM PLACE A 'P' IN THE 4T
H POSITION OF THE STRING
150 L=LEN(S$):REM NOW GET ITS LENGTH
160 ? :? :? "STRING CONTAINS -";S$
170 ? :? "ITS LENGTH IS-";L
180 REM ALL THE CHARACTERS UP TO THE NEW
ONE REAPPEAR
190 S$(1,1)="H":REM MAKE THE FIRST LETTER
 CAPITAL
200 L=LEN(S$):REM SEE IF THE LENGTH HAS C
HANGED
210 ? :? :? " STRING NOW CONTAINS-";S$
220 ? :? "ITS LENGTH IS-";L
230 S$(5,7)=" me":REM CHANGE THE LETTERS
ON THE 5th - 7th POSITIONS
240 L=LEN(S$)
250 ? :? :? "STRING NOW CONTAINS-";S$
260 ? :? "ITS LENGTH IS-";L
270 END
```

Line 240 gets the new length of S$.

Lines 250-260 print the contents of the string. As you can see, changing the fifth to seventh characters in the string lengthened the string. The new characters replace the old ones.

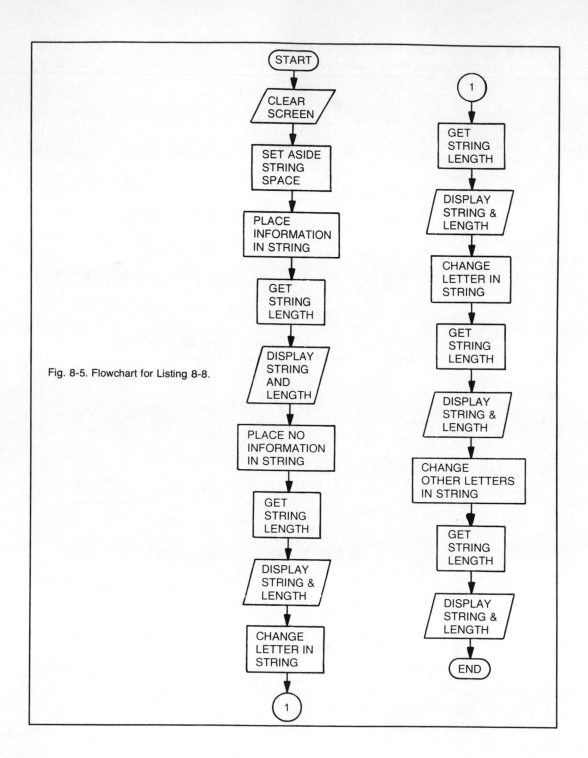

Fig. 8-5. Flowchart for Listing 8-8.

When you work with strings, use the double quotation marks only if you will replace characters in the string sequentially, starting with the first character of the string. If you will be placing characters in the string randomly, and you will be printing the entire string, replace the characters in the string with that number of spaces before setting the string to the double quotation marks (if S$ was dimensioned for eight bytes, we would clear it by making it equal to eight spaces-   S$="   "   .

Listing 8-9 shows you how to move letters around in a string.

Line 35 sets aside 60 bytes for A$ and one byte for B$. B$ will be used as a buffer or temporary storage area.

Line 40 sets the computer to graphics mode 18. This is mode 2 without a text window.

Line 50 sets A$ to the message we want printed.

Line 60 places the cursor at the left-most edge of the screen in row 5.

Line 70 prints the message to the screen. Since we are printing to the graphics window, use   6;   after   PRINT   . Graphics mode 2 only allows 20 characters on the screen in one line. Instruct the computer to   PRINT A$ from location 1 to location 20 inclusive.

Line 80 places the first character of A$ into B$. This is the temporary storage location.

Line 90 moves the remaining characters up one position in A$. Now the first character in A$

Listing 8-9. Ticker-Tape Program

```
10 REM LISTING VIII-9
20 REM TICKER TAPE
30 REM L.M.SCHREIBER FOR TAB BOOKS
35 DIM A$(60),B$(1):REM STORE THE MESSAGE
 HERE
40 GRAPHICS 18:REM GRAPHICS 2 WITHOUT TEX
T WINDOW
50 A$="THE DOW_JONES report at 12 noon is
 at&t up 3 points ........."
60 POSITION 0,5:REM PLACE THE CURSOR AT T
HE CORRECT POSITION
70 ? #6;A$(1,20):REM PRINT THE FIRST 20 L
ETTERS OF THE STRING
80 B$=A$(1,1):REM SAVE THE FIRST LETTER
90 A$(1,59)=A$(2,60):REM MOVE THE LETTERS
 UP ONE POSITION
100 A$(60,60)=B$:REM PUT THE FIRST LETTER
 LAST
110 FOR T=1 TO 50:NEXT T:REM TIMING LOOP.
..CHANGING THE 50 MAKES IT PRINT FASTER O
R SLOWER
120 GOTO 60
```

Listing 8-10. Sales Tax Program

```
10 REM LISTING VIII.10
15 TRAP 300
20 REM SALES TAX
30 REM BY L.M.SCHREIBER FOR TAB BOOKS
40 ? "}clear}"
50 ? "WHAT IS THE SALES TAX FOR YOUR STAT
E  NUMBER ONLY, NO LEADING DECIMALS OR
PERCENT SIGNS";
60 INPUT TAX
70 TAX=TAX/100:REM CHANGE NUMBER ENTERED
TO A DECIMAL
80 ? :? "WHAT IS THE COST OF THE ITEM(S)"
;
90 INPUT COST
100 STAX=INT((COST*TAX+5.0E-03)*100)/100:
REM ROUND TO NEAREST CENT AFTER MULTIPLYI
NG COST BY TAX
110 PRICE=COST+STAX:REM TOTAL PRICE IS TH
E COST PLUS THE TAX
120 ? :? "THE COST OF THE ITEM":? "INCLUD
ING SALES TAX IS-$";PRICE
300 END
```

has been replaced by the second, etc. If we left it this way, the fifty-ninth and sixtieth position would contain the same character.

Line 100 places the character stored in B$ into the last or sixtieth position of A$.

Line 110 is a *timing loop*. This causes the screen display to hesitate, giving us a chance to read the message on the screen. If we want the message to move slower, increase the 50 to a higher number, like 100. To speed the message up, change the 50 to a smaller number.

Line 120 sends the computer back to line 60. The process is repeated again.

The result of this program is a message that moves across the width of the screen. It will continue until the break key or system reset key is pressed.

INPUT

So far our variables and string variables have been assigned a value. However, you don't always know the values ahead of time. Listing 8-10 will compute the amount of sales tax to be added to an item and give the total purchase price. The program stops throughout and waits for you to enter an amount.

Line 50 asks for the sales tax. The program does not want leading decimals or percent signs. If the sales tax in your area is four percent, simply enter   4   and press return.

Line 60 will wait until the number has been entered. The input command tells the computer not to go on until a number is entered. The number has to be stored somewhere. Our program stores the number entered in the tax variable. The input command places ? on the screen to prompt you.

Line 70 divides the amount stored in the tax variable by 100. This converts the number to a decimal.

Line 80 asks you for the cost of the items purchased. The semicolon at the end of the print command holds the cursor on that line.

Line 90 contains an input. The computer will wait until the number has been entered. Since we are asking the user for the cost of the item, we will store the number entered in the cost variable.

Line 100 computes the tax on the item. The state tax is the cost of the item times the tax. Since we are dealing with money, we will want the purchase price rounded to the nearest penny. To do this add .005 to the tax. 5.0E-3 is the way ATARI BASIC represents the number .005. We then multiply the number by 100. This shifts the decimal point two places to the right. If the tax came out to .473, adding .005 would change it to .478. Multiplying it by 100 would move the decimal to the right. The number would be 47.8. If we take the integer of that number—that is, take only the whole number and ignore the decimal—we would have 47. Divide this by 100 and we have the tax of .47.

Line 110 adds the state tax to the cost of the item and stores it in the price variable.

Line 120 skips a line and prints the total cost of the item.

Each time you want the total cost of an item you could run this program.

If you are using the program in a store where items would be entered frequently, you would not want to rerun the program each time. You would not want to have to reenter the sales tax for your state each time, either. Change the program using Listing 8-11.

By adding the position statements to lines 80 and 120, the program does not scroll off the top of the screen. To erase the old answer, add four spaces and four backspaces to these lines. If you find that four spaces aren't enough, add a few more. Just be sure you have one backspace for each space. Tell the backspace in a print statement by pressing the escape key before you press the control key and the back-arrow key. The escape key must be pressed before each control key back-arrow sequence.

Line 130 prompts you with a question.

Line 140 will wait until you enter the answer. This time we are storing the entry in a string.

Line 150 checks the entry for a Y. If the first letter of A$ is a Y, the program will go back to line 80. This eliminates the need to reenter the sales tax for your state. The program would also go back to that line if you answered any word beginning with Y, since the program only checks the first letter of the entry.

Line 160 checks the first letter of ANSWER$ for an N. If it is not an N the program will go back to line 130. If it is an N, the program will end by wishing you a nice day.

When you reuse a string or numeric variable with an input statement, the variable will take on the new entry each time it is used. Pressing only the return key will clear a string variable and produce an error message if the program is looking at a particular location in the string. Clearing the string by pressing the return key sets its length to zero so the computer can't look at any of the characters in the string.

Listing 8-11. Sales Tax, Version 2

```
10 REM LISTING VIII.11
15 TRAP 300
20 REM SALES TAX VERSION 2
30 REM BY L.M.SCHREIBER FOR TAB BOOKS
35 DIM ANSWER$(5)
40 ? "}clear}"
50 ? "WHAT IS THE SALES TAX FOR YOUR STAT
E  NUMBER ONLY, NO LEADING DECIMALS OR
PERCENT SIGNS";
60 INPUT TAX
70 TAX=TAX/100:REM CHANGE NUMBER ENTERED
TO A DECIMAL
80 ? :? "WHAT IS THE COST OF THE ITEM(S)"
;
90 INPUT COST
100 STAX=INT((COST*TAX+5.0E-03)*100)/100:
REM ROUND TO NEAREST CENT AFTER MULTIPLYI
NG COST BY TAX
110 PRICE=COST+STAX:REM TOTAL PRICE IS TH
E COST PLUS THE TAX
120 ? :? "THE COST OF THE ITEM":? "INCLUD
ING SALES TAX IS-$";PRICE
130 ? :? "DO YOU HAVE ANOTHER SALE ";
140 INPUT ANSWER$
150 IF ANSWER$(1,1)="Y" THEN 80
160 IF ANSWER$(1,1)<>"N" THEN 130
170 ? :? "HAVE A NICE DAY"
180 END
300 END
```

Pressing only the return key for a numeric variable will also produce an error message.

Inputs can look cluttered and/or generate the wrong answers if they are not treated properly. In the last program, we added spaces and backspaces to remove the old answer from the screen. You should use this procedure whether you have a string or numeric variable. It will keep your programs clean and eliminate confusion.

Chapter 9

Storing
Related Information

An *array* is a set of locations used for storing and/or retrieving information. With ATARI BASIC, only numbers can be stored in an array. Figure 9-1 shows how an array is arranged. If a teacher wants to record the grades for her class and she knows there are 25 students and there will be eight tests in this quarter, to record this information, she would need an array 25 rows by 8 columns. Each element would hold one grade. The grades of each child would be stored in his or her own row and every test would have its own column.

In another program the array could hold a predetermined value for plotting points on the screen or determining various statistics. An insurance program could have an array that would contain various ages and the rate of insurance for each age group.

DIM

In the last chapter, the dimension statement was used to tell the computer how long a string would be. The dimension statement is also used to tell the computer how large an array you will be using. The format is: DIM A(4,8), B(7)   . The 4 in the A array is the number of rows the program will need and the eight is the number of columns. The next array is a one-dimension array. There are seven rows, but only one column.

Listing 9-1 (see flowchart, Fig. 9-2) is an example of a program using a one-dimension array.

Line 35 dimensions an array to seven elements, one for each day of the week.

Lines 50-70 print a message on the screen.

Line 80 skips a line, then asks the person using the program for the number of miles driven on the first day. The third statement in this line waits for the user to enter a number.

Line 90 places the number entered into the first element of the array.

Line 100 asks the user for the number of miles driven on the second day.

Line 110 stores this number in the second element of the array. Throughout this program, the number of miles driven will be entered into the miles variable.

Lines 120-210 repeat the same procedure: the user is asked for the miles driven on a specific day and the program waits for the number to be entered. The number is then stored in the correct element of the array.

Line 220 clears the total variable.

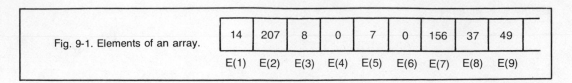

Fig. 9-1. Elements of an array.

14	207	8	0	7	0	156	37	49	
E(1)	E(2)	E(3)	E(4)	E(5)	E(6)	E(7)	E(8)	E(9)	

Lines 230-250 total the number of miles driven for the week. The variable X will increase from one to seven as the program passes through the loop.

Line 260 finds the average number of miles driven each day. By adding .5 to the number of miles driven after the total has been divided by seven, we can round the miles to the next highest integer.

Line 270 clears the screen one more time.

Lines 280-290 print the total number of miles driven on the trip and the average number of miles driven each day.

An array can be erased from a program with a **CLR** (clear) statement. If you try to obtain information from an array after the clear statement has been executed, you will get an error message and the program will stop. If you want to use the array again, you will have to redimension it. The clear statement will also set all the variables to zero and erase all the strings. The strings would have to be redimensioned also, if they were to be reused in the program. You would use a clear statement when you would be redimensioning an array in a program because of new data or information received from the user.

READ/DATA

The read and data commands are used together in a program. They do not have to be next to each other as program statements, but you cannot read something if you do not have data, and conversely, data is useless without a read statement. You can read numbers, characters, or letters. Data can be numbers, characters, or letters (words).

As with input, variables can only read numbers. String variables can read numbers, letters, or characters.

Listing 9-2 demonstrates how the computer can read and use data.

Line 35 dimensions C$ for twelve letters or characters. This is as many letters that this string can store. The computer will store the names of the colors in this string.

Line 50 reads the data from lines 140-150. The first time the computer gets to this line, it will read the first two pieces of information in the data lines. The variable C will hold the number, and C$ will contain the name of the color.

Line 60 sets the color of the screen to the new color. The variable C contains the number of the new color.

Line 70 gets the length of C$.

Line 80 finds the center of the word, and subtracts that amount from the center of the screen.

Line 90 prints the color stored in C$ on the center of the screen.

Line 100 is a timing loop. By making the computer loop in this line 250 times we give the person using the program a chance to see what is printed on the screen.

Line 110 removes the line of print from the screen.

Listing 9-1. Mileage

```
10 REM LISTING IX-1
20 REM MILEAGE
30 REM L.M.SCHREIBER FOR TAB BOOKS
35 DIM M(7):REM WE WILL BE STORING NUMBER
S FOR 7 DAYS
40 ? "}clear}":REM CLEAR SCREEN
50 POSITION 5,2:? "This program will calc
ulate the"
60 POSITION 5,3:? "average number of mile
s driven"
70 POSITION 5,4:? "on a 7 day trip."
80 ? :? " HOW MANY MILES WERE DRIVEN ON T
HE      FIRST DAY";:INPUT MILES
90 M(1)=MILES:REM PLACE THE MILES DRIVEN
IN THE FIRST ELEMENT OF THE ARRAY
100 ? :? " SECOND DAY";:INPUT MILES
110 M(2)=MILES
120 ? :? " THIRD DAY";:INPUT MILES
130 M(3)=MILES
140 ? :? " FOURTH DAY";:INPUT MILES
150 M(4)=MILES
160 ? :? " FIFTH DAY";:INPUT MILE
170 M(5)=MILES
180 ? :? " SIXTH DAY";:INPUT MILES
190 M(6)=MILES
200 ? :? " SEVENTH DAY";:INPUT MILES
210 M(7)=MILES
220 TOTAL=0:REM CLEAR THE VARIABLE
230 FOR X=1 TO 7
240 TOTAL=TOTAL+M(X):REM ADD THE DAYS
250 NEXT X:REM DO IT SEVEN TIMES
260 AVERAGE=INT(TOTAL/7+0.5):REM FIND THE
 AVERAGE-ROUND TO THE NEXT MILE
270 ? "}":REM CLEAR THE SCREEN AGAIN
280 POSITION 5,10:? "THE TOTAL MILES DRIV
EN WERE ";TOTAL
290 POSITION 5,14:? "THE AVERAGE MILES DR
IVEN IN A        DAY WERE ";AVERAGE
300 END
```

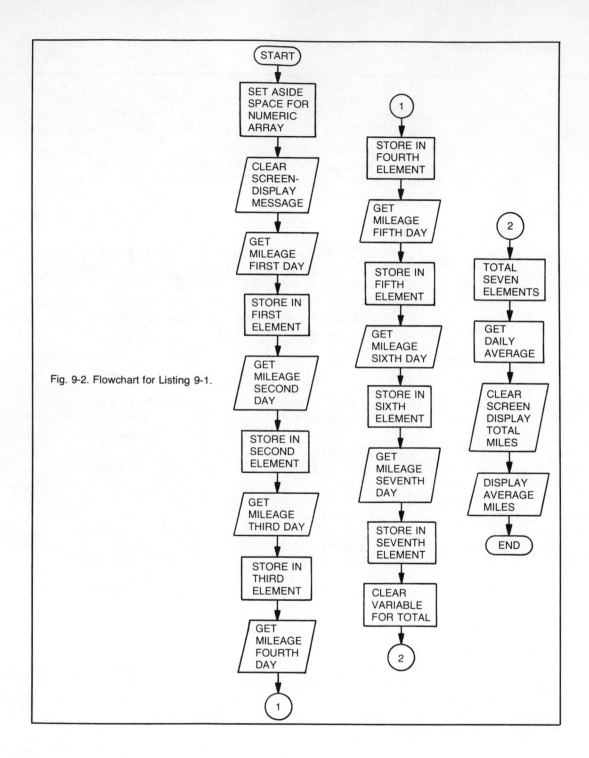

Fig. 9-2. Flowchart for Listing 9-1.

Listing 9-2. Colors

```
10 REM LISTING IX-2
20 REM COLORS
30 REM L.M.SCHREIBER FOR TAB BOOKS
35 DIM C$(12)
40 ? "}clear}":POKE 752,1:REM CLEAR SCREE
N-REMOVE CURSOR
50 READ C,C$:REM GET THE COLOR OF THE SCR
EEN AND THE COLOR
60 SETCOLOR 2,C,5:REM CHANGE THE COLOR OF
 THE SCREEN
70 L=LEN(C$):REM GET THE LENGTH OF THE CO
LOR
80 P=20-L/2:REM GET THE CENTER OF THE WOR
D
90 POSITION P,20:? C$
100 FOR X=1 TO 250:NEXT X:REM LEAVE IT ON
 THE SCREEN FOR A WHILE
110 POSITION 0,20:? "":REM REMOVE THE LI
NE OF PRINT-SHIFT DELETE
120 IF C=15 THEN RESTORE :REM START ALL O
VER
130 GOTO 50
140 DATA 0,GRAY,1,GOLD,2,ORANGE,3,RED,4,P
INK,6,PURPLE,7,BLUE,8,BLUE AGAIN,9,LIGHT
BLUE
150 DATA 10,TURQUOISE,11,BLUE-GREEN,12,GR
EEN,13,YELLOW-GREEN,14,ORANGE,15,LIGHT OR
ANGE
160 END
```

Line 120 checks the value stored in the variable C. When the computer has read the last number in the data lines, the value of C will be 15. When this happens, we want the computer to start reading the data from line 140 again. By having the restore statement in that line, the computer will set its pointer back to the first line containing data. If we did not check the value of C but simply had a restore command on that line, the computer would reset its pointer every time it came to this line and the program would only display the color gray.

Line 130 sends the computer back to line 50. This program will not end on its own. The only way to end it is by pressing the break or system reset key.

Lines 140-150 contain the data this program uses. The computer starts with line 140 and reads the information on that line. It will then go on to the next data line and continue to read the information on that line. If there were program statements between the lines of data, the computer would skip those lines, and look for the lines of data. If you tell the computer to read and there is no more data in the program, you will get an error message. If you have a remark on a line where there is data, and the program has to read past the last piece of information on that line, you will get an error message.

When you mix numbers with letters or characters, as this program has done, be sure that all the data is in the correct order. The C$ can read a number, but C cannot read a letter or character.

The information in the data line is read sequentially. The program will always start with the color gray and end with orange.

RESTORE

In the preceeding program we used the restore command to tell the computer to start again with the first piece of information. In this version of BASIC, you can also use the restore command to tell the computer which line you want it to start with by placing a number or a variable after the restore command.

CLEARING AN ARRAY

ATARI BASIC does not clear the values from an array when you run a program. If it did, the merge and chain features would be useless. A program can load and run a second program segment and use the values calculated in the first part of the program. The drawback is that each array element will have some information in it, much like the string arrays. If your program will be accessing information from an element of an array that may or may not have had information stored in it, you could *crash* (cause it to stop abruptly) your program. It is best to clear that array by setting each element of it to zero before you use it. Listing 9-3 shows you what can be stored in an array before you clear it.

Line 40 dimensions the array A to 12 elements. There are three rows and four columns.

Line 60 prints the contents of one element of the array. We chose the second row and the fourth column. You can change these to any you want within this array. If you have just turned the system on, or if the last program you ran was shorter than this program, no strange numbers will appear on the screen.

Lines 70-110 clear the elements of the array. The X variable will begin with one and increment to two, then three. The Y variable will begin with one and increment by one until it reaches four. Because of the way that this loop is set up, Y will do this three times. Line 90 sets the A element to 0. The location will be determined by the values of X and Y.

Lines 100-110 continue this loop until all the locations or elements of the array have been set to 0.

Line 120 prints the contents of the same location on the screen, leaving nothing in that element.

When you enter a new program the computer will still contain remnants of the old program. Using the clear command and redimensioning an array will not remove the old information from the computer's memory.

Listing 9-3. Clearing an Array

```
10 REM LISTING IX-3
20 REM CLEAR AN ARRAY
30 REM BY L.M.SCHREIBER FOR TAB BOOKS
40 DIM A(3,4):REM DIMENSION AN ARRAY
50 ? "}clear}"
60 POSITION 3,5:? "THE CHOSEN ELEMENT CON
TAINS ";A(2,4):REM SHOW WHAT IS IN THAT E
LEMENT
70 FOR X=1 TO 3:REM THERE ARE 3 ROWS
80 FOR Y=1 TO 4:REM THERE ARE 4 COLUMNS
90 A(X,Y)=0:REM CLEAR THAT ELEMENT
100 NEXT Y:REM DO ALL 4 COLUMNS
110 NEXT X:REM DO ALL 3 ROWS
120 POSITION 3,7:? "NOW IT HOLDS ";A(2,4)
:REM SHOW THAT IT IS CLEARED
130 END
```

USING STRINGS

Strings cannot be dimensioned into two-dimensional arrays. This can pose a problem if you want a list of words to choose from, or if you want to store words for later use. In the first example, you can use data lines to store the words. In Listing 9-4 we will use data lines as a two-dimensional array. The first word in each data line is a color written in English, the second word is its Spanish translation. Both words are read into two different strings. One string is printed on the screen. The program checks your answer with its answer in the other string.

Line 40 dimensions three different strings. E\$ will contain the English word, S\$ will contain the Spanish word and A\$ will get the answer from the user.

Line 55 reads the English word and the Spanish word from the first data line—line 150.

Lines 60-70 print the color on the screen in English.

Lines 80-90 prompt the user to enter the Spanish word.

Line 90 contains eight spaces and eight backspaces. This will remove the previous answer from the screen.

Line 100 waits for the person using the program to enter a word.

Line 110 compares the entered word with the word the program has in S\$. If the two springs are not the same, the computer will go back to line 90, erase the answer, and wait for the user to enter another word.

Line 120 checks E\$ for the word yellow. If E\$ contains that word, the program will end.

Line 130 will send the computer to line 50 where the screen will clear and the routine will be repeated.

In another program, you may want the student or teacher to enter spelling words. Since it would be cumbersome to have to keep changing data lines, you would want the person using the program to be able to enter the words directly. Listing 9-5 (see flowchart, Fig. 9-3) uses a two-dimensional array to keep track of the start and end locations of the words in the string. As the words are entered, they are added to the string.

Line 40 dimensions two strings and one array. WORD$ will be used to store all the words that will be entered. I$ is the temporary storage string for each word, and W is the array that will store the beginning and ending location of each word in the string WORD$.

Line 50 clears the screen and the variables LL and FL. LL will represent the Last Letter location, and FL will be the location of the First Letter of the word being placed in the string.

Lines 60-70 print the instructions on the screen. In this program, we give the user two ways to end the routine by entering twenty words into the program, or entering the code XXX to indicate you are done.

Lines 80-170 contain the routine for entering the new words. Line 80 uses the variable X to indicate which word is being entered. X will be equal to 1, but will not accept more than twenty words. It also prompts the person using the program to enter a word.

Line 90 prints the number of the word being entered, performs fifteen spaces and fifteen backspaces, and then waits for a word to be entered. The word entered will be stored in I$.

Listing 9-4. Spanish/English Color Test.

```
10 REM LISTING IX-4
20 REM SPANISH COLORS
30 REM BY L.M.SCHREIBER FOR TAB BOOKS
40 DIM E$(10),S$(10),A$(10)
50 ? "}clear}"
55 READ E$,S$:REM READ THE WORDS IN THE S
AME ORDER AS THE DATA LINES
60 POSITION 3,8:? "ENGLISH WORD IS "
70 POSITION 5,10:? E$
80 POSITION 23,8:? "SPANISH WORD IS"
90 POSITION 25,10:? "        ";:R
EM 8 SPACES - 8 BACKSPACES
100 INPUT A$
110 IF A$<>S$ THEN 90:REM TRY AGAIN IF WR
ONG
120 IF E$="YELLOW" THEN END :REM LESSON C
OMPLETE
130 GOTO 50:REM YOU GOT IT RIGHT
140 END
150 DATA RED,ROJO
160 DATA BLUE,AZUR
170 DATA GREEN,VERDE
180 DATA BLACK,NEGRO
190 DATA WHITE,BLANCO
200 DATA YELLOW,AMARILLO
```

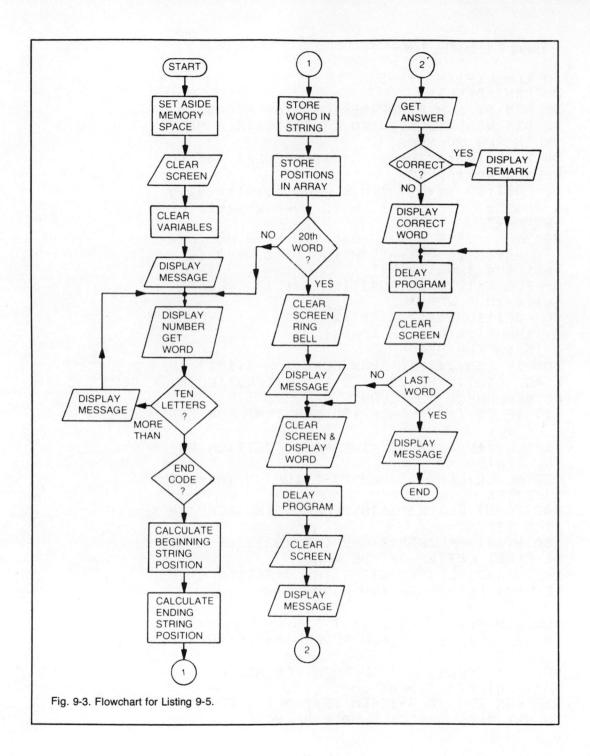

Fig. 9-3. Flowchart for Listing 9-5.

Listing 9-5. Spelling Test

```
10 REM LISTING IX-5
20 REM SPELLING
30 REM BY L.M.SCHREIBER FOR TAB BOOKS
40 DIM WORD$(205),W(20,2),I$(15):REM MAKE
 ROOM FOR 20 WORDS
50 ? "}clear}":LL=0:FL=0:REM CLEAR THE SC
REEN & VARIABLES
60 POSITION 5,5:? "This program will allo
w you to     enter up to twenty spelling
 words."
70 ? "   TYPE - xxx when you have no more
    words to enter and the last word is
 not the twentieth."
80 FOR X=1 TO 20:POSITION 5,15:? "PLEASE
ENTER YOUR WORD"
90 POSITION 5,17:? "#";X;"
";:INPUT I$:REM 15 SPACES
& 15 BACKSPACES
100 IF LEN(I$)>10 THEN POSITION 5,19:? "P
LEASE LIMIT THE WORD TO 10 LETTERS":GOTO
80:REM CHECK THE LENGTH OF WORD
110 IF I$="XXX" THEN 180:REM TEST FOR END

120 FL=1+LL:REM GET THE NEXT POSITION ON
THE STRING
130 LL=LL+LEN(I$):REM POSITION ON THE LAS
T LETTER
140 WORD$(FL,LL)=I$:REM PLACE THE WORD IN
 THE STRING
150 W(X,1)=FL:REM STORE THE POSITION OF T
HE FIRST LETTER OF THE WORD
160 W(X,2)=LL:REM STORE THE POSITION OF T
HE LAST LETTER OF THE WORD
170 NEXT X
180 REM NOW FOR THE TEST
190 ? "}}}":REM CLEAR SCREEN AND RING BEL
L TWICE
200 ? "   PRESS RETURN WHEN YOU ARE READY
TO    START";:INPUT I$
210 FOR Z=1 TO X-1:REM SUBTRACT 1 FROM X
TO GET THE CORRECT NUMBER OF WORDS ENTERE
D
```

```
220 POSITION 5,10:? "}ESCAPE 2}";WORD$(W(
Z,1),W(Z,2));
230 FOR T=1 TO 200:NEXT T:REM TIMING LOOP
 FOR A CHANCE TO READ WORD
240 ? "}":REM REMOVE THE WORD
250 POSITION 5,10:? "ENTER THE WORD":POSI
TION 5,12
260 INPUT I$:POSITION 5,14
270 IF I$=WORD$(W(Z,1),W(Z,2)) THEN ? "VE
RY GOOD!!!!!":GOTO 300
280 ? "WRONG - - THE WORD WAS"
290 ? WORD$(W(Z,1),W(Z,2))
300 FOR T=1 TO 200:NEXT T:REM ANOTHER TIM
ING LOOP
310 ? "}":NEXT Z
320 POSITION 4,12:? "YOU HAVE FINISHED TH
IS LESSON"
330 END
```

Line 100 tests the length of I$. If the word entered contains more than ten letters, the computer will be instructed to print a message to the user and go back to line 90.

Line 110 tests the word entered for the ending code. If the contents of I$ were equal to XXX, then the computer would go to the next part of the program. The computer is directed to line 190. The line above it is the remark line for the routine. Do not send a program to a remark line.

Line 120 finds the position of the first letter of the word in WORD$. If is the first word being entered, the variable LL would be equal to zero, and adding one to it would make the variable FL equal to one, which is the first location in WORD$. If the first word has already been entered, LL would contain the position of the last letter in the previous word in WORD$. Adding one to it would point to the location or position immediately following that word.

Line 130 makes the variable LL equal to the last position in WORD$ that the entered word will occupy. We know how long the word entered is; we add its length to the last location the previously entered word occupied and we know where this word will end.

Line 140 places the entered word into WORD$ using the starting and ending locations it calculated in the two previous lines.

Line 150 places the location of the first letter of the word into one element of the array. The variable X is set to the word number that has been entered. It will store the location of the letter in the corresponding element of the array.

Line 160 places the ending location of the word entered into the other element of the array. This location will also correspond with the number for the word entered.

Line 170 tells the computer to repeat this routine until the variable X is greater than 20.

Line 190 clears the screen and rings the bell on the computer twice to attract your attention to the screen.

Line 200 prints the message on the screen and waits until the return key has been pressed. I$ will not be checked after this input, so you do not have to enter anything.

Line 210 begins the test routine. It subtracts one from X to get the number of words that have been entered. If the program came to this line through line 170, X would be equal to 21. If the computer came to this line because the user entered XXX , X will be equal to one more than the number of words entered. In either case, we must subtract one to arrive at the actual number of words entered.

Line 220 rings the bell on the computer and prints the word in the fifth column of the tenth row. The first time the computer executes this routine, the Z variable will be set to one. The computer will look at the W array and take the values placed in the first two parts of the array. These values tell the computer where the word begins and ends. The computer can now print the word from WORD$ using these values.

Line 230 is a timing loop to give the person using the program a chance to view the word. If the word is not on the screen long enough, change 200 to a higher number. Changing 200 to a smaller number will cause the word to flash on the screen.

Line 240 clears the screen, removing the word.

Line 250 prompts the user to enter the word that was just flashed on the screen.

Line 260 waits for a word to be entered. The second part of this statement moves the cursor to a predetermined location on the screen. The program is ready for the next print command. This eliminates the need for two position commands, one for the correct answer and one for the wrong answer.

Line 270 checks the word the user has entered. If the word was spelled correctly, the computer will print VERY GOOD on the screen and go on to line 300.

Line 280 prints the response for an incorrect entry.

Line 290 prints the correct spelling of the word on the screen.

Line 300 is another timing loop.

Line 310 clears the screen for the next entry. The program will continue until all the words entered have been shown.

Line 320 tells the user that the program is over.

The technique used in this program—placing all the words continuously in one string—is called *packing* a string. You will have to decide which method, fielding or packing, is best suited for your programs.

Chapter 10

Repeating Part of the Program

You will often find parts of your program repeating themselves. To type the same instructions over and over again is tiring for you and a waste of memory for the computer. Bytes disappear very quickly even in the most memory-efficient programs.

One way to conserve memory is to place an instruction or set of instructions the computer will be repeating in a *loop*. A loop tells the computer to return to a certain set of instructions any number of times. In the past few chapters, you have used loops for timing routines and input, keeping the size of the programs down considerably.

USES FOR LOOPS

The computer can process information with remarkable speed. If the computer is also asked to print information on the screen as it processes it, chances are the computer's speed will be too fast for you to read the information. Sometimes listing a program is too fast.

If you are printing instructions for the user on the screen, or presenting a problem you want the user to read before it is removed, you will need to slow the computer down. A *timing loop* was used for this purpose in the Ticker Tape program and the Spelling program. Timing loops tell the computer to stay at a particular place in the program and do nothing but count from one number to another. The numbers are not displayed on the screen but serve to slow the printing process down to allow the user to read information on the screen.

Another loop was used in the Spelling program when the user was asked to enter the words. Without it, the program would have to contain twenty input commands, twenty prompt lines, and twenty decision lines, using memory needlessly. A series of inputs can usually be obtained most efficiently by using a loop.

Beware of looping to infinity! When you construct a loop you must design an exit from the loop, or you may wait forever for the computer to complete a calculation, read information, or time an activity, only to discover (after pressing the break key, of course) that the computer hasn't passed line 30! A loop with no exit is called an *endless loop*; they are useful in demonstration programs, where you want the same program to be repeated all day, or at the end of a program you want to end without the   READY   prompt appearing on the screen. The only way to exit an endless loop is by pressing the break key or system reset button.

GOTO

The GOTO command can be used in a loop. The number following the GOTO command is the line number the computer will process next. The line number can be an actual number, a variable, or an arithmetic equation.

30   GOTO 100

Following this command, the computer would execute program lines up to 30, then skip all the lines between 30 and 100. Line 100 is the next line the computer would execute, and unless it was directed back to the lines it skipped, the computer would never execute those lines.

30   GOTO QUESTION

QUESTION   is a variable. The computer will branch to the line the variable is equal to. If Question has not been set to a value it would be equal to zero. Unless you have a line 0, you will get an error message.

30   GOTO ANSWER+55

This situation arises when you want the program to branch to a routine dependent on the answer entered, or on some other calculation. The routines the computer could branch to start with line 55. The value in the answer variable will be added to 55 and the program will branch to the line whose sum is   ANSWER+55   . Again, if that line does not exist, you will receive an error message. Using this variation of a GOTO requires some planning and forethought.

Listing 10-1 (see flowchart Fig. 10-1) demonstrates the three ways the GOTO   command can be used:

Line 40 sets the Question variable to 50.

Lines 45-47 dimension the strings used in this program. Each string contains the maximum number of bytes it will need.

Line 48 sets up an array with the number of days each month can contain. The data for this array is the last line of the program.

Line 50 begins the program. After the screen is cleared, the program asks for the month (by number) you were born in.

Line 55 waits for you to enter this number. It will be stored in the month variable.

Lines 60-65 check this variable. If you entered a number greater than 12, or less than one the computer will be sent back to line 50.

Line 70 asks for your date of birth.

Lines 75-80 check the date entered for a valid input. If the date is invalid the computer will go back to line 70. The Month variable contains the number of the month entered, array D contains the correct number of days for each month in the correct order.

Line 85 checks the number stored in the Date variable one more time. If the date entered is greater than 20, the program will add one to the Month variable because this user was born under the next sign.

Listing 10-1. Zodiac Program

```
10 REM LISTING X-1
20 REM ZODIAC
30 REM BY L.M.SCHREIBER FOR TAB BOOKS
40 QUESTION=50:REM LINE THAT PROGRAM BEGI
NS
42 SIGN=1500:REM LINE THAT PRINTS INFORMA
TION ON THE SIGN
45 DIM SIGN$(11),SYMBOL$(9),CNTRL$(25),PL
ANET$(7),COLOUR$(14),STONE$(10)
47 DIM ELEMENT$(5),A$(1),D(12)
48 FOR X=1 TO 12:READ DATE:D(X)=DATE:NEXT
 X
50 ? "}clear}":POSITION 5,10:? "ENTER THE
  NUMBER OF THE MONTH THAN    YOU WERE BOR
N IN      ";:REM GET MONTH
55 INPUT MONTH:REM STORE IT IN MONTH
60 IF MONTH>12 THEN GOTO QUESTION:REM CHE
CK FOR A CORRECT NUMBER
65 IF MONTH<1 THEN GOTO QUESTION
70 POSITION 5,15:? "ENTER THE DATE OF YOU
R BIRTH    ";:INPUT DATE
75 IF DATE<1 THEN 70:REM CHECK FOR A GOOD
 DATE
80 IF DATE>D(MONTH) THEN 70
85 IF DATE>20 THEN MONTH=MONTH+1:REM BORN
 UNDER NEXT SIGN
90 IF MONTH=13 THEN MONTH=1:REM WRAP AROU
ND THE CALENDER
95 GOTO MONTH*100:REM CALCULATE THE LINE
FOR THE SIGN
100 SIGN$="CAPRICORN":SYMBOL$="GOAT"
110 CNTRL$="KNEES"
120 PLANET$="SATURN":STONE$="RUBY"
130 COLOUR$="RED-BLUE-GREEN"
140 ELEMENT$="EARTH"
150 GOTO SIGN
200 SIGN$="AQUARIUS":SYMBOL$="WATER BOY"
210 CNTRL$="LEGS"
220 PLANET$="URANUS":STONE$="GARNET"
230 COLOUR$="DARK RED"
240 ELEMENT$="AIR"
```

Listing 10-1. Zodiac Program. (Continued from page 77.)

```
250 GOTO SIGN
300 SIGN$="PISCES":SYMBOL$="FISH"
310 CNTRL$="FEET"
320 PLANET$="NEPTUNE":STONE$="AMETHYST"
330 COLOUR$="PURPLE"
340 ELEMENT$="WATER"
350 GOTO SIGN
400 SIGN$="ARIES":SYMBOL$="RAM"
410 CNTRL$="HEAD & FACE"
420 PLANET$="MARS":STONE$="AQUAMARINE"
430 COLOUR$="RED-GREEN"
440 ELEMENT$="FIRE"
450 GOTO SIGN
500 SIGN$="TAURUS":SYMBOL$="BULL"
510 CNTRL$="THROAT & NECK"
520 PLANET$="VENUS":STONE$="SAPPHIRE"
530 COLOUR$="BLUE"
540 ELEMENT$="EARTH"
550 GOTO SIGN
600 SIGN$="GEMINI":SYMBOL$="TWINS"
610 CNTRL$="SHOULDERS, LUNGS &  ARMS"
620 PLANET$="MERCURY":STONE$="EMERALD"
630 COLOUR$="GREEN"
640 ELEMENT$="AIR"
650 GOTO SIGN
700 SIGN$="CANCER":SYMBOL$="CRAB"
710 CNTRL$="STOMACH"
720 PLANET$="MOON":STONE$="AGATE"
730 COLOUR$="BLENDS"
740 ELEMENT$="WATER"
750 GOTO SIGN
800 SIGN$="LEO":SYMBOL$="LION"
810 CNTRL$="HEART"
820 PLANET$="SUN":STONE$="TURQUOISE"
830 COLOUR$="BLUE-RED"
840 ELEMENT$="FIRE"
850 GOTO SIGN
900 SIGN$="VIRGO":SYMBOL$="VIRGIN"
910 CNTRL$="INTESTINES"
920 PLANET$="MERCURY":STONE$="PERIDOT"
```

```
930 COLOUR$="RED-BROWN"
940 ELEMENT$="EARTH"
950 GOTO SIGN
1000 SIGN$="LIBRS":SYMBOL$="SCALES"
1010 CNTRL$="LOINS"
1020 PLANET$="VENUS":STONE$="CHRYSOLITE"
1030 COLOUR$="GREEN-BLUE"
1040 ELEMENT$="AIR"
1050 GOTO SIGN
1100 SIGN$="SCORPIO":SYMBOL$="SCORPION"
1110 CNTRL$="GENERATIVE ORGANS"
1120 PLANET$="MARS":STONE$="BERYL"
1130 COLOUR$="BLENDS"
1140 ELEMENT$="WATER"
1150 GOTO SIGN
1200 SIGN$="SAGITTARIUS":SYMBOL$="ARCHER"

1210 CNTRL$="THIGHS"
1220 PLANET$="JUPITER":STONE$="TOPAZ"
1230 COLOUR$="GOLD"
1240 ELEMENT$="FIRE"
1500 ? "}"
1510 POSITION 2,2:? "YOUR SIGN IS - ";SIG
N$
1520 POSITION 2,4:? "IT IS SYMBOLIZED IN
THE - ";SYMBOL$
1530 POSITION 2,6:? "TAKE CARE OF YOUR ";
CNTRL$
1540 POSITION 2,8:? "YOU ARE RULED BY ";P
LANET$
1550 POSITION 2,10:? "YOU SHOULD WEAR CLO
THES THAT ARE ":? COLOUR$
1560 POSITION 2,12:? "AND GEMS OF ";STONE
$
1570 POSITION 2,14:? "YOUR ELEMENT IS ";E
LEMENT$
1600 POSITION 2,17:? "PRESS RETURN TO CON
TINUE ";:INPUT A$
1610 GOTO QUESTION
1700 DATA 31,29,31,30,31,30,31,31,30,31,3
0,31
```

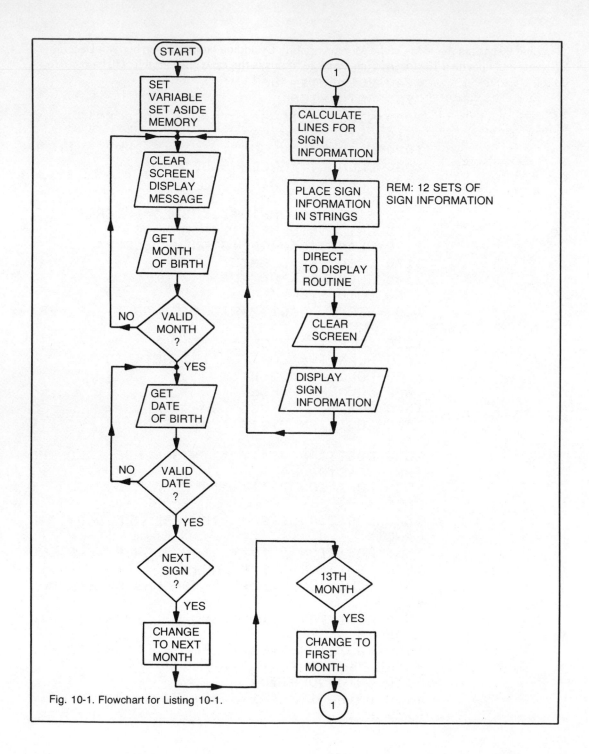

Fig. 10-1. Flowchart for Listing 10-1.

Line 90 checks the value of the Month variable. By adding one, a person born on December 27 would end up with a 13 stored in this variable. If this is the case, the variable will be reset to a one, for January. This is called a *wrap-around routine*.

Line 95 calculates the lines containing information for a person born under this sign. Each sign starts at a line number that is a multiple of 100. By multiplying the number stored in the Month variable by 100, the program can direct the computer to the correct set of lines.

Lines 100-150 contain information for the sign Capricorn. Pertinent information for this sign are stored in the strings dimensioned at the beginning of this program. Each string name refers to the information stored in it. We used the English spelling of colour because COLOR is a BASIC command. When all the strings have been set, the program directs the computer to line 1500.

All twelve sets of information are essentially the same. The string variables will contain information about that sign when the computer proceeds to line 1500.

Line 1500 clears the screen.

Lines 1510-1600 print the information stored in the strings:

SIGN$ is the sign of Zodiac.

SYMBOL$ is the symbol usually designating that sign.

CNTRL$ is the area of the body the sign is said to control.

PLANET$ is the planet that rules the sign.

COLOUR$ is the colors best suited for a person born under this sign.

STONE$ is the gem or stone for the sign.

ELEMENT$ is the element of nature ruling the sign.

Line 1600 waits for you to press the Return key. A timing loop here could be too long or too short, since the user may want to write down the information on the screen. An Input command leaves the information on the screen for any length of time.

Line 1610 sends the computer back to line 50 since that is the value stored in this variable.

FOR . . . NEXT LOOPS

A *For . . . Next loop* repeats a set of lines a given number of times.

```
20      FOR T=1 TO 100:NEXT T
```

This loop would start setting T to 1. The second command is NEXT T . The program tells the computer to start with the number one, then add one to the value of T and return to the FOR statement. It continues to go back and forth between For and Next until T is equal to 100. When T equals 101, it has exceeded the second value and goes on to the next program line.

If we place FOR T=1 TO 100 on one line and NEXT T on another line, the program would execute any and all lines between the For and the Next.

In the above example, we started with T equal to one and ended when it was equal to 100. Any variable and any starting and ending numbers can be used.

One common error when using the For . . . Next loop is to set a variable to 0 within the loop instead of before the computer starts the loop. An example of this would be a program where you give the user three tries to answer a problem. The variable that counts the number of wrong answers must be cleared before each question. If this variable is cleared within the loop, the program will never know when the three tries are up. Listing 10-2A demonstrates the use of For . . . Next loops (see Flowchart, Fig. 10-2).

Line 50 dimensions the strings used in this routine.

Line 60 prints the question on the screen.

Line 70 places the answer in ANSWER$.

Line 80 begins the For . . . Next loop. X will be equal to one, then two, then three, for the tries the user is given.

Line 90 clears the W variable. This variable tells the user how many tries it took to get the right answer.

Line 100 adds one to the number of tries. The program waits here for an input.

Line 120 checks the answer entered against the correct answer. If they do not match, the computer will print a message.

Line 110 checks the answer again. This time if the answer entered matches the answer stored in ANSWER$, the program will direct the computer to line 150.

Line 130 sends the computer back to complete the For . . . Next loop. After the loop has been completed, the computer will print the answer on the screen.

Line 140 routes the computer around line 150 when the user does not answer the question correctly, and the program would continue with line 160.

Line 160 ends the program.

Listing 10-2B is essentially the same as Listing 10-2A except in lines 80 and 90 (see flowchart 10-3). In Listing 10-2A, the For . . . Next loop began with line 80. Line 90 set the W variable to zero. Each time the loop was executed, this variable was reset to zero. If the user answered the problem correctly on the first or the third try, the results were the same:

VERY GOOD
YOU GOT IT IN 1 TRIES

The second listing changes these two lines. W is set to zero only once; it correctly counts the number of tries the user needed to answer the question correctly.

For . . . Next loops can also be used within each other. This is called *nesting*. An example of nesting loops is the Spelling program (Listing 9-5). The timing loop was nested within the loop that showed the word to be spelled. Listing 9-2B also nested one loop within the other when the array was cleared. Figure 10-1 shows the proper structure of nesting loops. Note that the inner loop is completed before the outer loop can go on to the next value. The inner loop is also completed each time the outer loop is executed. If you do not nest the loops properly, you can cause the program to *crash*, or give erroneous answers.

STEPPING

A For . . . Next loop does not have to add one to the variable every time it completes the loop. You can have the variable incremented by any amount by adding   STEP   to the command.

40   FOR Z=10 TO 100 STEP 5

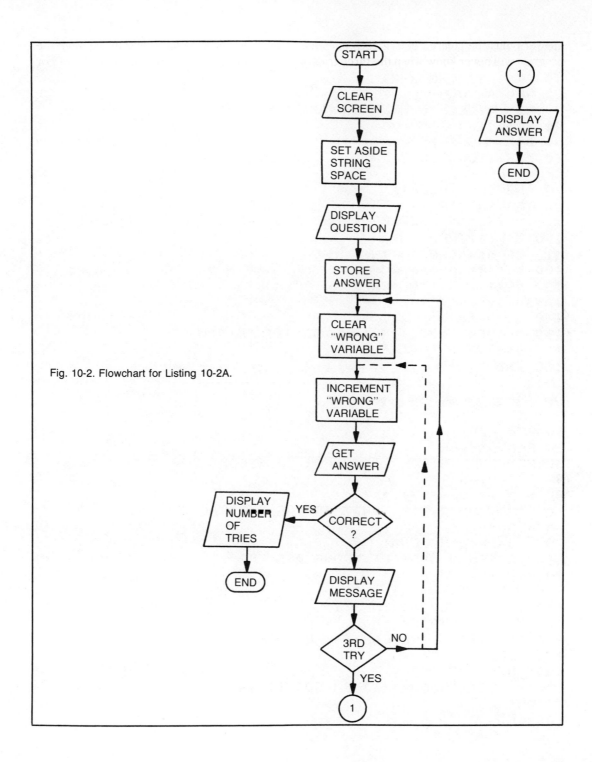

Fig. 10-2. Flowchart for Listing 10-2A.

83

Listing 10-2A. Answer

```
10 REM LISTING X-2A
20 REM ANSWER
30 REM BY L.M.SCHREIBER FOR TAB BOOKS
40 ? "}clear}"
50 DIM ANSWER$(7),A$(7)
60 POSITION 2,5:? "WHAT IS THE CAPITAL OF
 MONTANA"
70 ANSWER$="HELENA"
80 FOR X=1 TO 3
90 W=0:REM NUMBER OF WRONG ANSWERS
100 W=W+1:INPUT A$
110 IF A$=ANSWER$ THEN 150
120 ? "TRY AGAIN"
130 NEXT X:? "THE CAPITAL OF MONTANA IS "
;ANSWER$
140 GOTO 160
150 ? "VERY GOOD":? "YOU GOT IT IN ";W;"
TRIES"
160 END
```

Listing 10-2B. Answer, Version 2

```
10 REM LISTING X-2B
20 REM ANSWER
30 REM BY L.M.SCHREIBER FOR TAB BOOKS
40 ? "}clear}"
50 DIM ANSWER$(7),A$(7)
60 POSITION 2,5:? "WHAT IS THE CAPITAL O
 MONTANA"
70 ANSWER$="HELENA"
80 W=0:REM NUMBER OF WRONG ANSWERS
90 FOR X=1 TO 3
100 W=W+1:INPUT A$
110 IF A$=ANSWER$ THEN 150
120 ? "TRY AGAIN"
130 NEXT X:? "THE CAPITAL OF MONTANA IS
;ANSWER$
140 GOTO 160
150 ? "VERY GOOD":? "YOU GOT IT IN ";W;"
TRIES"
160 END
```

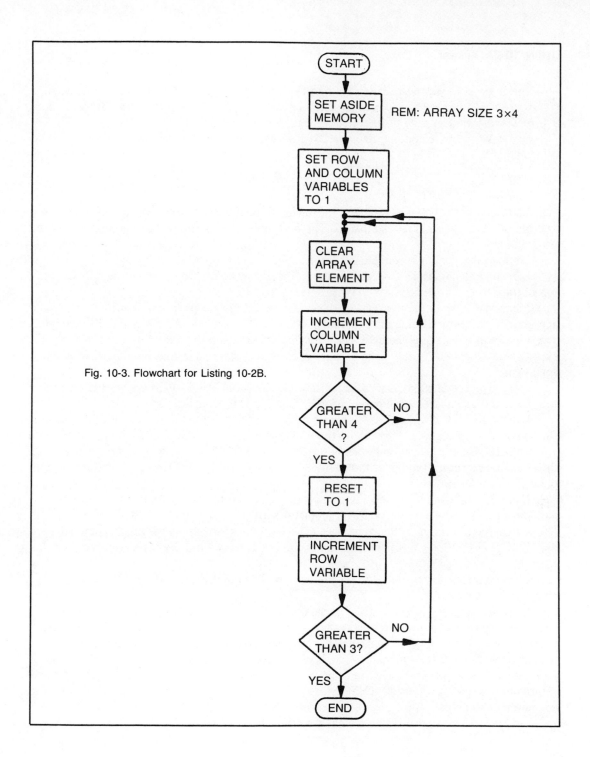

Fig. 10-3. Flowchart for Listing 10-2B.

```
50        . . .
60        NEXT Z
```

The Z variable will be equal to 10 the first time the computer executes line 40. When it comes to line 60, five will be added to the variable, making it 15. The program will continue adding five to Z every time it gets to line 60 until Z is greater than 100.

If you want the computer to count backwards, use a negative number after the Step command.

$$50 \text{ FOR } G = \text{TO } 50 \text{ STEP } -5$$

The computer will make Q equal to 150 the first time it executes the line. The second time Q will be 145, etc. When Q is less than 50, the computer will continue with the next line of the program.

Listing 10-3 contains examples of For . . . Next loops.

Line 40 dimensions T$ to five characters. This string holds the target that will fly over the top of the screen.

Lines 41-45 print the directions on the screen. Once again, the directions will be left on the screen until the person using the program presses the Return key. At this point, T$ is empty.

Line 50 places some characters in T$. This combination of characters (an asterick, two slashes and a hyphen) is the target. The screen is also cleared in this line and the cursor is removed.

Line 55 places hits and misses on the screen. The variables H and M are set to zero at this time. When these scores have been updated, this line will print the new score.

Line 60 sets the Y variable to 19. This is the column number on the screen for the position of the rifle. The program then tells the computer to   GOSUB   line 600. A   GOSUB   command is similar to a   GOTO   , but the program will tell the computer to return to this location automatically with a   GOSUB   (discussed in detail in Chapter 12).

Lines 70-100 contain nested For . . . Next loops. The first loop begins with line 70. The variable P1 will be the position of the target on the screen. We will move the target from right to left. The screen location on the right is 34. The columns decrease as we move to the left. We use   STEP -1 to decrease the value of P1 every time the computer executes this loop.

Line 80 prints the target, T$, on the screen. The column changes but the row number remains the same.

Line 90 is a timing loop that also checks the keyboard to see if a key has been pressed. The computer will remain at line 90 counting from 1 to 25. Every time it adds one to TL, it will check location 764 in its memory to see if a key has been pressed. The variable K will store the number the computer has in that memory location. It will then check the variable K against 255. If K is not 255, a key has been pressed, and the computer is directed to the subroutine at line 500. After it returns to this line, it will   GOTO   line 100. If a key has been pressed, we want the computer to exit this For . . . Next loop.

Line 95 continues the For . . . Next loop the computer began in line 90.

Listing 10-3. Target

```
10 REM LISTING X-3
20 REM TARGET
30 REM BY L.M.SCHREIBER FOR TAB BOOKS
40 DIM T$(5)
41 ? "}":POSITION 7,7:? "TARGET SHOOT is
a rifle game.        PRESS the RIGHT ARROW
to move the      rifle to the";
42 ? " right. PRESS the LEFT      ARROW to
move the rifle to the left. PRESS the SPA
CE BAR (      ) to shoot."
43 POSITION 16,13:? "GOOD LUCK!!"
45 POSITION 2,16:? "PRESS RETURN TO CONTI
NUE";:INPUT T$
50 T$="*//- ":? "}clear}":POKE 752,1
55 POSITION 2,0:? "HITS ";H:POSITION 25,0
:? "MISSED ";M
60 Y=19:GOSUB 600
70 FOR P1=34 TO 0 STEP -1:REM TARGET WILL
 MOVE FROM RIGHT TO LEFT
80 POSITION P1,5:? T$;:REM DRAW THE TARGE
T ON THE SCREEN
90 FOR TL=1 TO 25:K=PEEK(764):IF K<>255 T
HEN GOSUB 500:GOTO 100:REM CHECK IF THE P
LAYER PRESSED A KEY
95 NEXT TL
100 NEXT P1
110 GOTO 50
500 POKE 764,255:IF K=6 OR K=7 THEN 503
501 IF K=33 THEN 700
502 RETURN
503 IF Y<3 AND K=6 THEN RETURN
504 IF Y>34 AND K=7 THEN RETURN
505 FOR P=20 TO 23:POSITION Y,P:? "   ";:
NEXT P:REM CLEAR OLD GUN
510 IF K=6 THEN Y=Y-1:GOTO 550
520 Y=Y+1
550 IF Y<2 OR Y>35 THEN RETURN
600 FOR P=20 TO 23:POSITION Y,P:? "}B} }V
}";:NEXT P:RETURN :REM 'Y' WILL NOT CHANG
E PLACE IT OUTSIDE THE LOOP
700 POP :REM THIS ROUTINE WILL NOT RETURN
```

Listing 10-3. Target. (Continued from page 87.)

```
705 FOR B=22 TO 5 STEP -1:REM COUNT BACKW
ARDS UP THE SCREEN
707 POSITION Y+1,B+1:? " ";:REM ERASE LAS
T BULLET
710 POSITION Y+1,B:? "}T}";:REM PLACE THE
 CONTROL 'T' INSIDE THE GUN AND SHOOT AT
TARGET
715 NEXT B
719 REM COMPARE THE POSITION OF THE LAST
BULLET WITH THE POSITION OF THE TARGET-SC
ORE 1 FOR A HIT
720 IF Y+1>=P1 AND Y+1<=P1+3 THEN POSITIO
N P1,5:? "****":H=H+1:GOTO 750
725 REM ADD ONE TO THE MISSES
730 POSITION P1-1,3:? "MISSED":M=M+1
750 FOR TL=1 TO 100:NEXT TL:GOTO 50
```

Line 100 continues the For . . . Next loop that began in line 70. Notice that as P1 decreases from 34 to 0, the For . . . Next loop in lines 90-95 will be executed at every value of P1.

Line 110 sends the computer back to line 50. The target has moved across the screen and the user chose not to shoot at it.

Line 500 is the beginning of the subroutine line 90 can send the computer to. Lines 50-110 are one loop. There is no way the computer can get to this line of the program unless it is directed to it from line 90. This line resets memory location 764 to 255. It has now cleared the key value from its memory. This line also checks the value of the K variable for a six or a seven. If K contains either, the computer will branch to line 503. If K does not contain those values, the computer will continue to the next line.

Line 501 checks the value of K for 33. If K is 33 the space bar has been pressed, and the user has fired at the target. The computer is directed to line 700 for the fire routine.

Line 502 sends the computer back to line 90 if the key pressed was not one of the arrow keys or the space bar.

Line 503 begins the routine for the arrow keys. This line checks the left side of the screen if the arrow key left has been pressed. The Y variable stores the column position of the rifle. Since we do not want the rifle to go off the screen, or Y to have a negative value, we send the computer back (Return) if the left arrow key has been pressed and the rifle is in the second column.

Line 504 checks the right side of the screen if the right arrow has been pressed. Again, we do not want a cursor out of range error, so we tell the computer to Return if the rifle is printed in the 35th position on the screen.

Line 505 clears the rifle from the old position on the screen before the rifle can be printed in the new position.

Line 510 once more checks the value of K. If the left arrow key has been pressed, the value of Y will be decreased by one, and the computer will be directed to line 550.

Line 520 increases the value of Y by one. Since the only way the computer could go to these lines is if the value of K is six or seven, we do not have to retest K in this line. In the last line we tested K for a six. If the computer got thus far the value of K must be seven.

Line 550 tests Y once more for values too large or too small. If the value of Y is out of range, the program will direct the computer back to the line that it came from.

Line 600 draws the rifle in the new position and then returns to the line it came from.

Line 700 pops the line the program would return to off its stack. A *stack* is a place in the computer's memory where it remembers the line it came from. This routine will not let the program return to the line that sent it. We do not want an error 10 - argument stack overflow error, so we pop the line number off the stack. We will discuss stacks and POP commands in detail in Chapter 12.

Line 705 begins another For . . . Next loop. This time we place the bullet on the screen. It will start at the bottom of the screen and continue up to the line the target is on. The rows on the screen decrease as we travel up the screen, so this loop will count backwards.

Line 707 erases the last bullet. The first time through this loop, there will be no bullet to erase. The next times through the loop there will be a bullet to erase. The Y variable is increased by one before the bullet is erased. The variable holds the place of the rifle on the screen. The bullet would be in the next position, between the two lines that create the rifle. B is the row. We start with 22, which is one row off the bottom of the screen. When we add one to B we are in the bottom row. Use a semicolon whenever you print in the bottom row of the screen, or your picture will scroll.

Line 710 prints the bullet on the screen. We will use the graphics character, control T for the bullet.

Line 715 continues the For . . . Next loop.

Line 720 compares the position of the target with the position of the bullet. P1 is the position of the target. The target is four characters long. If the position of the bullet, which is one more than Y, is equal to the position of the target, or is not greater than the last character of the target (P1 plus 3) we have hit the target. The target will be replaced with four asterisks. The H variable will be increased by one and the computer will be sent to line 750.

Line 730 will be executed if the bullet is not within the range specified for the target. MISSED will be printed above the target and the variable M will be increased by one.

Line 750 contains another timing loop. The computer is directed back to line 50.

Listing 10-4 is a routine for shuffling cards. You may want to use it in any program where you will be using information, numbers, or words randomly, and do not want to repeat the same one twice.

This method replaces the item chosen with the last one in the stack, takes the last one and places it in the location chosen, then decreases the number of items the computer can choose from. The locations that the information is moved to cannot be disturbed because the computer will not be allowed to choose those locations.

Line 40 dimensions CARD$ to 13. The numbers and letters that appear on the cards will be stored here. Card is a one-dimensional array that stores all 52 cards by number.

Listing 10-4. Shuffle

```
10 REM LISTING X-4
20 REM SHUFFLE
30 REM BY L.M.SCHREIBER FOR TAB BOOKS
40 DIM CARD$(13),CARD(52)
50 CARD$="A234567890JQK"
60 FOR X=1 TO 52:CARD(X)=X:NEXT X:REM NUM
BER THE CARDS
70 REM 'C' IS A TEMPORARY STORAGE VARIABL
E
80 FOR X=52 TO 1 STEP -1
90 C1=INT(RND(1)*X)+1:REM CHOOSE A CARD F
ROM 1 TO THE NUMBER LEFT IN THE DECK
100 C=CARD(C1):REM SWAP THE CARDS STORE T
HE CARD IN LOCATION C1 IN THE VARIABLE C
110 CARD(C1)=CARD(X):REM TRANSFER THE CAR
D FROM LOCATION X TO C1
120 CARD(X)=C:REM PLACE THE CARD REMOVED
FROM C1 INTO LOCATION X
130 NEXT X
140 ? "}clear}":REM PRINT THE FIRST 5 CAR
DS
150 FOR X=1 TO 5
160 C=CARD(X):C1=CARD(X):REM GET THE CARD
 & THE PLACE IN THE STRING
165 IF C1>13 THEN C1=C1-13:GOTO 165
170 IF C1=10 THEN ? "1";
175 ? CARD$(C1,C1);:REM PRINT THE VALUE O
F THE CARD
180 IF C>13 THEN 200:REM IT'S NOT A DIAMO
ND
190 ? "}.}":GOTO 260
200 IF C>26 THEN 220:REM IT'S NOT A HEART

210 ? "},}":GOTO 260
220 IF C>39 THEN 240:REM IT'S NOT A SPADE

230 ? "};}":GOTO 260
240 ? "}P}":REM IT'S A CLUB
260 NEXT X
270 END
```

Line 50 places the numbers and letters of the cards into the string. The Ace is the lowest card and the king is the highest.

Line 60 is a For . . . Next loop. The computer will count from 1 to 52. Each time it will place the value of X into the Card array. Every element of Card will contain a number from 1 to 52.

Line 80 starts the For . . . Next loop that will shuffle the cards. We want to start with a full deck, so make X equal to 52 and count backwards.

Line 90 picks one of the cards. The computer will be allowed to choose one number from one to the value of X. The first time the computer executes this line, it can choose any of the 52 cards, the second time any of 51, etc. The number of the card the computer picks is stored in C1.

Line 100 places the value of Card at location C1 into the variable C. We will use C as a temporary storage variable.

Line 110 takes the card at the bottom of the pile and places it in the location we just removed a card from. X will always represent the bottom of the pile. The first time, the card is taken from location 52, the second time from 51, etc. Since X is always decreasing, we will not take a card twice.

Line 120 transfers the card in the C variable to the bottom of the pile. Again, X will be decreasing, so the number placed in the last element of the array cannot be chosen or replaced once X has decreased.

Line 130 tells the computer to continue this routine until all the cards have been moved.

Line 140 clears the screen.

Line 150 begins another For . . . Next loop. This time we want only the first five cards in the array printed on the screen.

Line 160 takes the value of the X element of the array and places it in C and C1. C1 will be the number or letter of the card.

Line 165 checks C1. If C1 is greater than 13, C1 will be decremented by 13 until it is less than or equal to 13.

Line 170 checks the value of C1 again. If it is 10, the computer will print a one on the screen, and use a semicolon to hold the cursor there for the rest of the card. CARD$ can only contain one letter or number for each card—the ten card is an exception to the number/suit pattern.

Line 175 prints the number or letter of the card on the screen. Use the semicolon here, also, to keep the cursor on the same line so the computer can print the suit symbol.

Lines 180-240 test the value of C. This number will indicate which suit should be printed on the screen. If C is greater than 13, the suit is not a diamond, so the computer will continue with line 200. If C is less than or equal to 13, we tell the computer to print the diamond. The lines continue to test C for its value in increments of 13 until it prints the correct card symbol. After the symbol has been printed, the program directs the computer to line 260.

Line 260 continues the For . . . Next loop until five cards have been dealt.

This routine can be changed for any number of elements in the array. It can also be used in routines that will shuffle the words to be displayed, as in a Spelling program.

Chapter 11

Making Decisions

Programs are not always straightforward calculations of accumulated information. When we figured out the area of a room, or placed names in our directory, the program ran from start to finish without any consideration of the information entered by the user. It processed everything in the order it was instructed.

Some of the programs we've seen so far did take into consideration the entries. The Spelling program (Listing 9-5) allowed the user to stop the first routine by entering **XXX** . When the computer must choose between different program paths, we are talking about *logic or decision making statements*. The computer must decide which path to take. This decision is determined by information that has been entered, or calculated in the first part of the program.

IF . . . THEN

The very simplest decision-making statement is an If . . . Then statement. If the first part of the statement is true, Then the program continues with the statement. These statements are often used after an input statement to check the answer entered for erroneous answers. Other times it is used after a computation to decide on the path the computer must take in the program. Listing 11-1 shows an example of If . . . Then statements (see flowchart, Fig. 11-1).

Line 40 sets the vertical and horizontal locations. The V variable is the vertical location, or the column. The H variable is the horizontal location or the row.

Line 50 clears the screen and erases or turns off the cursor.

Line 60 prints the ball in the center of the screen. Use **control T** for the ball.

Line 70 looks at a location in the computer's memory. This location stores the value of the key that has been pressed. If no key has been pressed, the number 255 will be stored there. The computer will not go past this line if no key has been pressed. If this location contains a number other than 255, the first part of the statement would be false and the computer would go on to the next line.

Line 80 places the number stored in memory location 764 into the variable K.

Line 90 resets memory location 764. If we did not reset this location, the number placed in K would remain there also. The computer does not place 255 in that location if a key is not being

Listing 11-1. Ball

```
10 REM LISTING XI.1
20 REM BALL
30 REM BY L.M.SCHREIBER FOR TAB BOOKS
40 V=12:H=20:REM SET THE VERTICAL AND HOR
IZONTAL LOCATIONS
50 ? "}clear}":POKE 752,1:REM CLEAR SCREE
N AND TURN CURSOR OFF
60 POSITION H,V:? "}T}":REM PLACE THE BAL
L INTO THE CENTER OF THE SCREEN
70 IF PEEK(764)=255 THEN 70:REM LOOP BACK
 TO THIS LINE IF A KEY HAS NOT BEEN PRESS
ED
80 K=PEEK(764):REM GET THE KEY PRESSED
90 POKE 764,255:REM CLEAR THE KEY
100 IF K=6 THEN 200:REM MOVE THE BALL TO
THE LEFT
110 IF K=7 THEN 250:REM MOVE THE BALL TO
THE RIGHT
120 IF K=14 THEN 300:REM MOVE THE BALL UP


130 IF K=15 THEN 350:REM MOVE THE BALL DO
WN
150 GOTO 70:REM NOT A VALID ENTRY
200 H=H-1:IF H<2 THEN H=2:REM CHECK FOR T
HE EDGE OF THE SCREEN
210 POSITION H+1,V:? " ";:REM ERASE THE O
LD BALL
220 GOTO 400:REM PRINT THE BALL ROUTINE
250 H=H+1:IF H=40 THEN H=39:REM 39 IS THE
 RIGHT EDGE
260 POSITION H-1,V:? " ";:REM ERASE THE O
LD BALL
270 GOTO 400
300 V=V-1:IF V=-1 THEN V=0:REM -1 IS OFF
THE SCREEN
310 POSITION H,V+1:? " ":REM ERASE THE OL
D BALL
320 GOTO 400
350 V=V+1:IF V=24 THEN V=23:REM 23 IS THE
 LAST LINE
```

Listing 11-1. Ball. (Continued from page 93.)

```
360 POSITION H,V-1:? " ":REM ERASE THE OL
D BALL
400 POSITION H,V:? "}T}";:REM PRINT THE N
EW ONE
410 GOTO 70:REM GET THE NEXT KEY
```

pressed. It is just a location that stores the number of the last key pressed. Your program must reset the location to 255.

Line 100 tests the value of K for six. Six is the number for the left arrow key. If the left arrow key has been pressed, the program will direct the computer to line 200.

Line 110 tests the value of K for seven. Seven is the number for the right arrow key. If the right arrow key has been pressed, the program will direct the computer to line 250.

Line 120 tests the value of K for 14. This is the number for the up arrow key. If the up arrow key has been pressed, the program will direct the computer to line 300.

Line 130 tests the value of K for 15. 15 is the value of the down arrow key. If this key has been pressed, the program will direct the computer to line 350.

Line 150 sends the computer back to line 70. If the key pressed was not an arrow key, the K variable will contain a value other than those tested for in the previous lines. Since we want to use only the four arrow keys, we will send the computer back to line 70 and let it wait there until another key has been pressed.

Line 200 begins the routine that moves the ball left. One is subtracted from H. The computer checks the value of H and if it is less than two, it is reset to two. This way, the ball will not be placed off the screen.

Line 210 erases the old ball. In the last line we subtracted one from H. To erase the old ball, add one to H and print a space. The V variable is not affected by moving the ball to the left.

Line 220 directs the computer to line 400.

Line 250 begins the routine that moves the ball right. By adding one to H we will be able to print the ball in the next location in that row. The value of H is tested for 40.   39 is the last column of the screen. If the variable contains a 40, it must be reset to 39.

Line 260 erases the ball from its previous position on the screen. Since we calculated the new position by adding one to the value of H, the computer will subtract one from H to determine where the ball was last printed. V will not change when the ball is moved to the right.

Line 270 directs the computer to line 400.

Line 300 begins the routine that moves the ball up the screen. V tells the computer which row to print the ball in. To move the ball up subtract one from V. The computer then tests V for a negative one. The top row on the screen is zero. If V is less than zero, it will be reset to zero, keeping the ball on the screen.

Line 310 erases the ball from its old position. This time one is added to the value V and H does not change.

Line 320 directs the computer to line 400. Line 350 begins the routine to move the ball down. One is added to V. V is tested for 24. The last row on the screen is 23. If V contains 24, it will be reset to 23.

Line 360 erases the old ball from the screen. Again, V is adjusted for the old position and H does not change.

Line 400 prints the ball in the new position. All the routines direct the computer to this line.

Line 410 sends the computer back to line 70 where it waits for another key to be pressed.

Because the values of the variable are tested, there is no way the ball can be directed off the screen. The program also ignores the wrong keys.

In the last program, the If...Then statements checked the contents of variables. Strings can also be tested in a similar way.

The Then part of an If...Then statement can be a variable or an arithmetic equation. It can also be another program statement.

```
50        IF V=3 THEN 540:REM SEND COMPUTER TO A LINE NUMBER.
50        IF V < > 3 THEN PRINT "WRONG":REM ANOTHER PROGRAM STATE-
          MENT.
50        IF V=6 THEN GOTO PLACE:REM PLACE IS A VARIABLE. YOU MUST
          HAVE A 'GOTO' BEFORE IT.
50        IF V=7 THEN GOTO A*B:REM A*B IS AN ARITHMETIC EXPRESSION THE
          PRODUCT WILL BE THE LINE NUMBER THAT THE COMPUTER WILL
          GOTO.
```

When you use a variable or an arithmetic expression as the line number, be sure the variable has a value assigned to it, and that the program will not compute a line that does not exist. The program must also have a GOTO command between the Then and the line number.

EXITS

Another use for If...Then statements is to exit a loop. Two examples where you would use If...Then as an exit are:

When you are getting information from the user, but do not determine ahead of time the exact number of entries the user will enter. In the Spelling program (Listing 9-5), the user could enter up to 20 words, but it is possible to enter only one word. The code XXX signifies the end of the word list. The program checks each entry to see if it is the final entry. When the code is entered, the program will leave the routine it is in and direct the computer to the spelling routine.

In another program you may have data you want the computer to read. The amount of data will vary. A similar code can be used to signify the end of that group of data.

ELSE

ATARI BASIC does not allow the use of an Else command in an If...Then statement. In other BASIC formats, Else is used to direct the computer to follow one instruction if the first part of the statement is true, and another if it is false.

For example, in a program that will show the tax imposed on your income if your earnings are above a certain level, where incomes below $25,000 are taxed at 15 percent, and incomes above $25,000 are taxed at 17 percent, other BASIC formats allow:

```
215   IF A$="Y" THEN T=.15 ELSE T=.17
```

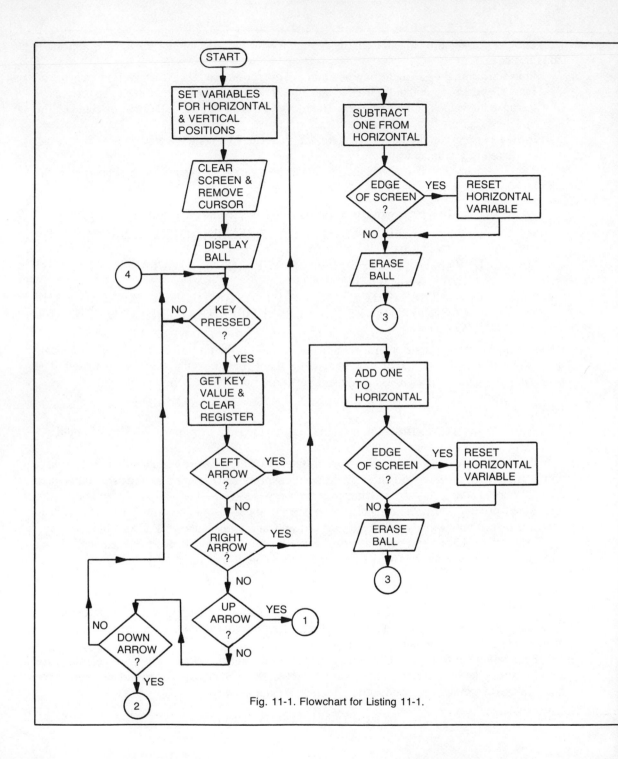

Fig. 11-1. Flowchart for Listing 11-1.

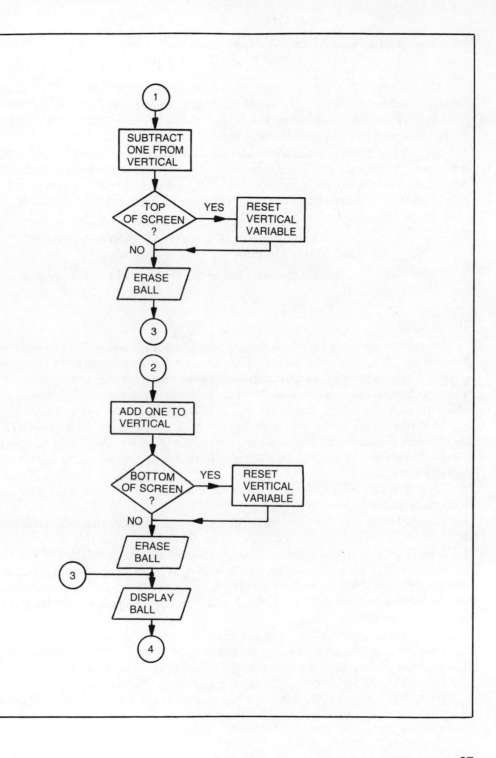

97

but this must be done in ATARI BASIC as:

215　　T=.17:IF A$="Y" THEN T=.15

This, in effect, works the Else part of the statement before the If . . . Then statement. The variable is set for the higher tax. Should the income be less than $25,000, the variable will be reset to the lower tax. GOTO is not necessary because T will be properly set in either case and the program will continue with the next line.

Since the program can use variables as line numbers, the same principle can apply to GOTO statements. If there are two possible routines that can be used, each dependent on an entry or calculation, you can set the variable to one of the routines, check the entry, and change the variable if the computer should use the other routine. The GOTO statement would send the computer to the correct routine.

400　　ANSWER =500: IF C=3 THEN ANSWER=450
410　　GOTO ANSWER

ANSWER　　　　contains the line number the program will branch to. It will be changed only if C is equal to 3.

ON . . . GOTO

In some programs you may have several routines that can be used, but all will never be used at the same time, or in the same order. When we want the computer to go to a routine only when certain conditions are met, we are using *selective branching*. One example is a program containing several games or learning modules. When the program is run the screen contains a menu from which the user can choose a program or unit. (Listing 11-2; see also flowchart in Fig. 11-2).

Line 40 dimensions the strings used in this program. A$ holds the answer, STATE$ holds the names of the states, PR$ holds the answers to the questions, AN$ is the temporary storage area for the answer, TS$ holds the state printed on the screen, and Q$ is used in the question printed on the screen.

Line 50 clears STATE$. Since this string has been fielded, we don't want any garbage between the states.

Line 60 begins a For . . . Next loop. A$ holds the name of the state when it is read from the data line.

Line 70 gets the length of the state and places the state into STATE$. The For . . . Next loop was started with 0 for a purpose; each state field is 14 bytes long. By multiplying X by 14 and adding 1 we get the location for the first character of that state in STATE$. By starting with 0, we get 1 for the first location ($1 \times 14 + 1 = 1$). Multiplying X by 14 and adding the length to it gives us the last location for that state.

Line 80 continues the For . . . Next loop.

Line 85 clears the string holding the answers for all units of this program. This line also clears out the old answers from the unit completed in the course of the program.

Line 90 clears the screen and prints the first line of the menu.

Lines 100-130 print the units you can choose from. Line 130 prints four spaces and backspaces before waiting for an input. The number entered will be stored in the A variable.

Listing 11-2. Selective Branching Demonstration

```
10 REM LISTING XI.2
20 REM SELECTIVE BRANCHING
30 REM BY L.M.SCHREIBER FOR TAB BOOKS
40 DIM A$(20),STATE$(700),PR$(1000),AN$(2
0),TS$(14),Q$(12)
50 STATE$(1)=" ":STATE$(700)=" ":STATE$(2
)=STATE$
60 FOR X=0 TO 49:READ A$:REM GET THE STAT
ES
70 L=LEN(A$):STATE$(X*14+1,X*14+L)=A$:REM
 PUT THEM IN THE STRING
80 NEXT X
85 PR$(1)=" ":PR$(1000)=" ":PR$(2)=PR$:?
"}clear}"
90 POSITION 4,10:? "PLEASE CHOOSE A UNIT
FROM 1 TO 3"
100 POSITION 8,12:? "1) STATES & CAPITALS
"
110 POSITION 8,14:? "2) STATE ABBREVIATIO
NS"
120 POSITION 8,16:? "3) STATE FLOWERS"
130 POSITION 19,18:? "    ";;:INPUT A:
REM 4 SPACES & BACKSPACES
140 ON A GOTO 200,300,400
150 GOTO 130:REM INCORRECT RESPONSE
199 REM STATES & CAPITALS
200 RESTORE 1100:Q$="CAPITAL"
210 GOTO 410
299 REM ABBREVIATIONS
300 RESTORE 1200:Q$="ABBREVIATION"
310 GOTO 410
399 REM FLOWERS
400 RESTORE 1300:Q$="FLOWER"
410 FOR X=0 TO 49:READ A$
420 L=LEN(A$):PR$(X*20+1,X*20+L)=A$
430 NEXT X
450 C=0:FOR X=50 TO 1 STEP -1:S=INT(RND(1
)*X)+1:TS$=STATE$((S-1)*14+1,S*14)
455 AN$=PR$((S-1)*20+1,S*20)
460 ? "}"
470 POSITION 3,5:? "What is the ";Q$
```

```
480 ? "of ";TS$
490 POSITION 10,10:? "
 ";:INPUT A$
495 L=LEN(A$):FOR Z=L+1 TO 20:A$(Z,Z)=" "
:NEXT Z
500 IF A$=AN$ THEN POSITION 15,15:? "VERY
 GOOD":C=C+1:GOTO 515
510 POSITION 15,15:? "NO, IT'S ";AN$
515 FOR ZZ=1 TO 500:NEXT ZZ
520 PR$((S-1)*20+1,S*20)=PR$((X-1)*20+1,X
*20):PR$((X-1)*20+1,X*20)=AN$
530 STATE$((S-1)*14+1,S*14)=STATE$((X-1)*
14+1,X*14):STATE$((X-1)*14+1,X*14)=TS$
540 NEXT X
560 ? "}clear}":POSITION 5,15:? " YOU GOT
 ";C;" CORRECT."
570 GOTO 85
580 END
1000 DATA NEBRASKA,SOUTH DAKOTA,NORTH DAK
OTA,MINNESOTA,KANSAS,IOWA,MISSOURI
1010 DATA TEXAS,OKLAHOMA,ARKANSAS,ALABAMA
,MISSISSIPPI,LOUISIANA,TENNESSEE
1020 DATA NEW MEXICO,ARIZONA,UTAH,IDAHO,C
OLORADO,MONTANA,WYOMING,NEVADA
1030 DATA WASHINGTON,HAWAII,OREGON,CALIFO
RNIA,ALASKA,MAINE,VERMONT,KENTUCKY
1040 DATA RHODE ISLAND,NEW HAMPSHIRE,MASS
ACHUSETTS,CONNECTICUT,DELEWARE
1050 DATA NEW YORK,MARYLAND,NEW JERSEY,PE
NNSYLVANIA,WEST VIRGINIA,FLORIDA
1060 DATA NORTH CAROLINA,VIRGINIA,SOUTH C
AROLINA,GEORGIA,MICHIGAN,WISCONSIN
1070 DATA ILLINOIS,INDIANA,OHIO
1099 REM CAPITALS START HERE
1100 DATA LINCOLN,PIERRE,BISMARK,ST. PAUL
,TOPEKA,DES MOINES,JEFFERSON CITY
1110 DATA AUSTIN,OKLAHOMA CITY,LITTLE ROC
K,MONTGOMERY,JACKSON,BATON ROUGE
1120 DATA NASHVILLE,SANTA FE,PHOENIX,SALT
 LAKE CITY,BOISE,DENVER,HELENA
1130 DATA CHEYENNE,CARSON CITY,OLYMPIA,HO
```

```
NOLULU,SALEM,SACRAMENTO,JUNEAU,AUGUSTA
1140 DATA MONTPELIER,FRANKFORT,PROVIDENCE
,CONCORD,BOSTON,HARTFORD,DOVER,ALBANY
1145 DATA ANNAPOLIS,TRENTON,HARRISBURG,CH
ARLESTON,TALLAHASSEE,RALEIGH,RICHMOND
1150 DATA COLUMBIA,ATLANTA,LANSING,MADISO
N,SPRINGFIELD,INDIANAPOLIS,COLUMBUS
1199 REM ABBREVIATIONS START HERE
1200 DATA NE,SD,ND,MN,KS,IA,MO,TX,OK,AR,A
L,MS,LA,TN,NM,AZ,UT,ID,CO,MT,WY,NV
1210 DATA WA,HI,OR,CA,AK,ME,VT,KY,RI,NH,M
A,CT,DE,NY,MD,NJ,PA,WV,FL,NC,VA,SC
1220 DATA GA,MI,WI,IL,IN,OH
1299 REM FLOWERS
1300 DATA GOLDENROD,PASQUEFLOWER,WILD PRA
IRIE ROSE,LADY SLIPPER,SUNFLOWER
1310 DATA WILD ROSE,HAWTHORN,BLUEBONNET,M
ISTLETOE,APPLE BLOSSOM,CAMELIA
1320 DATA MAGNOLIA,MAGNOLIA,IRIS,YUCCA FL
OWER,SAGUARO,SAGO LILY,SYRINGE
1330 DATA COLUMBINE,BITTERROOT,INDIAN PAI
NTBRUSH,SAGEBRUSH,RHODODENDRON
1340 DATA HIBISCUS,OREGON GRAPE,GOLDEN PO
PPY,FORGET-ME-NOT,PINE CONE
1350 DATA RED CLOVER,GOLDENROD,VIOLET,PUR
PLE LILAC,MAYFLOWER,MOUNTAIN LAUREL
1360 DATA PEACH BLOSSOM,ROSE,BLACK-EYED S
USAN,VIOLET,MOUNTAIN LAUREL
1370 DATA RHODODENDRON,ORANG BLOSSOM,FLOW
ERING DOGWOOD,AMERICAN DOGWOOD
1380 DATA CAROLINA JESSAMINE,CHEROKEE ROS
E,APPLE BLOSSOM,VIOLET,VIOLET,PEONY,SCARL
ET CARNATION
```

Line 140 uses the On . . . GOTO command. There are three different line numbers after GOTO. If A is one, the computer will choose the first line number and go to line 200. If A is two, the computer will go to line 200. If A is three, the computer will go to line 400. If A is 0 or a number greater than three, there are no line numbers the computer proceeds to the next line. The line following an On . . . GOTO command should return the computer to the beginning of the program, the menu, or to the input line. Otherwise, it will continue with whatever instructions are on the next line.

Line 199 is a remark to tell us what the next routine will do. Never send a program to a

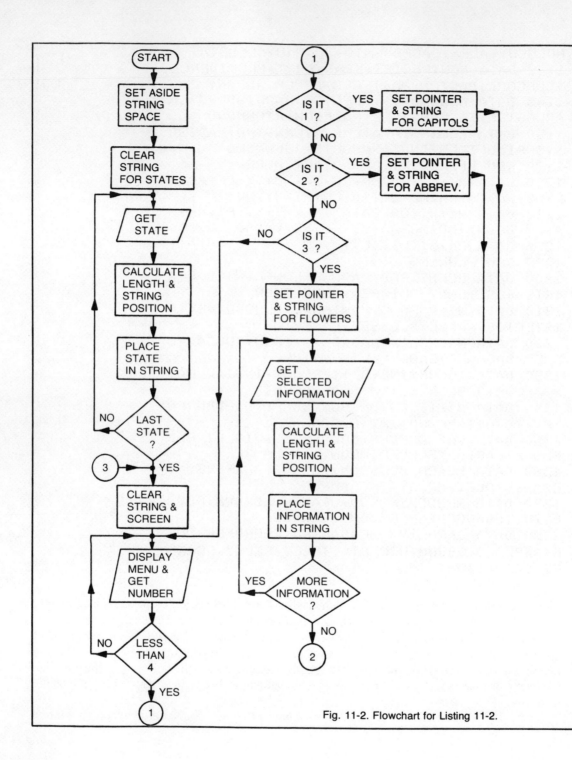

Fig. 11-2. Flowchart for Listing 11-2.

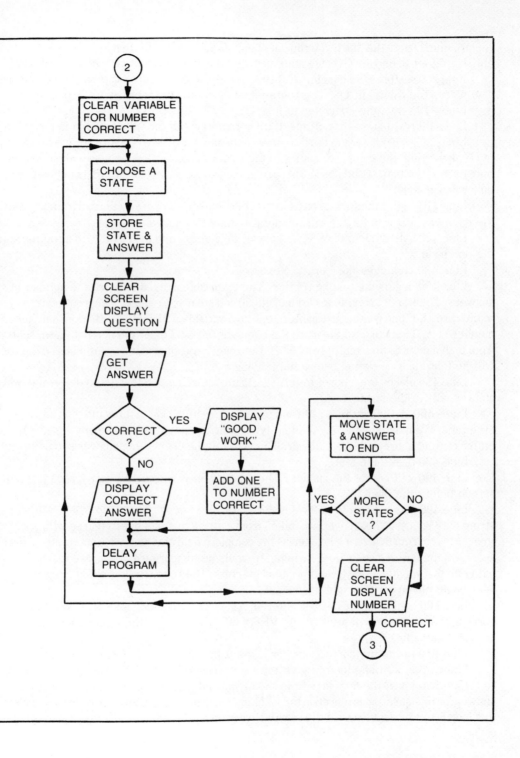

2

CLEAR VARIABLE
FOR NUMBER
CORRECT

CHOOSE A
STATE

STORE
STATE &
ANSWER

CLEAR
SCREEN
DISPLAY
QUESTION

GET
ANSWER

CORRECT
?

YES

DISPLAY
"GOOD
WORK"

MOVE STATE
& ANSWER
TO END

NO

DISPLAY
CORRECT
ANSWER

ADD ONE
TO NUMBER
CORRECT

YES

MORE
STATES
?

NO

DELAY
PROGRAM

CLEAR
SCREEN
DISPLAY
NUMBER

CORRECT

3

103

remark line. Delete the line if you run out of memory, but you will then have to search through the entire program to find the GOTO's statements for that line. A remark can be deleted at any time.

Line 200 restores the data line to 1100. This is the line the first capital appears on. This line also places the capital in Q$. The routine that asks the questions will use this string.

Line 210 sends the computer to line 410.

Lines 299-310 are similar. Line 1200 is restored and the abbreviation is placed in Q$.

Lines 399-410 are for the third routine. This time Line 1300 is restored, and flower is placed in Q$. Each time the computer comes to the restore command, it points its data pointer to that line. Each set of answers begins at a particular line, so we can restore the data depending on which unit was chosen.

Line 410 begins the For . . . Next loop. This time the computer will read from whichever line the data was restored to. A$ will temporarily hold the answer.

Line 420 gets the length of A$ and places the information into PR$ with a routine similar to the one used with the states.

Line 430 continues the For . . .Next loop.

Line 450 begins the testing routine. The C variable is used to store the number of correct answers. The For . . . Next loop begins with 50 and steps backwards. This routine is very similar to the card-shuffling routine in Chapter 10. The S variable will contain a random number up to the number of X. TS$ will hold the state the computer picks. To get the correct state, subtract one from the value of S, then multiply by 14 and add one. S-1 is placed in parentheses so the computer will do that math operation before multiplying S by 14.

Line 455 places the answer into AN$. Again, the value of S is used to determine where the answer falls in the string.

Lines 460-470 clear the screen and print the question. The user could pick any one of three programs. We must have a way of identifying which question should be answered. Q$ contains either capital, abbreviation, or flower. This will tell the user which answer should be entered.

Line 480 prints the state.

Line 490 will accept the answer. There are twenty spaces and backspaces printed on the screen before the input.

Line 490 puts the length of the answer in A$. The For . . . Next loop which follows pads the string with spaces. The answer was taken from a string that had been cleared with spaces. Each answer taken from that string is taken as the complete field of twenty characters. If we did not add spaces to the entered answer, the computer would be comparing a string twenty characters long with one that might be only two or eight characters. The two strings would never match and the user could never get the right answers.

Line 500 compares the answer entered, A$, with the correct answer, AN$. If the answer is correct, the computer will print: **VERY GOOD** on the screen, add one to the value of C and go to line 515.

Line 510 prints the correct answer if the user entered an incorrect answer.

Line 515 is a timing loop to give the user a chance to read what is on the screen.

Line 520 takes the last answer in the string and places it in the location just shown. The answer for this question is placed in the last location of this string. Since X is decreasing each time this loop is executed, the last location will always be one less than it was the previous time. Since the computer can only choose a number up to the value of X, it will only choose each state and answer once.

Line 530 does the same thing for the state. The state just chosen will be replaced with the last state in the string. The last state will be replaced with the state just chosen.

Line 540 continues the For . . . Next loop.

Line 560 prints the number of questions the user answered correctly.

Line 570 sends the computer back to the menu. Since line 85 clears the PR$, and this takes some time; we do not need a timing loop before going back.

Line 580 is a precautionary measure. Since the entire program is a closed loop, we do not need an end statement, but it is better to include one to separate the program from the data.

Lines 1000-1380 contain the data used in the program. Lines 1000-1070 contain the states. The program uses these lines when it reads the states into STATE$.

Lines 1100-1150 contain the capitals of all the states. If these capitals are in the wrong order, or one is missing, the program will generate wrong answers.

Lines 1200-1220 contain the two-letter abbreviations for all the states. Again, be sure these are entered correctly.

Lines 1300-1380 contain the state flowers for all the states. This data must be entered accurately for the program to work correctly.

The data in the last three sets can be reused as many times as the user chooses the routine utilizing that data.

Chapter 12

Reusing Part of a Program

In Chapter 11 we discussed routines used selectively by the program. These routines could be used more than once, but only after the entire routine was completed and the program had displayed the menu. What happens if we have a routine used by several parts of the same program? If this routine will be used by the main part of the program, and we expect to come back to the point we left, we will need some way to keep track of where we are and where we are going. This could be done by setting a variable to a line number and returning to that line when you have finished the routine. You could also set a series of If . . . Then statements, or list the routine in memory wherever you needed it. Each of these methods waste time and memory.

GOSUB . . . RETURN

The best way to handle a routine you will call often is to replace the routine with one subroutine. A *subroutine* is part of the program that can be used at any time in the program. When the computer finishes with the subroutine, it returns to the part of the program it came from.

You will often use a timing routine at several points in your program. You can use one timing routine as a subroutine and use it from any point in your program. If, for example, you have a routine that plays a certain melody, and you want to use this routine several times in your program, you would make the music routine a subroutine.

When the computer finds a GOSUB command, it remembers its line number by placing it in an area of memory called a *stack*, and goes to the line number indicated after the GOSUB. It executes the lines in the subroutine until it encounters a Return command which tells the computer to go back to the line it came from and continue with the program. Try Listing 12-1 (see flowchart, Fig. 12-1).

Line 40 clears the screen and prints a message on the screen.

Line 50 contains a GOSUB. The computer will go to line 800, complete that routine, then return to this line. When the computer RETURNs, it will proceed with the other statement on this line and print the message on the screen.

Line 60 asks for the number of the month and stores this number in month variable.

Line 70 goes to the subroutine first. When it returns, the computer prints the prompt: DATE   on the screen and waits until the date has been entered.

Listing 12-1. Days

```
10 REM LISTING XII.1
20 REM DAYS
30 REM BY L.M.SCHREIBER FOR TAB BOOKS
40 ? "}clear}":POSITION 4,4:? "THIS IS A
DEMONSTRATION OF A SUBROUTINE"
50 GOSUB 800:? "PLEASE ENTER TODAY'S DATE
"
60 ? "MONTH (NUMBER ONLY) ";:INPUT MONTH
70 GOSUB 800:? "DATE ";:INPUT DATE
80 GOSUB 800:? "YEAR ";:INPUT YEAR
90 TDAYS=0:REM CLEAR TOTAL NUMBER OF DAYS

95 IF MONTH=1 THEN 150
100 FOR AD=1 TO MONTH-1
110 READ DAYS
120 TDAYS=TDAYS+DAYS
130 NEXT AD
140 IF YEAR/4=INT(YEAR/4) THEN IF MONTH>2
   THEN TDAYS=TDAYS+1:REM CHECK FOR LEAP YE
AR
150 TDAYS=TDAYS+DATE
160 GOSUB 800:POSITION 2,15:? "TODAY IS T
HE ";TDAYS;"th DAY OF THE YEAR."
170 END :REM DON'T LET THE PROGRAM RUN IN
TO THE DATA
200 DATA 31,28,31,30,31,30,31,31,30,31,30
,31
800 FOR X=10 TO 100 STEP 10
810 SOUND 0,X,12,10:REM MAKE THE SOUND
820 FOR Z=1 TO 50:NEXT Z:REM HEAR THE SOU
ND
830 SOUND 0,0,0,0:REM TURN IT OFF
840 NEXT X
850 RETURN :REM GO BACK TO THE LINE YOU C
AME FROM
```

Line 80 uses the same subroutine and then waits for the user to enter the year.

Line 90 clears the TDAYS variable. This variable adds the number of days that have passed during the current year, and we want to make sure we start with 0.

Line 95 checks the month variable for a one. If it equals one, the computer skips the lines of the program that total the days in the months, because no months have passed.

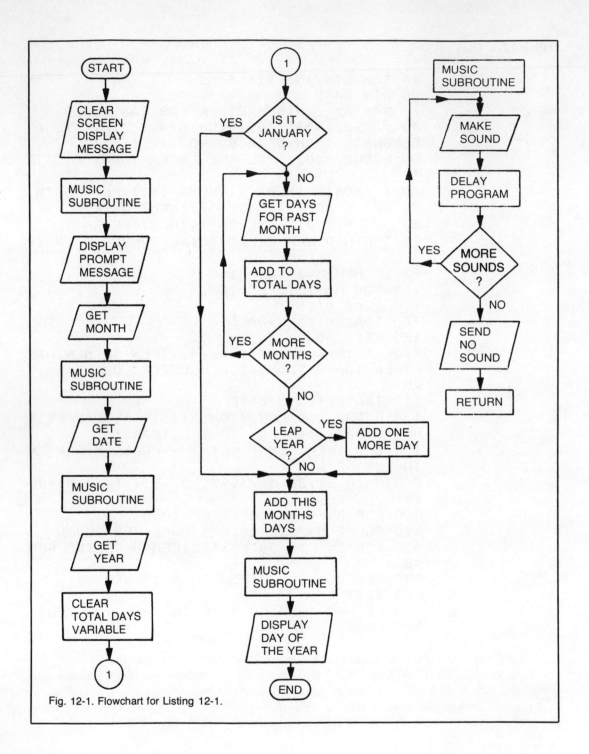

Fig. 12-1. Flowchart for Listing 12-1.

Line 100 begins the For . . . Next loop that totals the number of days that have passed. The program stops one month before the month that has been entered, because all those days have not passed.

Line 110 reads the value into the days variable. The corresponding data line contains the number of days each month has.

Line 120 totals the number of days that have passed. The value of the DAYS variable is added to TDAYS.

Line 130 continues the For . . . Next loop.

Line 140 checks for a leap year by dividing the year by four. If the year is a whole number, it is a leap year. The statement checks to see if we have passed February. If the month entered is greater than two, the computer will add one to the total number of days.

Line 150 adds the value of the Date variable to the total number of days that have passed.

Line 160 uses the subroutine in line 800. The second part of this statement prints which day of the year today is.

Line 170 ends the program.

Line 200 contains the number of days for each month.

Lines 800-840 form the subroutine for the sound. The computer will count by ten's starting with ten.

Line 810 sends the value of X to the sound generator.

Line 820 is a timing routine so we can hear the sound.

Line 830 turns the sound off.

Line 840 continues this For . . . Next loop.

Line 850 tells the computer to return to the line it came from.

A variable used in the main program should not be used in any subroutine unless you know for certain you will not need the value stored in that subroutine later in the program. If you are using a variable for a counter within a subroutine, it should be reset to zero as you enter the subroutine. If it is not reset each time it will continue to count from the last number it counted to.

ON . . . GOSUB/RETURN

Like the On . . . GOTO command you can selectively branch to a subroutine from the main program. With an On . . . GOSUB command, the subroutine you enter is determined by the value of the variable. The computer remembers the line the GOSUB was on, executes the subroutine, and returns to the next instruction.

Be sure all subroutines end with a return statement, or the computer will continue with the lines following the subroutine until it comes to the end of the program, finds another return, or crashes. Also, if you place your subroutines at the end of the program, be sure an end statement is between the end of the program and the subroutines. If the program does not end, it will continue into the subroutines until it finds a return statement. At that point, it will crash with an error—16—return error.

POP

There are a few occasions when you will want to exit a subroutine without returning to the line you came from. You may find it necessary to go to another line or routine.

Each time the computer begins a GOSUB routine, it places the location of the line it is leaving in an area of its memory called a stack. When the computer comes to a return command, it checks the last address on its stack, removes it, and goes to that line. If you leave a subroutine without using a return statement the computer will not remove the address from its stack. If you constantly send the computer to subroutines and exit them without return statements, you will confuse the computer and cause errors or crash. You may also run out of stack space.

When you must go to another subroutine rather than return to the main part of the program, use the POP command to remove the address from the stack. We used POP in Chapter 10 in Listing 10-2B. POP is also demonstrated in Listing 12-2.

Line 40 dimensions A$ to 1, and SC to two elements. A$ will be used for the input. SC will store the scores for two players.

Line 45 sets P to two, the number of players; the roll variable is set to 500, the line number where the subroutine that rolls the dice begins. Both elements of the SC array are set to zero. We will print the contents of these elements before placing any numbers in them, so we need to clear them.

Line 50 clears the screen and prints both players on the screen. The two tabs between the number 1 and the second player space the words on the screen properly.

Line 55 adds the value of TS to the value stored in the P element of the array. It then prints the scores of both players on the screen. P will always be a one or a two. This is the line the program sends the computer to after a person stops rolling the dice or loses.

Line 56 tests the values of both elements of the array to see if either player scored over 500 points. The game ends when one player's score is more than 500.

Line 60 sets the P variable for the other player. To alternate two numbers in a program, subtract one of the numbers from the sum of the two numbers you want to alternate. The result will always be the other number. This line also sets the TS variable to zero. This variable stores the total score for the player who is rolling the dice. The next command places the number of the player on the screen.

Line 62 waits for the return key to be pressed. A$ will not be checked after the return key is pressed.

Line 65 removes any message printed for the last player on the screen.

Line 70 tells the computer to go to the subroutine stored in the roll variable: line 500.

Line 80 is the line the computer returns to. It asks the player if he wants another turn. The computer waits here until something is entered.

Line 90 checks the contents of A$. If it contains the letter Y the computer is directed to line 70. Since A$ was dimensioned for one character, the user could enter any word beginning with a Y and be given another turn.

Line 100 checks the contents of A$ for an N. If the letter entered was not an N, the computer returns to line 80. This loop will be continued until A$ contains either an N or a Y.

Line 110 sends the computer to line 55. The person playing this game has decided to stop rolling the dice, so the program directs the computer back to the line that totals the score.

Line 120 ends the program. By placing and end statement between the program and the subroutine, the program can't continue into the subroutine without being directed there.

Listing 12-2. Dice

```
10 REM LISTING XII.2
20 REM SNAKE-EYES
30 REM BY L.M.SCHREIBER FOR TAB BOOKS
40 DIM A$(1),SC(2)
45 P=2:ROLL=500:SC(1)=0:SC(2)=0:REM CLEAR
   THE ARRAY BEFORE ADDING ANY SCORES
50 ? "}clear}":POSITION 3,3:? "PLAYER #1
   PLAYER #2"
55 SC(P)=SC(P)+TS:POSITION 5,5:? SC(1);"
     ":POSITION 25,5:? SC(2);"     ";
56 IF SC(1)>500 OR SC(2)>500 THEN 700
60 P=3-P:TS=0:POSITION 3,9:? "PLAYER #";P
   :POSITION 3,10
62 ? "PRESS RETURN TO ROLL THE DICE":INPU
   T A$
65 POSITION 2,19:? "":REM 4 ESCAPE SH
   IFT-DELETES
70 GOSUB ROLL
80 POSITION 2,20:? "PLAY AGAIN (Y-N)";:IN
   PUT A$
90 IF A$="Y" THEN 70
100 IF A$<>"N" THEN 80
110 GOTO 55
120 END
500 POSITION 5,15:? "DICE=       ";:
    REM 6 SPACE & 6 BACKSPACES
510 D1=INT(RND(1)*6)+1:D2=INT(RND(1)*6)+1

515 POSITION 11,15:? D1;"  ";D2
520 IF D1=1 AND D2=1 THEN POP :POSITION 2
    ,20:? "SNAKE-EYES YOU LOSE":SC(P)=0:TS=0:
    GOTO 55:REM NO MORE TURN
525 IF D1=1 OR D2=1 THEN POP :POSITION 2,
    20:? "ONE EYE - LOSE THIS TURN":TS=0:GOTO
     55:REM LOSE THIS TURN
530 TS=TS+D1+D2
540 POSITION 5,17:? "RUNNING SCORE
    ";:? TS:REM 6 SPACES & 5 BACKSPACES
550 RETURN
700 POSITION 10,22:? "GAME OVER!!!!":END
```

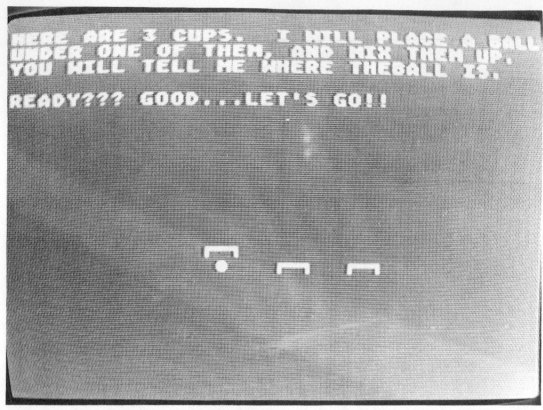

Fig. 12-2. Screen display for Listing 12-3, cups program.

Line 500 begins the dice rolling subroutine. This line prints: DICE and erases the previous roll.

Line 510 picks a random number for each die. The number can be any number from one to six, inclusive.

Line 515 prints both dice on the screen.

Line 520 checks the dice for a one. If both contain a one, you have snake-eyes, and lose your total score and everything you have gained in the game. The contents of your element is set to zero, and the TS variable is set to zero. The stack is POPped because the person playing will not be given the option of rolling again. The computer is directed, instead, to line 55 where the scores for both players are displayed.

Line 525 checks for a one on the dice. If you roll a one, only the accumulated points for that roll are lost. The stack is POPped because the turn is over, and the TS variable is set to zero. The computer is directed to line 55 where it can print the scores of both players on the screen.

Line 530 adds the points on both dice to the accumulated points for this turn.

Line 540 prints the total score on the screen. The previous number of points are erased with spaces and backspaces before the new score is printed.

Line 550 returns the computer to the line it came from.

Line 700 is the end of the program. The computer is directed to this line when one score is more than 500.

Listing 12-3 demonstrates selective subroutines.

Line 40 dimensions the strings used in this program. Try to reuse strings whenever possible to save memory.

Lines 50-90 print the menu on the screen. This program contains three games for the user to choose from.

Line 100 directs the computer to one of three subroutines depending on the value of A. If A is greater than three or less than one, the computer will go on to the next line.

Line 110 directs the computer to line 90 for a new entry. This part of the program continues to loop until the user has entered a valid number.

Line 150 begins the first game—cups. The menu is removed from the screen.

Lines 160-180 print the directions on the screen.

Line 190 removes the cursor from the screen, and places the graphics for the cup into C$. S1$ contains three spaces to erase the cup from the screen.

Line 200 draws the three cups on the screen.

Line 210 erases the first cup, draws it one row higher, and places the ball under it. Use   control T   for the ball. The TT variable is set to 100 and the computer is sent to a subroutine beginning at line 1000. TT is used in the subroutine which will be accessed by all three games. The length of time the computer spends in that subroutine depends on the value stored in TT.

Line 220 places the cup over the ball. This simulation is done by erasing the cup in row 14 and redrawing it in row 15. When the cup is redrawn, the ball will be erased and it will appear the cup was placed over the ball.

Line 230 chooses a number from one to three. This number determines which cup the ball is under.

Lines 240-270 contain the For . . . Next loop that erases and redraws the cups on the screen ten times.

Line 280 turns the cursor on and asks the user which cup the ball is under. The computer waits until a number is entered before going on to the next line. The number entered is stored in variable B.

Line 285 checks the value of B. If it is less than one or greater than three, the program sends the computer back to the previous line.

Line 290 checks the value of B. If it is equal to C the user has chosen the correct cup.   THAT'S RIGHT   is printed on the screen. The computer is directed around the next line.

Line 300 tells the user which cup the ball was under if the number entered was not correct. Both this message and the previous message will be printed in the same position. This position was set in the last line.

Line 310 asks the user if he wants to play again. The question asks for a Y or N entry.

Line 320 checks the first position of C$ for the letter Y.

Line 330 checks the first letter of C$ for an N. If the first character is not an N, the computer returns to line 310 and waits for another entry.

Line 340 returns the computer to the line that sent it to this subroutine. The menu will reappear on the screen.

Line 350 begins the subroutine for the hurky game.

Lines 360-380 print the directions for this game on the screen.

Line 390 chooses a number for the column and row hurky will be hiding in. H is the column and V is the row. Hurky can be in any column or row from one to ten.

Line 400 places the row of dots in DOT$. Make the dots with   control T   . The OH and OV variables contain the values for the old row and old column. When the program starts, the values are set to one.

Lines 410-430 draw the grid the hurky is hiding in. The GT variable is the column where the grid starts.

Lines 440-460 place the numbers across the bottom of the grid. GT is the column the numbers will be printed on.

Lines 465 place the directions on the screen.

Line 470 clears the bottom three rows on the screen.

Line 475 prints a message and waits for the column number and row number to be entered. Both numbers can be entered with one input statement. Enter one number, a comma, then the second number. The computer stores the first number entered in HH and the second number in HV.

Line 477 clears the symbol from the old location. The first time the computer comes to this line, the OH and OV values are one. The dot will be placed in that location on the grid. By multiplying the values of OV and OH by two and adding eight, the program determines the location on the grid guessed last.

Line 480 places a cross in the location the user guessed. The same formula is used to determine the placement of the marker on the grid.

Line 490 clears the last hint from the screen and starts to print the message.

Line 485 checks the variable for the column HH and the variable for the row HV with those where the hurky is hiding. If the user has guessed the exact location, the program directs the computer to line 600.

Lines 500-530 print the direction the user should move to find hurky.

Line 560 stores the values of HH and HV in OH and OV so the marker can be erased after the next guess. The program directs the computer back to line 475 and another guess.

Lines 600-605 print a message on the screen. By printing the message, going to the timing subroutine, erasing the message and going again to the subroutine, we are able to flash the message on the screen.

Line 610 gives the user the option of playing again.

Lines 620-640 check the first character in C$ for a Y or an N. A Y repeats the game, and N returns the user to the menu. Any other letter repeats the question.

Line 650 begins the game for flipping a coin. The screen is cleared, and directions are printed.

Line 660 erases the cursor for cleaner graphics and animation.

Listing 12-3. Trap 300

```
10 REM LISTING XII.3
15 TRAP 300
20 REM GUESS
30 REM BY L.M.SCHREIBER FOR TAB BOOKS
40 DIM C$(3),DOT$(19),H$(17),S$(17),S1$(1
0),S2$(3),T$(17)
50 ? ">clear>":POSITION 4,10:? "PLEASE CH

OOSE A UNIT FROM 1 TO 3"
60 POSITION 12,12:? "1) CUPS"
70 POSITION 12,14:? "2) HURKY"
80 POSITION 12,16:? "3) FLIP"
90 POSITION 19,18:? "         ";:INPUT A
:REM 5 SPACES & 5 BACKSPACES
100 ON A GOSUB 150,350,650
110 GOTO 50
150 ? ">clear>":REM REMOVE THE MENU
160 ? "HERE ARE 3 CUPS.  I WILL PLACE A B
ALL UNDER ONE OF THEM, AND MIX THEM UP.
 YOU WILL TELL ME WHERE THE";
170 ? "BALL IS."
180 ? :? "READY??? GOOD...LET'S GO!!"
190 POKE 752,1:C$=">QRE>":S1$="   "
200 POSITION 15,15:? C$:POSITION 20,15:?
C$:POSITION 25,15:? C$
210 POSITION 15,15:? S1$:POSITION 15,14:?
 C$:POSITION 16,15:? ">T>":TT=100:GOSUB 1
000
220 POSITION 15,14:? S1$:POSITION 15,15:?
 C$
230 C=INT(RND(1)*3)+1:REM GET THE NUMBER
OF THE CUP
240 FOR X=1 TO 10
250 POSITION 15,15:? S1$:POSITION 20,15:?
 S1$:POSITION 25,15:? S1$
260 POSITION 15,15:? C$:POSITION 20,15:?
C$:POSITION 25,15:? C$
270 NEXT X
280 POKE 752,0:POSITION 10,20:? "WHERE IS
 THE BALL(1,2,3)  ";:INPUT B:REM 2 SPAC
ES & 2 BACKSPACES
```

Listing 12-3. Trap 300. (Continued from page 115.)

```
285 IF B<1 OR B>3 THEN 280
290 POSITION 10,21:IF B=C THEN ? "THAT'S
RIGHT!!!":GOTO 310
300 ? "IT WAS UNDER CUP ";C
310 POSITION 5,22:? "DO YOU WANT TO PLAY
AGAIN (Y-N)";:INPUT C$
320 IF C$(1,1)="Y" THEN POSITION 1,20:? "
":GOTO 190:REM PRINT 3 ESCAPE-SHIFT-DE
LETEs
330 IF C$(1,1)<>"N" THEN 310
340 RETURN
350 ? "}clear}"
360 ? "HURKY IS VERY SHY.  HE LIVES IN A
    10 X 10 GRID.  TRY TO FIND HURKY BY
 ENTERING THE COLUMN AND ROW ";
370 ? "NUMBER    WHERE YOU THINK HE IS LI
KE THIS - 3,4.IF YOU DID NOT GUESS WHERE
HURKY IS,  YOU WILL BE TOLD ";
380 ? "WHICH WAY TO GO."
390 H=INT(RND(1)*10)+1:V=INT(RND(1)*10)+1
:REM H IS THE COLUMN AND V IS THE ROW
400 DOT$="}T T T T T T T T T T}":OH=1:OV=
1:REM OH IS PREVIOUS COLUMN - OV IS THE
410 GT=10:FOR X=9 TO 18:POSITION GT-3,X:?
 11-(X-8):REM Start in the 9th row and pu
t the grid on the screen.
420 POSITION GT,X:? DOT$
430 NEXT X
440 C=1:FOR GT=10 TO 29 STEP 2:REM Put th
e numbers along the bottom too.
450 POSITION GT,X:? C;:C=C+1
460 NEXT GT
465 POSITION 19,8:? "N";:POSITION 4,13:?
"W";:POSITION 31,13:? "E";:POSITION 19,X+
1:? "S";:REM directions
470 POSITION 2,21:? "":REM clear the b
ottom three rows-3 ESCAPE-SHIFT-DELETEs
475 POSITION 5,21:? "Where am I hiding
   ";:INPUT HH,HV:REM set the colum
n and row in one INPUT
477 POSITION OH*2+8,11-(OV-8):? "}T}";:RE
```

```
M CLEAR THE LST GUESS
480 POSITION HH*2+8,11-(HV-8):? "}S}";:RE
M SHOW THE NEW GUESS
485 IF HH=H AND HV=V THEN 600:REM check f
or a match
490 POSITION 5,23:? "                    ";:POS
ITION 5,23:? "GO ";:REM CLEAR THE CLUE LI
NE
495 REM COMPARE WHERE HURKY IS AGAINST TH
E ANSWER AND GIVE THE NEXT CLUE
500 IF V<HV THEN ? "SOUTH ";
510 IF V>HV THEN ? "NORTH ";
520 IF H<HH THEN ? "WEST";
530 IF H>HH THEN ? "EAST";
560 OH=HH:OV=HV:GOTO 475:REM STORE THE PO
SITION JUST ENTERED AND TRY AGAIN
595 REM FLASH THE MESSAGE
600 TT=100:FOR TL1=1 TO 5:POSITION 5,23:?
 "YOU FOUND ME!!!";:GOSUB 1000
605 POSITION 5,23:? "                    ";:G
OSUB 1000:NEXT TL1
610 POSITION 2,21:? "DO YOU WANT TO PLAY
AGAIN (Y-N)    ";:INPUT C$
620 IF C$(1,1)="Y" THEN 390
630 IF C$(1,1)<>"N" THEN 610
640 RETURN
650 ? "}":? "I WILL FLIP A COIN. YOU MUST
  GUESS    WHAT IF WILL BE.   ENTER AN 'H'
FOR    HEADS - A 'T' FOR TAILS "
660 POKE 752,1
670 N=INT(RND(1)*2)+1:REM THINK OF A NUMB
ER - 1=HEADS 2=TAILS
680 H$="        H          ":S$="
     ":S1$="                ":S2$="
":T$="        T          "
681 REM H$ IS }FMG} ESCAPE-CNTRL-DOWNARRO
W- 3 BACKSPACES }V} H }B} ESCAPES-CNTRL-D
OWNARROW 3 BACKSPACES }GNF}
682 REM S$ IS }FMG} ESCAPE-CNTRL-DOWNARRO
W- 3 BACKSPACES }GNF} ESCAPE-CNTRL-DOWNAR
ROW 3 SPACES
```

Listing 12-3. Trap 300. (Continued from page 117.)

```
683 REM S1$ IS 3 SPACES ESCAPE-CNTRL-DOWN
ARROW 3 BACKSPACES }UUU} ESCAPE-CNTRL-DOW
NARROW 3 BACKSPACES 3 SPACES
684 REM S2$ IS }UUU} IN REVERSE VIDEO
685 REM T$ IS }FMG} ESCAPE-CNTRL-DOWNARRO
W- 3 BACKSPACES }V} T }B} ESCAPES-CNTRL-D
OWNARROW 3 BACKSPACES }GNF}
690 TT=10:FOR X=1 TO 5
700 POSITION 10,10:? H$:GOSUB 1000
710 POSITION 10,10:? S$:GOSUB 1000
720 POSITION 10,10:? S1$:GOSUB 1000
730 POSITION 10,11:? S2$:GOSUB 1000
740 POSITION 10,10:? S$:GOSUB 1000
750 POSITION 10,10:? T$:GOSUB 1000
760 POSITION 10,10:? S$:GOSUB 1000
770 POSITION 10,10:? S1$:GOSUB 1000
780 POSITION 10,11:? S2$:GOSUB 1000
790 POSITION 10,10:? S$:GOSUB 1000
800 NEXT X
900 POSITION 10,15:? "WHAT IS IT (H-T)
";:INPUT C$:IF C$<>"T" AND C$<>"H" THE
N 900
905 DOT$=T$:IF N=1 THEN DOT$=H$
910 POSITION 10,10:? DOT$
915 IF N=1 AND C$="H" THEN 930
920 IF N=2 AND C$="T" THEN 930
925 GOTO 950
930 POSITION 10,20:? "VERY GOOD!!!"
950 POSITION 2,22:? "DO YOU WANT TO PLAY
AGAIN (Y-N) ";:INPUT C$
960 IF C$="Y" THEN POSITION 10,15:? "
":GOTO 670:REM PRINT 9 ESCAPE-SHIFT-D
ELETEs
970 IF C$<>"N" THEN 950
980 RETURN
990 END
1000 FOR TL=1 TO TT:NEXT TL:RETURN :REM T
IMING SUBROUTINE
```

Line 670 picks a random number. If the computer chooses a one, the coin will flip to heads, if it chooses a two, the coin will flip to tails.

Line 680 places the graphics characters into the correct strings. These strings will be printed when the coin is flipped.

Line 690 begins the For . . . Next loop that prints the coin while it is being flipped.

Lines 700-790 print a string, then go to the subroutine, giving the user enough time to view the coin while it flips. The TT variable is set to ten. Try changing its value to see the effect a larger or smaller number will have.

Line 900 waits for the user to call the coin. H should be entered for heads, and T for tails.

Lines 905-910 print the correct side of the coin on the screen. Here is an example of setting a string to a set of characters then comparing a value. If the value of N is one, the contents of DOT$ will be changed.

Lines 915-920 check the entry in C$ against the face value of the coin (1=heads, 2=tails). A correct entry sends the computer to line 930.

Line 925 sends the computer to line 950. The answer entered was wrong since it did not match on the two previous lines.

Line 930 prints the appropriate praise.

Line 950 gives the user the option of playing again or returning to the menu.

Lines 960-980 check the contents of C$. If a Y was entered, the game continues. If an N was entered, the menu will be printed on the screen. An incorrect entry repeats the question.

Line 1000 is the timing loop. In this program, the second number of the loop can be changed to any number by setting the TT variable before the program sends the computer to this subroutine.

Chapter 13

Arithmetic Functions

ATARI BASIC can perform any standard arithmetic function: addition, subtraction, multiplication, division, raising to a power, etc. When the computer solves an equation, it follows these priority rules:

1. parentheses
2. raising to a power
3. multiply and/or divide
4. addition and/or subtraction.

If you want a subtraction operation completed before multiplication, you must place the numbers and/or variables in parentheses. Below are some examples of the way the computer would solve various types of equations.

$$4+2*3-8=2$$
$$8*(53-8)+9=369$$
$$47-2^2+(4*5)=63.00000004$$

As you can see ATARI BASIC does not raise numbers to a power correctly. The correct answer to the last equation is 63.

In any equation, variables can be substituted for the numbers. If a value has been assigned to the variable, the computer will use that value. If no value has been assigned, the computer will use a zero.

INT

In this chapter we will discuss the five most frequently used special functions. When you want a whole number without the fractional part (the numbers after the decimal point), you will use the INT (integer) command. This command ignores any numbers following the decimal point and the variable becomes a whole number, E.g., X=INT(10/3). X would be equal to 3.

Program Listing 13-1 uses the INT command to figure the number of coins to be given as change.

Line 40 clears the screen and tells the player the computer has $5.00.

Line 50 asks the user how much money will be spent, and waits for an input. The amount spent will be stored in the Spend variable.

Listing 13-1. Change

```
10 REM LISTING XIII.1
20 REM CHANGE
30 REM BY L.M.SCHREIBER FOR TAB BOOKS
40 ? "}clear}":POSITION 2,5:? "YOU HAVE $
5.00"
50 POSITION 2,7:? "HOW MUCH DO YOU WANT T
O SPEND      ";:INPUT SPEND
60 IF SPEND>5 THEN 50:REM DON'T SPEND MOR
E THAN YOU HAVE
70 CHANGE=5-SPEND:REM GET THE AMOUNT LEFT

80 ? :? "YOU HAVE $";CHANGE;:IF CHANGE*10
=INT(CHANGE/0.1) THEN ? "0";
85 ? " LEFT"
90 CHANGE=CHANGE*100:REM MAKE IT ALL PENN
IES
95 DOLLARS=INT(CHANGE/100):REM GET THE NU
MBER OF DOLLARS
100 IF DOLLARS<>0 THEN CHANGE=CHANGE-DOLL
ARS*100:REM REMOVE THE DOLLARS
110 QUARTERS=INT(CHANGE/25):IF QUARTERS<>
0 THEN CHANGE=CHANGE-QUARTERS*25
120 DMES=INT(CHANGE/10):IF DMES<>0 THEN C
HANGE=CHANGE-DMES*10
130 NICKEL=INT(CHANGE/5):IF NICKEL<>0 THE
N CHANGE=CHANGE-NICKEL*5
140 PENNIES=CHANGE
150 ? :? DOLLARS;" DOLLAR(S)",QUARTERS;"
QUARTER(S)":? DMES;" DIME(S)",NICKEL;" NI
CKEL(S)":? PENNIES;" PENNIES"
```

Line 60 checks the amount entered. If more than $5.00 has been entered, the computer is sent back to line 50.

Line 70 subtracts the amount spent from $5.00 and stores it in the Change variable. This is the amount of change the user would receive.

Line 80 tells the user how much change the user has. If the cents ended with a zero, like $1.20, the computer would print only 1.2 as the amount in Change. The program checks the value of ten times the amount in Change (moves the decimal one place to the right) against the integer of Change times 10. If the number ends with a zero the result of multiplying the number times ten will be the same as taking the integer of the number multiplied by 10.

Line 85 prints the last word in the message.

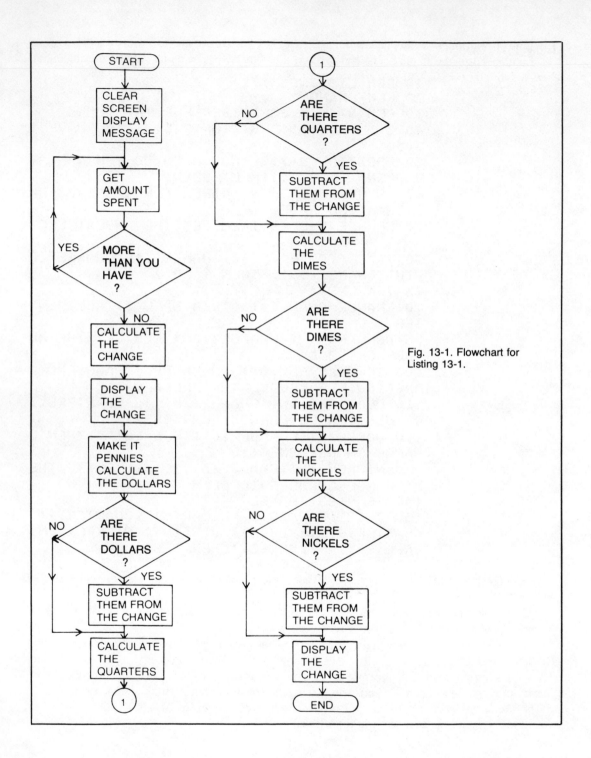

Fig. 13-1. Flowchart for Listing 13-1.

Line 90 multiplies the amount stored in Change by 100. This converts the amount to pennies.

Line 95 stores the amount of dollars in the Dollars variable. The dollar value is the amount of change divided by 100. The integer command stores only the dollars in the variable.

Line 100 tests the value of dollars for a zero. If it is a zero, we will know no dollars have been removed and the amount stored in Change is less than a dollar. In this case the computer goes to the next line. If dollars have been removed, the computer must reduce the amount stored in Change by that amount. Multiplying the value of Dollars by 100 and subtracting that amount from Change removes the dollars from Change.

Line 110 finds the number of quarters in Change by dividing the value stored there by 25. The next statement in the line tests the value of Quarters for the amount of quarters removed. If there were quarters in the change, the program removes them from the value stored in Quarters by multiplying that value by 25 and subtracting the result from the value stored in Change.

Line 120 finds the number of dimes in Change by dividing the value stored in DMES by 10. This variable cannot be DIMES because it contains the DIM command. By changing it to DMES we do not confuse the computer. The next statement in the line tests the value stored in DMES to see if any dimes have been removed. By multiplying the value stored in DMES by ten and subtracting that number from the value stored in Change, we arrive at the amount of change left.

Line 130 finds the number of nickels by dividing the value stored in Change by five. The line further tests the Nickel variable to see if any nickels were removed. The computer removes the number of nickels by multiplying the number of nickels removed by five and subtracting that amount from the amount stored in Change.

Line 140 takes the remaining Change and stores it in the Pennies variable.

Lines 150-160 print the amount of change you would receive in dollars, quarters, dimes, nickels, and pennies.

Notice that in every line the value stored in Change was divided by a value, the computer was told to take the integer of the value.

ABS

The ABSolute command gives the value of a number without the sign. The absolute of −3 and of +3 is 3. It is used when you need to know the difference between two numbers without regard to the sign. Listing 13-2 is a good example of the absolute command. The program tells a child user how many spaces a marble is away from a hole without telling the child if the number should be bigger or smaller.

Line 40 clears the screen and erases the cursor.

Line 50 draws a straight line across the screen. Use   control N   for the line.

Line 60 draws the sides of the holes. Use   control B, space,   and   control   V for the holes. The For . . . Next loop spaces the holes evenly on the screen.

Line 70 numbers the holes. The C variable increases and is used to number the holes. X increases by three in the For . . . Next loop, so it would be impractical to use it to number the holes.

Line 80 chooses a random number from one to twelve. This number will be used in the example.

Listing 13-2. Bounce

```
10 REM LISTING XIII.2
20 REM BOUNCE
30 REM BY L.M.SCHREIBER FOR TAB BOOKS
40 ? "}clear}":POKE 752,1
50 FOR X=0 TO 39:POSITION X,10:? "}N}";:N
EXT X:REM DRAW THE GROUND
60 FOR X=2 TO 35 STEP 3:POSITION X,11:? "
}B V}":NEXT X:REM DRAW THE HOLES
70 C=1:FOR X=2 TO 35 STEP 3:POSITION X+1,
12:? C:C=C+1:NEXT X:REM NUMBER THEM
80 H=INT(RND(1)*12)+1:REM THINK OF THE MA
GIC HOLE
90 C=1:FOR X=2 TO 35 STEP 3:POSITION X+1,
9:? "}T}":GOSUB 500:POSITION X+1,9:? " ":
IF C=H THEN 120:REM BALL DOWN
100 POSITION X+2,5:? "}T}":GOSUB 500:REM
BOUNCING UP
110 POSITION X+2,5:? " ":C=C+1:NEXT X:REM
 COUNT THE HOLE IT IS OVER
120 POSITION X+1,10:? " }T}":GOSUB 500:P
OSITION X+1,10:? " ":REM DROP IT IN-SPACE
 ESCAPE-CNTRL-BACKARROW }T}
130 POSITION X+1,10:? "}N}";:REM COVER IT
 OVER
132 REM NOW START TO PLAY
135 H=INT(RND(1)*12)+1:REM THINK OF THE M
AGIC HOLE
137 REM LET HUMAN GUESS WHICH HOLE WILL O
PEN
138 POSITION 2,9:? "
                 ":REM CLEAR ALL BALLS
140 POSITION 2,15:? "THE BALL CAN ONLY FA
LL THROUGH ONE OF THESE HOLES. GUESS WHIC
H ONE    ";:INPUT G
145 REM BOUNCE TO THAT HOLE
150 C=1:FOR X=2 TO 35 STEP 3:POSITION X+1
,9:? "}T}":GOSUB 500:IF C=G THEN 180
160 POSITION X+1,9:? " ":POSITION X+2,5:?
 "}T}":GOSUB 500
170 POSITION X+2,5:? " ":C=C+1:NEXT X
180 IF G<>H THEN 250:REM CHECK THE GUESS
```

```
- TRY AGAIN IF IT IS NOT RIGHT
185 POSITION X+1,9:? " "
190 POSITION X+1,10:? " }T}":GOSUB 500:P
OSITION X+1,10:? " ":REM IT'S RIGHT-LET T
HE BALL IN-SPACE ESC-CNTRL-BKAR
200 POSITION X+1,10:? "}N}";
205 POSITION 5,20:? "":REM CLEAR THE LIN
E BEFORE PRINTING THE MESSAGE-ESCAPE-CNTR
L-DELETE
210 FOR TL=1 TO 5:POSITION 5,20:? "YOU GO
T IT":GOSUB 500:POSITION 5,20:? "
  ":GOSUB 500:NEXT TL
220 GOTO 135:REM GO THINK OF ANOTHER NUMB
ER
250 N=ABS(H-G):REM SUBTRACT THE GUESS FRO
M THE HOLE
260 POSITION 5,20:? "YOU ARE ";N;" SPACES
 AWAY":GOTO 140:REM TELL HUMAN HOW FAR AW
AY - BUT NOT WHICH WAY
500 FOR ZZ=1 TO 50:NEXT ZZ:RETURN :REM LE
AVE IT ON THE SCREEN
```

Lines 90-110 bounce the ball across the screen. C is used to count again, after being set to one before the For . . . Next loop. The loop counts by three, keeping the ball consistent with the holes. Use   control T   to print the ball. Adding one to the value of X will place the ball over the hole. After the ball is printed, the program directs the computer to the timing subroutine. This gives the user a chance to see the ball in each position on the screen. The ball is erased from that position and C is compared to the number chosen in the previous line. If both numbers are the same, the computer goes to line 120. If the two variables are not equal, the computer continues with the next line. That line prints the ball four rows above the line, and goes to the timing subroutine. The next line erases the ball, adds one to the counter and continues the loop. The ball needs to be printed only in the two positions to give the illusion of bouncing. If you change the length of time in the timing loop, the ball will bounce faster or slower.

Line 120 erases the top of the hole and places the ball in that position. After the timing subroutine, the ball is erased and the program continues.

Line 130 prints the cover of the hole in the position the ball was in. This creates the illusion of the ball falling into the hole.

Line 135 begins the part of the program where in the user guesses where the next hole is. The computer chooses a number from one to twelve.

Line 138 prints a row of spaces above the line. This clears all the balls from the previous game.

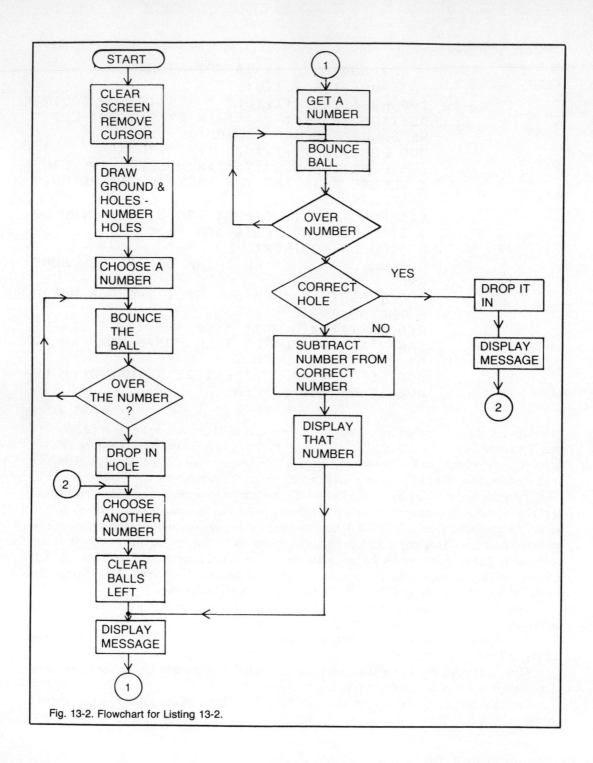

Fig. 13-2. Flowchart for Listing 13-2.

Line 140 prints a message on the screen and waits for a number to be entered. Be sure to include the four spaces and backspaces. This line will be reused throughout the game. The last number entered must be erased from the screen.

Lines 145-170 bounce the ball across the screen. The ball always starts above the first hole and stops over the number of the hole entered. This routine is similar to the one used in the demonstration, however, instead of comparing the count to the random number, the count is compared to the number entered. If both variables are equal, the program directs the computer to line 180.

Line 180 compares the number entered to the number the computer chose. If the numbers do not match, the computer goes to line 250.

Lines 185-200 drop the ball through the hole. Lines 190 and 200 are identical to lines 120 and 130. These lines could be made into one subroutine.

Line 205 clears any message on row 20.

Line 210 flashes the message   YOU GOT IT   on the screen.

Line 220 sends the computer back to line 135 for another game.

Line 250 uses the absolute command. The user's guess is subtracted from the number the computer chose. Since we only want the program to state the number of holes the user is away from the correct hole, and not let the user know whether the guess was high or low, we have the computer disregard the remainder's sign, and only print the absolute value of the variable.

Line 260 prints this information on the screen and goes back to line 140 for another guess.

Line 500 is the subroutine used as a timing loop throughout the program.

SQR

The SQuaRe command finds the square root of a number or variable. Unlike its counterpart, this command does compute the correct value. Its format is:

```
100 X=SQR(V):REM THE SQUARE ROOT OF 'V' IS STORED IN 'X'
```

RND

RND is the most frequently used special function. It has been used in every program choosing a random number. The number the computer chooses is between the values of zero and one. Try Listing 13-3 (see flowchart in Fig. 13-3).

Lines 40-70 choose and print a random number. The numbers printed on the screen are always less than one, but always greater than zero. Each time that the program is run, a different set of numbers will be printed.

Lines 90-120 print a number greater than zero. Line 100 multiplies the number by five. The number printed is now more than zero, but less than five, because the computer is multiplying a decimal value that is less than one by five.

Lines 140-170 print the integer of the number chosen. The integer command is usually used with the RND command. It is very rare to need a number with the decimal in a program. The numbers printed in this routine will be from zero to four.

Lines 190-220 add one to the number chosen. By adding one to the number, we will get a number from one to five. Any value can be added to the random number. The value added will

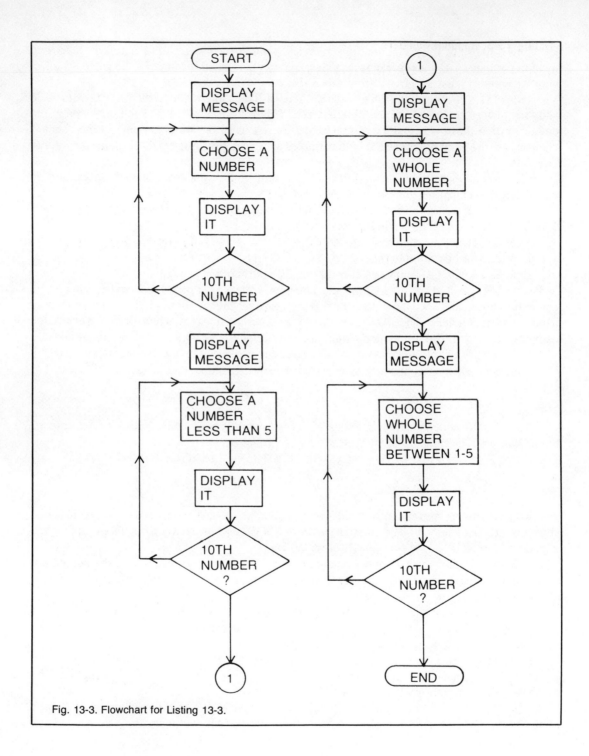

Fig. 13-3. Flowchart for Listing 13-3.

Listing 13-3. Random Numbers

```
10 REM LISTING XIII.3
20 REM RANDOM
30 REM BY L.M.SCHREIBER FOR TAB BOOKS
40 ? "RANDOM":FOR X=1 TO 10:REM GIVE 10 S
AMPLE NUMBERS
50 N=RND(1):REM GET A RANDOM NUMBER
60 ? N,:REM SHOW IT
70 NEXT X
80 REM NOW SHOW IT WITH A MULTIPLE
90 ? :? "MORE THAN 0":FOR X=1 TO 10
100 N=RND(1)*5
110 ? N,:REM IT'S MORE THAN 0 BUT LESS TH
AN 5
120 NEXT X
130 REM NOW WITH THE INTEGER COMMAND
140 ? :? "INTEGER":FOR X=1 TO 10
150 N=INT(RND(1)*5):REM ANY NUMBER BETWEE
N 0 AND 4
160 ? N,
170 NEXT X
180 REM NOW ADD 1
190 ? :? "ADD 1 TO NUMBER":FOR X=1 TO 10
200 N=INT(RND(1)*5)+1:REM ANY NUMBER BETW
EEN 1 AND 5 INCLUSIVE
210 ? N,
220 NEXT X
230 END
```

increase the number by that value. The numbers from zero to one less than that number will never be chosen, e.g., X=INT(RND(1)*20)+5 will only return numbers from five to twenty-four.

SGN

The SiGN command sets a variable to -1 if the variable it checks is negative, and to zero if the variable is positive. It can be used when you are not interested in the actual value, but are checking for a negative or positive result. An example is a checking account program that would need to know if the balance in the account is above zero.

Listing 13-4 checks temperatures for a month and finds the warmest and coldest days of the month.

Lines 50-70 store the number of the month in the Month variable, then reads the number of days in each month until it comes to the month entered. The number of days in that month are stored in the Days variable.

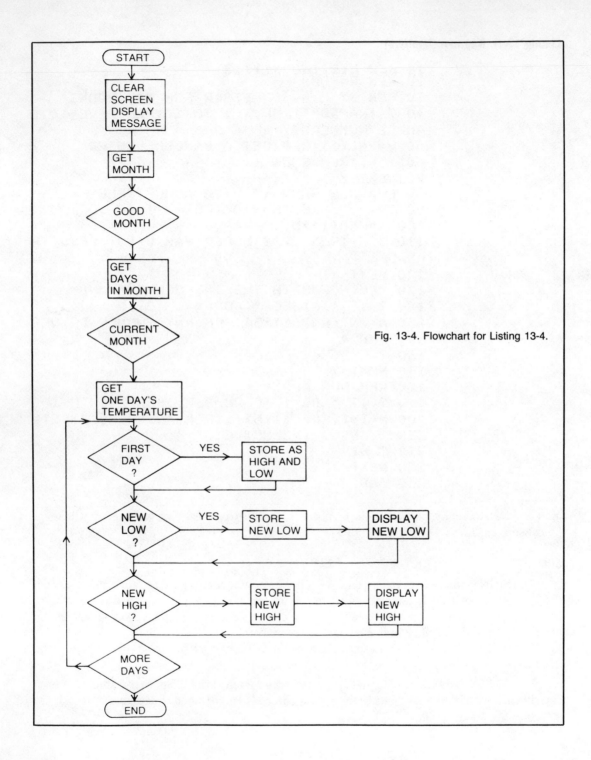

Fig. 13-4. Flowchart for Listing 13-4.

Listing 13-4. Negative Numbers

```
10 REM LISTING XIII.4
20 REM NEGATIVES
30 REM BY L.M.SCHREIBER FOR TAB BOOKS
40 ? "}clear}"
50 ? "ENTER THE NUMBER OF THE MONTH
":INPUT MONTH
60 FOR X=1 TO MONTH:READ DAYS:REM READ TH
E NUMBER OF DAYS
70 NEXT X
80 FOR X=1 TO DAYS
90 POSITION 2,10:? "WHAT WAS THE TEMPERAT
URE":? "  FOR ";MONTH;"-";X;"   ";:INP
UT TEMP:REM 3 SPACES & BACKSPACE
100 IF X=1 THEN LOW=TEMP:HIGH=TEMP:REM FI
RST DAYS SET THE RECORDS
110 IF SGN(TEMP-LOW)=-1 THEN POSITION 10,
20:? "NEW LOW TEMPERATURE ";TEMP;"   ";LO
W=TEMP
120 IF SGN(HIGH-TEMP)=-1 THEN POSITION 10
,22:? "NEW HIGH TEMPERATURE ";TEMP;"   ";:
HIGH=TEMP
130 NEXT X
150 END
500 DATA 31,28,31,30,31,30,31,31,30,31,30
,31:. DAYS IN THE MONTH
```

Lines 80-130 get the temperature for each day of the month. Line 100 sets the Low and High variables to the same value on the first day.

Line 110 uses the Sign command. The value stored in Low is subtracted from the value in Temp. If the difference is a negative number, there is a new low temperature. We are not concerned with how many degrees colder it was, just the fact that it was colder. The new low temperature is printed on the screen, and that temperature is stored in Low.

Line 120 subtracts Temp from High. Again, if the result is negative, the new high will be printed on the screen and the value of Temp will be stored in High.

Chapter 14

Working with Strings

Storing information in a string gives you easy access to the information, lets you move the information around within the string, and lets you use only the parts of the string you need.

As you learned in Chapter 9, a string is made up of consecutive characters. Each character occupies one byte of memory. All strings must be dimensioned before they can be used in a program. One of the features of ATARI BASIC is that the string can be dimensioned to any length needed for a program as long as you have enough memory to support the string. The program we will develop in this chapter allows a teacher to enter the names of students in a class and scores for each student's tests. The program will also total the scores and print the report card markings for each student on the screen. The program assumes that the first and last names of the students will not exceed 20 characters. Listing 14-1 uses many of the techniques presented in the previous chapters.

Lines 100-120 print the menu on the screen. The user can choose to enter the names of the students, enter the test scores, or print the students' scores. The N variable stores the number of the unit entered.

Lines 125-130 check the value of the variable. If the number entered is too large or too small, the program directs the computer back to line 120.

Line 135 uses selective branching. The number entered determines the routine the computer goes to.

Line 150 begins the routine to enter the students' names. The SC variable is cleared. SC holds the number of each test being entered. Since we are setting up a new class, the number of tests entered are zero. The S variable holds the number of students in this class.

Line 155 checks the amount of free memory. F holds the amount of free memory. Since we are allocating 20 bytes of memory per student for the name, we must be sure we have enough memory to handle all the students. If there is insufficient memory, that message will be printed and the program will return to line 150.

Line 160 dimensions the amount of memory needed for the students names. We can use this command more than once in a program if the variables being dimensioned are different.

Line 165 clears student$. The names of the students will not occupy every byte in the string, so the string must be cleared before it can be used.

Listing 14-1. Student Test Scorekeeper

```
10 REM LISTING XIV.1
20 REM STUDENTS TESTS
30 REM BY L.M.SCHREIBER FOR TAB BOOKS
100 CLR :DIM A$(20),CLAS$(20):? "}":POSIT
ION 4,5:? "PLEASE ENTER A NUMBER"
105 POSITION 6,8:? "1.  ENTER NAMES OF ST
UDENTS"
110 POSITION 6,10:? "2.  ENTER TEST SCORE
S"
115 POSITION 6,12:? "3.  PRINT STUDENTS S
CORES"
120 POSITION 10,14:? "     ";:INPUT N:
REM 4 SPACES & BACKSPACES
125 IF N<1 THEN 120
130 IF N>3 THEN 120
135 ON N GOTO 150,500,700
150 SC=0:? "}clear}":POSITION 3,10:? "HOW
 MANY STUDENTS IN THIS CLASS";:INPUT S
155 F=FRE(S):IF F<S*20 THEN ? "INSUFFICIE
NT MEMORY":GOSUB 1200:GOTO 150
160 DIM STUDENT$(S*20):REM SET ASIDE MEMO
RY FOR THE STUDENTS
165 FOR X=1 TO S*20:STUDENT$(X,X)=" ":NEX
T X:REM CLEAR OUT THE STRING
170 POSITION 3,12:? "HOW MANY TEST SCORES
 WILL YOU BE      ENTERING FOR EACH STUDE
NT   ";:INPUT TS
175 F=FRE(S):IF F<TS*3*S THEN ? :? "INSUF
FICIENT MEMORY FOR THAT NUMBER OF STUDENT
S":GOSUB 1200:GOTO 170
180 DIM TEST$(TS*3*S):FOR X=1 TO TS*3*S:T
EST$(X,X)="},}":NEXT X:REM CLEAR THIS STR
ING TOO
190 ? "}":POSITION 4,3:? "PLEASE NAME THI
S CLASS";:INPUT CLAS$
200 FOR X=1 TO S:POSITION 4,6:? "STUDENT
";X
205 POSITION 4,8:? "":POSITION 4,8:? "NA
ME ";:INPUT A$:REM PRINT ESCAPE-CNTRL-DEL
ETE
210 STUDENT$(X*20-19,X*20)=A$
```

Listing 14-1. Student Test Scorekeeper. (Continued from page 133.)

```
215 NEXT X
220 L1=LEN(CLAS$):L2=TS*3*S
230 GOTO 1100
500 GOSUB 1000
535 SC=SC+1:IF SC>TS THEN ? "ALL TESTS HA
VE BEEN ENTERED":GOSUB 1200:GOTO 100
540 SE=SC*3:SB=SE-2:REM OFFSET FOR STARTI
NG & ENDING LOCATIONS FOR THE TEST
545 FOR L=1 TO S:POSITION 5,10:? STUDENT$
(L*20-19,L*20)
550 POSITION 5,12:? "TEST SCORE (NUMBERS)
    ";:INPUT SCORE
555 IF SCORE>100 OR SCORE<0 THEN 550:REM
CHECK IF SCORE IS LEGAL
560 TB=(L-1)*TS*3:A$=STR$(SCORE):TEST$(TB
+SB,TB+SE)=A$:NEXT L
565 L2=TS*3*S:GOTO 1100
700 GOSUB 1000:IF SC=0 THEN 100
705 ? ">clear}":? "DO YOU WANT TO GET A C
LASS AVERAGE OR THE STUDENTS AVERAGES (C-
S)  ";:INPUT A$
710 IF S$(1,1)="C" THEN 750
715 IF A$(1,1)<>"S" THEN 705
720 TB=0:FOR L=1 TO S:POSITION 5,8:? STUD
ENT$(L*20-19,L*20)
725 TOTAL=0:FOR X=1 TO SC:SE=X*3:SB=SE-2:
TOTAL=TOTAL+VAL(TEST$(TB+SB,TB+SE)):NEXT
X:TB=TB+TS*3
730 AVE=TOTAL/SC+0.5:AVE=INT(AVE)
735 POSITION 5,10:? "AVERAGE IS
";AVE:REM 5 SPACES & BACKSPACES
740 ? "PRESS RETURN FOR NEXT AVERAGE";:IN
PUT A$
745 NEXT L:? ">clear}":? "DO YOU WANT THE
 CLASS AVERAGE (Y-N)  ";:INPUT A$:IF A$
(1,1)="N" THEN 100
750 ? ">clear}":? "WHICH TEST DO YOU WANT
 A CLASS AVERAGE OF (1-";SC;")  ";:INPU
T T
755 IF T>SC THEN 750
760 SE=T*3:SB=SE-2:TOTAL=0:FOR L=1 TO S:T
```

```
B=(L-1)*TS*3:TOTAL=TOTAL+VAL(TEST$(TB+SB,
TB+SE)):NEXT L
765 AVE=TOTAL/S+0.5:AVE=INT(AVE)
770 ? "THE CLASS AVERAGE FOR TEST #";T;"
IS";AVE
775 ? "DO YOU WANT ANOTHER CLASS AVERAGE
(Y-N)     ";:INPUT A$
780 IF A$(1,1)="Y" THEN 750
785 IF A$(1,1)<>"N" THEN 755
790 GOTO 100
1000 ? "}clear}":POSITION 2,4:? "PLACE TH
E PROPER CASSETTE IN THE"
1002 ? "RECORDER AND PRESS THE PLAY BUTTO
N     AND RETURN"
1005 OPEN #7,4,0,"C:"
1010 GET #7,L1:GET #7,S:GET #7,TS:GET #7,
SC:CLOSE #7
1015 DIM STUDENT$(S*20),TEST$(TS*3*S)
1020 L2=TS*3*S:OPEN #7,4,0,"C:"
1025 FOR L=1 TO L1:GET #7,V:CLAS$(L,L)=CH
R$(V):NEXT L
1030 FOR L=1 TO S*20:GET #7,V:STUDENT$(L,
L)=CHR$(V):NEXT L
1035 FOR L=1 TO L2:GET #7,V:TEST$(L,L)=CH
R$(V):NEXT L:CLOSE #7
1040 POSITION 2,8:? "TAPE FOR ";CLAS$
1042 ? "IF WRONG TAPE, ENTER 'W'":? "ENTE
R 'R' FOR RIGHT TAPE   ";:INPUT A$
1045 IF A$="W" THEN POP :GOTO 100
1050 IF A$<>"R" THEN 1040
1055 RETURN
1100 ? "}clear}":? "REWIND THE CASSETTE":
? "PRESS BOTH BUTTONS ON THE RECORDER"
1105 OPEN #7,8,0,"C:"
1110 PUT #7,L1:PUT #7,S:PUT #7,TS:PUT #7,
SC:CLOSE #7
1115 OPEN #7,8,0,"C:"
1120 FOR L=1 TO L1:PUT #7,ASC(CLAS$(L,L))
:NEXT L
1125 FOR L=1 TO S*20:PUT #7,ASC(STUDENT$(
L,L)):NEXT L
```

Listing 14-1. Student Test Scorekeeper. (Continued from page 135.)

```
1130 FOR L=1 TO L2:PUT #7,ASC(TEST$(L,L))
:NEXT L:CLOSE #7
1135 GOTO 100
1200 FOR ZZ=1 TO 900:NEXT ZZ:RETURN
```

Line 170 enters the number of test scores that will be entered for each student. The number of tests are stored in the TS variable.

Line 175 checks the amount of free memory available. If there is not enough, a message will be printed and the program will direct the computer to line 170. Fewer tests will have to be entered for this class.

Line 180 dimensions TEST$ to allow three bytes per test per student. The For . . . Next loop places a character in each byte when it clears the string. When this program stores the information in the string on tape, it will stop at the last character. It is important that there is a character in *every* byte of the string. Use   control comma   for the character to fill in bytes.

Line 190 places the name of the class into CLAS$. This way, a teacher could have a tape for each subject or class taught.

Lines 100-215 place the name of each student into STUDENT$. The name of each student is temporarily stored in A$. The part of the string that will contain the student's name is computed by multiplying the student's number (X) by 20, and subtracting 19. This is the first byte of the string segment that will contain A$. By multiplying the student's number by 20, the computer knows where the last byte is for the name.

Line 220 stores the length of CLAS$ in the L1 variable, the length of TEST$ is stored in L2.

Line 230 sends the computer to the line that will save these names onto a cassette.

Line 500 begins the routine to enter the scores of the students. This routine starts with a subroutine. If you look at Fig. 14-1, you will see that the second and third routines need to load the names of the students before continuing with the rest of the routine. Both routines use the same subroutines to save memory.

Line 535 adds one to the number of tests stored. If the number is more than the number entered when the tape was set up, there is no more room in the string for the test scores. A message will be printed and the program will return to the menu.

Line 540 computes the location in the string where the first character or number of the score will be placed, and the last place it could be stored. The location in the string is dependent on which test is being entered. SE contains the ending position and SB the beginning.

Lines 545-560 are the For . . . Next loop that prints the name of each student on the screen, the test number, and waits for the test score to be entered. The score will be stored in the Score variable. The score entered will be checked to make sure it is not greater than 100 or less than 0. If the teacher allows scores greater than 100 (extra credit on tests, etc.), this number will have to be adjusted to allow for those exceptions. The student's position in the string is calculated by multiplying the number of test scores that could be entered by three times one less than the student's number. The value of Score cannot be stored in a string as a variable. It is converted into a string with the STR$ command, and stored in A$. The first location and last location of TEST$ is calculated by adding the displacement values, SB and SE, to the student's location in TEST$. The score can now be stored in TEST$.

Line 565 sets L2 to the length of TEST$. The program directs the computer to the routine at line 1100 so the scores entered can be stored on tape.

Line 700 begins the routine that displays the scores of the students. First the program directs the computer to the subroutine that gets the scores from the cassette tape. It checks to see if there are scores on the tape. If there were no scores entered (SC=0), the program returns to the menu.

Line 705 clears the screen and asks the user to enter an S or a C. An S should be entered for the student's averages; a C to receive the class average for a particular test.

Lines 710-715 check the letter entered, and direct the computer to the proper routine.

Line 720 sets TB to zero. This variable is used to reference the test scores in TEST$. The For . . . Next loop prints the name of the student. Again, we use a formula to find the name of each student in the string.

Line 725 sets the Total variable to zero. This variable will be used to total the scores for the student. The For . . . Next loop in this line is used to add the scores together. SC is the total number of scores that have been entered. SE is the last location of the test scores for this test. By subtracting two, the first place of the test score is calculated. *Remember:* there are three places for each test. Total is equal to the previous total for this student plus the VALues of TEST$ from the first location of this test score to the last location. This loop continues until all the scores have been totalled. TB is incremented by the number of tests that had spaces reserved times three. Now TB is the reference point for the test scores for the next student.

Line 730 finds the average for the student. The Total is divided by the number of scores entered, plus 0.5. Adding .5 to a number rounds the number to the next value. Since we want the average to be a whole number, we take the integer of the average.

Line 735 prints the average on the screen.

Line 740 waits until the return key has been pressed. This holds the information on the screen until the user is ready to go on.

Line 745 continues the For . . . Next loop. After this loop is completed, the screen clears, and the user is given the opportunity to ask for a class average. Entering N returns the program to the menu.

Line 750 begins the second part of this routine. After the screen clears, the user is asked which test he wants the class average for. Since SC contains the number of tests entered, the program will always print the number of tests entered.

Line 755 checks the number entered against the number of tests recorded. If a number greater than the number of tests is entered, the program will repeat the question.

Line 760 adds one test from each student together. SE is the end position for the test score. By subtracting two, the first position of that test score is calculated. The value of Total is set to zero. In the For . . . Next loop, TB is the reference point for the position in the string for the score for each student. By subtracting one from the student number and multiplying that number times the number of tests that could be entered by three, we arrive at the starting location for that student's scores. By adding the beginning position to TB and the ending position to TB, we can

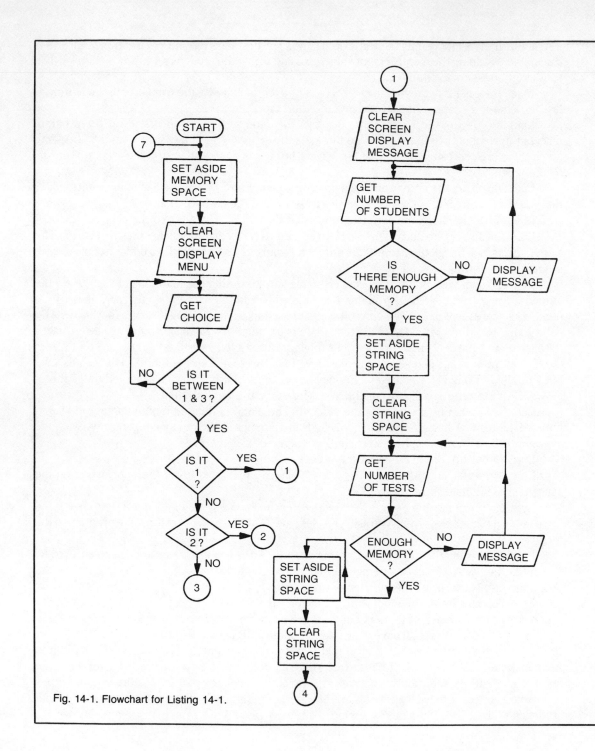

Fig. 14-1. Flowchart for Listing 14-1.

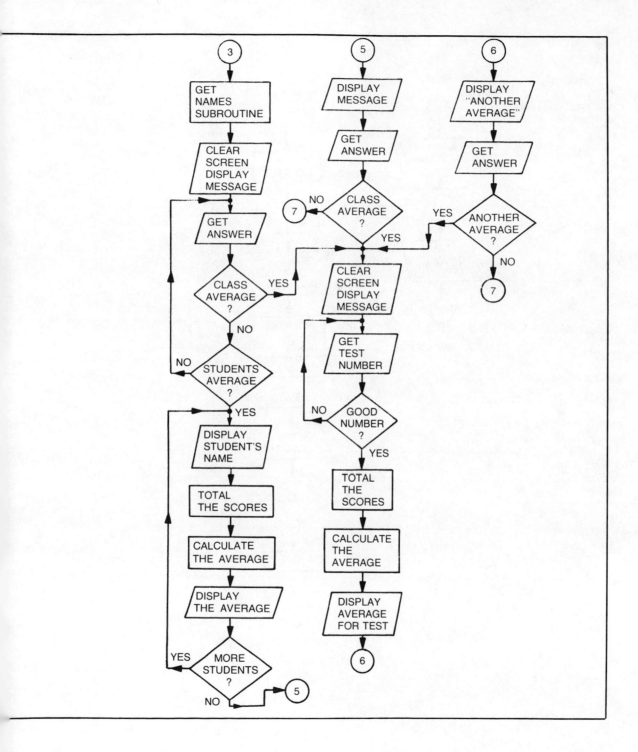

139

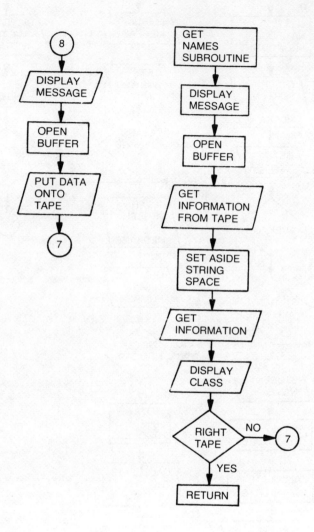

Fig. 14-1. Continued from page 139.

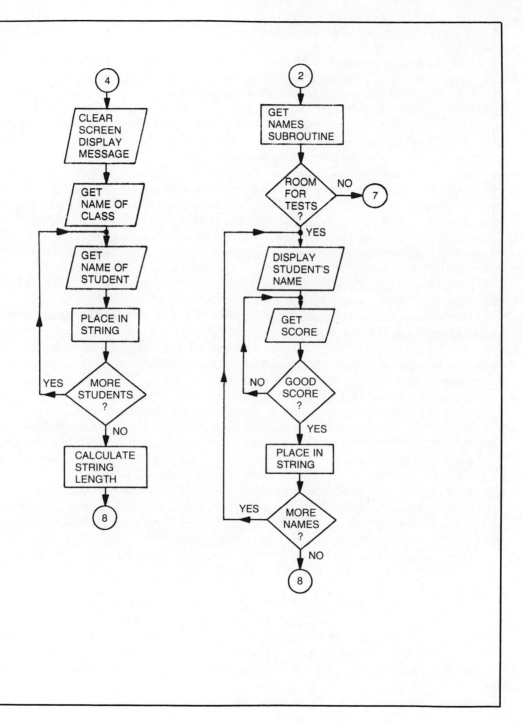

get the score for that particular test. The loop continues until all the students' scores have been totalled.

Line 765 divides the Total by the number of students, and adds .5. Again, we add .5 to round the average. The average is the integer of the average.

Line 770 prints the class average for a particular test.

Lines 775-790 allow the user to request another class average or return to the menu.

Lines 1000-1002 print a message on the screen. This is the subroutine that gets the data from the cassette tape. The screen clears and you are instructed to place the correct cassette into the program recorder and press the play button.

Line 1005 opens the port to the cassette for reading. The number seven indicates which buffer will be used, the four means the computer will be reading the information from the tape, the zero is a dummy value, the "C:" means the information will be coming from the cassette.

Line 1010 gets the information from the tape. The GET command tells the computer it will be receiving information. The number seven is the buffer it will be coming through, and each variable will contain the number the computer received.   CLOSE   7   tells the computer to stop listening.

Line 1015 dimensions STUDENT$ to the number of students times 20 and TEST$ to the number of tests times three times the number of students.

Line 1020 sets L2 to the length of TEST$. Buffer 7 is opened again. The computer will read more information on the cassette. The computer can only listen to one byte at a time.

Line 1025 contains the For . . . Next loop that gets the name of the class stored on the cassette. It places the character of the number it received into the string. The command CHR$ converts a number into the character it represents.

Line 1030 gets the names of the students in the same manner. Each number the computer receives will be converted into the letter or character it represents.

Line 1035 gets the test scores for all the students. The buffer is closed and the tape recorder will shut off.

Lines 1040-1055 prints the name of the class just entered on the screen. If the wrong tape was entered, the computer will POP the return address off the stack and go back to the menu. If the correct tape was entered, the program will return to the routine it came from.

Line 1100 is the subroutine that puts the information on the cassette. You are instructed to rewind the cassette and press both buttons on the recorder. Follow the directions that came with your program recorder for the proper location for starting your tape.

Line 1105 opens buffer 7 to move the information to the tape. The eight means the computer will be writing to the tape. The zero is a dummy value, and "C:" tells the computer to write to the cassette.

Line 1110 puts the information stored in these variables onto the cassette tape. Notice that line 1010 is nearly identical to this line. The variables must be stored on the tape in the same order they will be READ from the tape. Close the buffer and the computer stops writing to it.

Line 1115 opens the buffer again. The values are put on the tape in two separate routines because the program must close the buffer and dimension STUDENT$ and TEST$ when it reads the tape.

Line 1120 puts the name of the class onto the tape. The computer cannot store a string on the tape; it can only store numbers. Each letter in the string has an ASCII value, which is stored on the cassette. The computer takes each letter and places its ASCII equivalent on the tape.

Lines 1125-1130 use the same method to put the students' names and test scores on the tape. After all the information is put on the tape, the buffer will be closed.

Line 1135 directs the computer back to the menu.

Line 1200 is the subroutine the program uses when it pauses.

This program shows you how to manipulate strings. The routines let you enter names and test scores by combining the old information in the string with the new information being entered. The routine that prints the averages shows you how to split strings and use only the information you need. The program also uses four very important string functions: CHR$, VAL, ASC, and STR$.

ASC

One of the features of ATARI BASIC is its ability to store information on a cassette tape. This is very handy if you have files you want to use and keep for a program, but you don't have a disk drive. The computer can, however, only place numbers on the cassette tape. It cannot place strings or letters onto a tape.

Look again at lines 1120-1130. These lines put the name of the class, the names of the students, and their scores on the cassette. This information was in a string. In each case, the program found the length of the string before it entered this subroutine, and, starting with the first letter of the string, converted the letter to its ASCII value before putting it on the tape. *ASCII* is a numeric equivalent of a character. Every number, character, letter, and graphic has an ASCII value. The command for getting the ASCII value of a character is   ASC(character). The character must be a string. If you want to get the ASCII value of just one letter or character, place that character in quotation marks, e.g.,   A=ASC("C")   . A would become 67.

CHR$

Now that we have all the information transferred to the tape, we will want to be able to get it back into the computer. To put the information back into the string, we reverse the process. Look at lines 1025-1035. When we get the information from the cassette, we place it into a variable. To put it back into the string, we convert the value in the variable to its letter or character by getting the character for that value. CHR$(7) is the command to get the character of a value. The information in the ASCII table is used in reverse. Note: every number from zero to 255 has a corresponding character.

STR$

When you entered the test scores, you entered each score into the Score variable. This is a numeric variable. We wanted to store this value in TEST$. The command TEST$=SCORE   would cause an error message, since a string cannot equal a variable. Line 560 shows you how to convert a variable into a string. The command STR$ takes the value of the variable and makes it a string. Now we can place the test score into TEST$.

VAL

When we want to add the test scores we cannot use the strings. The computer cannot add TEST$(1,3) + TEST$(4,6). To the computer, anything in a string is a *character* that may or may not be a number. Characters cannot be added, subtracted, multiplied, or divided. Line 725 converts the characters in the string into numbers with the VALue command. This command looks at the contents of the string; if it is a number, it places the value of the string into a variable, or treats the value of the string as a variable. If the string contains a number and letters, the computer will only return the numbers, provided that the numbers were first in the string:

C$="14 MAIN ST."
A=VAL(C$)

The variable A would become 14. If the street name was first, an error message would have been generated.

Listing 14-2. Alphabet

```
10 REM LISTING XIV.2
20 REM ALPHABETIZE
30 REM BY L.M.SCHREIBER FOR TAB BOOKS
40 DIM WORD$(110),W$(10)
50 ? "}":FOR X=1 TO 110:WORD$(X,X)=" ":NE
XT X:REM CLEAR THE GARBAGE
60 FOR X=1 TO 110 STEP 10:REM FIRST LOCAT
ION OF EACH WORD IN THE STRING
70 READ W$
80 WORD$(X,X+9)=W$
90 NEXT X
100 FOR X=1 TO 100 STEP 10:REM ALPHABETIZ
E THE WORDS
105 FOR X1=X+10 TO 110 STEP 10:REM SECOND
 WORD
110 IF WORD$(X1,X1+9)<WORD$(X,X+9) THEN W
$=WORD$(X1,X1+9):WORD$(X1,X1+9)=WORD$(X,X
+9):WORD$(X,X+9)=W$
120 NEXT X1:NEXT X
130 FOR X=1 TO 110 STEP 10
140 ? WORD$(X,X+9)
150 NEXT X
160 END
200 DATA MONOPOLY,DETECTIVE,EXECUTIVE,POS
SESSIVE,RESTRICT,SELECTIVE,COMEDIAN
210 DATA }},LIBRARIAN,ERASURE,BIOLOGY
```

T$="3 Tablespoons"
T=VAL(T$)∗3

In this example T would become 9.

In addition to changing strings to numbers, characters, etc., there is one instance when the computer can view the string numerically. In Listing 14-2, the computer will arrange a group of words alphabetically. We do not have to change the strings to ASCII code to do this, and when comparing strings, the computer does not stop at the first letter. This routine could be incorporated in the first program to alphabetize the names of the students.

Line 40 dimensions WORD$, and W$. All the words that will be alphabetized are stored in WORD$. There are eleven words, each ten characters long. W$ is a temporary buffer for the words.

Line 50 clears the screen and clears the random characters from the string.

Lines 60-90 read the words from the data lines. X is increased by increments of ten during this loop. Because X is increased by ten, it will also point to the first location in WORD$ for the word that has been read.

Lines 100-120 contain two nested For . . . Next loops. The first word in WORD$ is compared to every word in the string. If any word is less than the first word, it is placed in W$, and the two words exchange places. The second word is compared in the same way, however, it is not compared to the first word, since that comparison has already occurred. The loop continues until every word in WORD$ is compared to the remaining words in that string.

Lines 130-150 print the words in alphabetical order on the screen. The two hearts in the data line are first, because their ASCII value is less than any letter. If two words begin with the same letter, the second letter of that word will be compared.

Chapter 15
Finding and Trapping Errors

The most necessary steps in programming are testing and debugging your program. When you write a program, you are familiar with its functions, what answers or input are expected, and how the program is supposed to work. The best test for a program is to let someone who is unfamiliar with the program sit at the computer and try it. It's amazing how many errors can appear when someone else is using your program. Of course, there are some errors the program cannot check for. If you enter 50 instead of 5, you would not expect the program to ask, ARE YOU SURE? after every question. On the other hand, there are ways to check for errors before or after they happen, have the program recover from the error and avoid having the user experience an error at line 100 message.

TRAP

The trap command does exactly what it sounds like: it traps an error and allows the program to recover from it. Go back through some of the programs in this book. One very common error is to type a letter instead of a number when the program asks you for an input. In Listing 15-1, the program is looking for the the number that represents a month rather than the name of the month. The trap command at the beginning of line 50 returns the program to this line if a number is not entered. Try to enter JUNE instead of 6 . The program will not crash, but go back to line 50 and wait for a correct input.

Trap is placed at the beginning of Line 50 because it needs to be reset after each use. If it were on Line 45, the program would repeat line 50 only once. If a word was entered the second time, the program would crash.

If your program needs to trap another input later in the program, you will need to reset the Trap command at that point in the program. Otherwise, the program will go to the line number in the last Trap command it encountered. Also, the Traps should not be set until after all the other parts of the program have been debugged. If you set a Trap for an input, and somewhere in the program you have a cursor out of range error, the computer only knows that when it comes to an error it should go to a particular line number, so it will go there.

If, for example, you have Trapped all your input, and feel you do not need to use the Trap in the remaining routines, you can stop it by setting it to 40000.

Any errors that occur after this line will be prominently displayed on the screen.

TESTING FOR ERRORS

As you write your program, you should test every routine and subroutine as they are added to the program. Every possible situation should be taken into account, and, since this is not always possible, try to test for the extreme situations: the largest value you expect, then a larger value, the smallest value that should be entered, then an even smaller value. Decimals, negative numbers, and letters should be Trapped or checked in the program. Check that the For . . . Next loops exit when and where they should. If there is another exit from the loop, does it branch to the correct routine? Does the GOSUB command return to the correct line, and if a program goes to a subroutine because of an If . . . Then statement, is the program correctly branched around the unnecessary lines?

If you are testing a routine that is not working correctly, you should first try setting the break points at the line you think is causing the error. Also set a break point before you enter the routine.

A *break point* is set by placing   STOP   in the line. Check the variable for accuracy before the program enters the routine by printing it as direct statements. Type   CONT   . When the program stops again, check the variables. If the variables were correct when the program entered the routine, and now are incorrect, the error is occurring somewhere between the two stop commands. Set a new break point *between* the two in the program and try it again. Keep dividing the area between the correct line and the incorrect line until you can pinpoint the error. Of course, if at the second stop the variables were correct, the error occurs after this line. Move the break point to the end of the routine and try again. After you correct the error, remove all stops. It is a good practice to remove only one or two breakpoints at a time and continue to check the program for accuracy.

Sometimes the program is operating correctly, but it is not running smoothly. It is taking too long to arrive at the answer, the screen does not look clean, the messages are garbled. These are weak points of the program. If it appears the program is running too slow, try to tighten the code

Listing 15-1. Trap

```
10 REM LISTING XV.1
20 REM TRAP
30 REM BY L.M.SCHREIBER FOR TAB BOOKS
40 ? "}clear}":? "THIS DEMONSTRATES THE '
TRAP'"
50 TRAP 50:POSITION 3,5:? "ENTER THE NUMB
ER OF THE MONTH THAT    YOU WERE BORN IN
       ";
60 INPUT MONTH
70 END
```

or instructions by placing more than one statement on a line. (Watch out for If . . . Then and GOSUB statements. They can cause problems when tightening code.) Place subroutines near the top of the program. ATARI BASIC starts at the top of the program and works its way down when looking for a line number. It will find line 10 much faster than line 1000.

PLAYING COMPUTER

Sometimes the best way to find an error that does not readily appear by using the previous methods is with a pencil and paper. Make a list of the variables being used. Write down the line number you are starting with and the value of the variables at that time. As you work each line of the program, change the variables the way the computer would. Calculate the equations and check the lines the program would direct the computer to. When you go to a subroutine, mark the line on the paper, work the subroutine, and return to that line. Many errors are made by reusing a variable in a subroutine you are using in the main program. The program returns to the main part of the program with a different value and causes an error later in the program. Othertimes, you find the program has been directed to another line and never returns to the original line at all! By working the program as the computer would, it is easy to spot such mistakes. This method can also alert you to routines used within the program that could be made into subroutines.

Chapter 16

Sights and Sounds

The best feature of the ATARI computer is its graphics and music capabilities. No other microcomputer on the market today can match the built-in functions of this computer. When used to fullest potential, they enchance any program you may write.

MODES

Most computers have only one or two graphics modes—text and graphics, or text, high resolution graphics, and low resolution graphics. These can sometimes be mixed, but on some systems they cannot. The ATARI has 14 modes, nine easily accessible from BASIC. The other five can also be accessed from BASIC if you have a good understanding of the computer's operating system. This chapter will deal with the modes that can be set with BASIC.

If you look very carefully at your screen, you will see that every character is made up of tiny dots (Fig. 16-1). These dots are called *pixels*. The fewer pixels turned on at one time, the finer the resolution and the better the graphics.

Mode 0 is the text mode. Each character is made up of an 8×8 dot matrix. You can place 40 characters in a line and have 24 lines of text on the screen. This mode can use the built-in graphics characters discussed in the earlier chapters. It is a crude, but very acceptable, way of mixing text with graphics.

Mode 1 provides a larger color print. The letters are larger because each character uses a 16×8 dot matrix. Four differently colored letters or characters can appear on the screen. By changing the characters between the quotation marks to lower and/or reverse video you change the color of the character on the screen.

Mode 2 has even larger print. These characters use a 16×16 dot matrix. As with mode 1, the characters can appear in any four colors by changing the format in the print statement. The larger letters in these two modes are easier to read, and are especially good when designing programs for young children. The only drawback is that the lowercase letters cannot be used with the uppercase letters. (The solution is in the next chapter!)

Mode 3 is a low-resolution graphics mode. Up to four colors can be displayed on the screen. One of these four colors will be the background color. Each point is an 8×8 dot matrix. No text can be displayed on the screen except for the lower four lines in the text window.

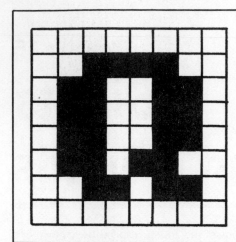

Fig. 16-1. Pixels or dots used to form the letter Q.

Modes 4 and 5 offer slightly higher resolution. Each point is a 4×4 dot matrix. You can have 80 points on a line and 40 or 48 lines on the screen. In mode 4 you can only display two colors, where mode 5 lets you use four colors. If you do not need four colors, mode 4 is the better choice since it uses less memory.

Modes 6 and 7 are higher resolution. Each point is a 2×2 dot matrix, giving you 160 points on a line and 80 or 96 lines on the screen. This is a good mode for many graphics applications. Again, mode 6 uses less memory than mode 7 because it supports only two colors while mode 7 has four.

Mode 8 is the highest resolution available on the ATARI. Each point can be turned on or off. There are 320 points on a line and 160 or 192 lines on the screen. This mode uses the most memory and line mode 8 can only display one color and luminance.

Each mode except for mode 0 offers you the use of a text window—four lines of mode 0—at the bottom of your screen. If you prefer to use the entire screen for your graphics, add 16 to the mode number:

```
10   GRAPHICS 20:REM MODE 4 WITH NO TEXT WINDOW
```

Occasionally you may hear of a reference to modes 9-11. These modes do not appear as legitimate modes on the earlier ATARI computers. They can be made available through the GTIA chip. This chip can be purchased from your local computer store.

Once you have decided on the graphics mode that will best suit your program, you will want to place the characters or designs on the screen. If you are working in mode 1 or 2, the easiest and the most direct way is to print the characters on the screen. If you print in these modes you will see your message at the bottom of the screen.

The computer must be told to print the message in the graphics area, or it will print in its most logical place—the text window. Where else should text go?

The ATARI computer has eight Input/Output Control Blocks (IOCBs) used for storing and transferring information. Some of these blocks are reserved by BASIC for a particular operation. IOCB 6 is used to transfer information to the graphics portion of the screen. Run Listing 16-1.

150

Listing 16-1. Graphics Demonstration

```
10 REM LISTING XVI-1
20 REM GRAPHICS DEMO
30 REM BY L.M.SCHREIBER FOR TAB BOOKS
40 GRAPHICS 2:REM NO NEED TO CLEAR THE SC
REEN - SETTING THE GRAPHICS DOES IT
50 POSITION 5,1:? #6;"HELLO"
60 END
```

Line 40 places the computer in graphics mode 2. This mode displays large colored letters and leaves a text window at the bottom of the screen. There is no need to clear the screen when the program changes modes. The screen is cleared automatically.

Line 50 uses the position command to place the message in the fifth column, first row. #6 tells the computer to transfer the message through this buffer. This buffer has been reserved by BASIC for the graphics screen. The message appears in yellow on the screen. Try displaying the message using reverse video, lower letters, and reverse lower letters. The message will appear in a different color each time.

Try the same program with different graphics modes. You will notice that the graphics modes 4 through 7 display either a yellow and blue block or two yellow blocks. As the resolution gets finer, the blocks move to the top and left of the screen. In order to see anything on the screen in mode 8, the position has to be changed to 25, 11. Instead of yellow or blue blocks, only two white dots appear on the screen.

The graphics command automatically opens the screen editor to IOCB 6.

COLOR

The value following the color command determines what will be plotted on the screen. In modes 1 and 2, the value will produce a character in one of four colors. Any number from 0 to 255 can be used in this mode. However, since the computer only recognizes 64 characters in these modes, the character will be dependent on which character set you are using at the time—the uppercase letters and numbers or lowercase letters and graphics (see Listing 16-2).

Line 40 sets the computer to mode 1, the smaller colored letters.

Lines 50-80 plot the character specified after the color command in four different locations. In each line the number after Color is different.

When you run this program, you should see a diagonal line of A's in four different colors. Add POKE 756,226 to line 40.

40 GRAPHICS 1:POKE 756,226

Now the screen will display a diagonal line of lowercase a's on a screen filled with yellow hearts. POKE 756,224 restores the uppercase letters, or press the system reset button.

Modes 3-8 are not text modes. The computer will recognize only two or four colors in these modes. The color value will be 0-3. If the value is larger, the computer will reduce the number to a

Listing 16-2. Four Colors

```
10 REM LISTING XVI-2
20 REM SHOW AN 'A' IN FOUR DIFFERENT COLO
RS
30 REM BY L.M.SCHREIBER FOR TAB BOOKS
40 GRAPHICS 1:REM NO NEED TO CLEAR THE SC
REEN - SETTING THE GRAPHICS DOES IT
50 COLOR 65:PLOT 5,5
60 COLOR 97:PLOT 6,6
70 COLOR 193:PLOT 7,7
80 COLOR 225:PLOT 8,8
90 END
```

number within the range. The color shown on the screen will be determined by the value stored in the color register. COLOR tells the computer which color register to use.

SETCOLOR

The command SETCOLOR changes the color in a particular color register. The color registers store a value that corresponds this to a particular color. This command works with the Color command. There are five color registers (0-4). Each color register can be set to any one of sixteen colors and eight different brightnesses. The format for this command is:

SETCOLOR 0, 8, 10

where 0 is the color register, eight is the color and ten is the brightness. The Table 16-1 shows which color registers are used in the various graphics modes, and the colors with their corresponding numbers.

The luminance or brightness increases with its value. A zero value is almost black, and 14 is nearly white. The brightness number must be an even number.

When a new value is placed in a color register, everything on the screen drawn or printed with that color register changes colors to reflect the new value in that register. This includes the background color as well as the characters or drawings on the screen (see Listing 16-3 and Fig. 16-2).

Line 40 sets the computer to graphics mode 2 with no text window. The X variable will be used later in the program to change the color in a color register.

Line 50 prints the message to the graphics portion of the screen. Even though there is no text window, the program still needs the 6 to print to the screen. The message will be displayed in three different colors.

Line 60 checks to see if the start button has been pressed on the computer. When it is pressed, the location 53279 will hold a 6. If that location does not hold a 6, the computer will subtract the value of X from 15, use the new value of X when it changes the color in the color register, and proceed to the timing loop. This line will be repeated until the start button has been pressed. Each time this line is executed the value of X will alternate between 5 and 10. This will make the word *continue* flash on the screen. When the start button is pressed, the computer will proceed to the next line.

Table 16-1. Default Colors for Graphics Modes/Decimal Values for Colors Used in SETCOLOR.

Graphics Mode	Color Default	Setcolor Register		Color	Decimal Value
0	light blue	Setcolor 1,x,x	character	white/	
	dark blue	Setcolor 2,x,x	background	black	0
	black	Setcolor 4,x,x	border	gold	1
				orange	2
1 and 2	orange	Setcolor 0,x,x	character	red/orange	3
	green	Setcolor 1,x,x	character	pink	4
	blue	Setcolor 2,x,x	character	lilac	5
	red	Setcolor 3,x,x	character	purple	6
	black	Setcolor 4,x,x	character	dk. blue	7
				lt. blue	8
3, 5, 7	orange	Setcolor 0,x,x	point plotted	turquoise	9
	green	Setcolor 1,x,x	point plotted	pale blue	8
	blue	Setcolor 2,x,x	point plotted	blue-green	10
	black	Setcolor 4,x,x	background, border	green	11
				green/	
4 and 6	orange	Setcolor 0,x,x	point plotted	yellow	12
	black	Setcolor 4,x,x	background, border	yellow/	
				green	13
8	light blue	Setcolor 1,x,x	point plotted	orange/	
	dark blue	Setcolor 2,x,x	background	green	14
	black	Setcolor 4,x,x	border	pale	
				orange	15

Line 70 clears the screen.

Line 80 prints the message THE END on the screen in different colors. If there was a program, the program would start here.

Line 90 is an endless loop. It keeps the message on the screen until the system reset button is pressed.

Listing 16-3. Flash

```
10 REM LISTING XVI-3
20 REM FLASH
30 REM BY L.M.SCHREIBER FOR TAB BOOKS
40 GRAPHICS 18:X=5:REM NO TEXT WINDOW
50 POSITION 2,5:? #6;"PRESS start TO
   CONTINUE"
60 IF PEEK(53279)<>6 THEN X=15-X:SETCOLOR
   2,X,4:FOR ZZ=1 TO 200:NEXT ZZ:GOTO 60
70 GRAPHICS 18:REM CLEAR SCREEN
80 POSITION 2,5:? #6;"THe enD"
90 GOTO 90:REM LOOP UNTIL SYSTEM RESET IS
   PRESSED
```

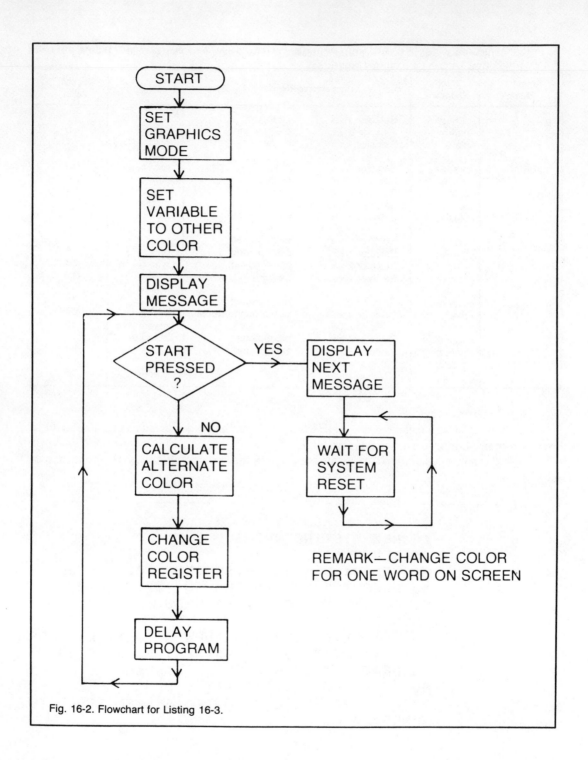

Fig. 16-2. Flowchart for Listing 16-3.

If you do not choose a specific color for each register, ATARI BASIC will assign the following colors to the five color registers:

Color Register	Default Color
0	orange
1	green
2	dark blue
3	red
4	black

PLOT

This command displays a point in a particular place on the screen, The screen is layed out like a grid, with 0,0 being the upper left-hand corner and the highest number of columns, the highest number of rows in the bottom right-hand corner. In graphics mode 4, this would be 79,39. Remember: the columns and rows start with 0 and must end with one less than the total number of points. The plot command uses the color set in the *last* color command it executed. Try Listing 16-4:

Line 40 sets the computer to graphics 5—medium resolution in four colors. There will be a text window at the bottom of the screen.

Line 50 sets color register 0 to light orange, color register 1 to light violet, color register 2 to medium turquoise, and color register 4 to medium blue. Color register 3 is not used in this mode.

Line 60 takes the color stored in color register 0 and plots a point in the eighth column and eighth row. The register the computer looks at is one less than the number following color.

Listing 16-4. Plots

```
10 REM LISTING XVI-4
20 REM PLOTS
30 REM BY L.M.SCHREIBER FOR TAB BOOKS
40 GRAPHICS 5
50 SETCOLOR 0,2,10:SETCOLOR 1,6,10:SETCOL
OR 4,8,4:SETCOLOR 2,10,6
60 COLOR 1:PLOT 8,8
70 PLOT 10,5
80 PLOT 12,9
90 COLOR 2:PLOT 16,10
100 PLOT 24,5
110 PLOT 30,27
120 COLOR 3:PLOT 77,30
130 PLOT 34,40
140 PLOT 65,2
150 COLOR 0:PLOT 26,13
160 END
```

Lines 70-80 plot two more points with the color stored in register 0—light orange.

Line 90 changes the color the computer will use when plotting the next points. The computer will now use the color stored in register 1—violet.

Lines 100-110 use the same color. The computer will continue to use violet until it receives another color command.

Lines 120-140 change the color the computer uses to the color stored in color register 2—medium turquoise. This color will also be used as the background color in the text window.

Line 150 plots a point in the 26th column and the thirteenth row. It uses the color stored in color register 4. Since this is the background color for the graphics display, this point will not show up on the screen.

DRAWTO

The DRAWTO command is used with the plot command. The plot command places a color in one location on the screen. The DRAWTO command draws a line from the point specified in the plot command to the point indicated in the DRAWTO command. If the row or column is the same in both commands, the line will be straight. If both row and column are different, the line will be jagged. The higher the resolution, the less jagged the line will appear.

Listing 16-5 generates designs on the screen using the plot and DRAWTO commands (see Fig. 16-3). Try it in different modes and compare the design differences.

Line 40 begins a For . . . Next loop. The value of S tells the computer how much to increment or add to the value of X in the next For . . . Next loop. The smallest value S can be is 2, the largest is 10.

Line 50 chooses a random number for the color used in the design. The color can be any value from 0 to 15. The color register 0 will be set to that color. The luminance or brightness of the color will remain the same throughout the program. COLOR 1 tells the computer to plot with the color stored in color register 0.

Line 55 chooses a random point on the screen. P will be the column. It can be any number from 0 to 159 (there are 160 columns in graphics mode 7). P1 is the row; it can be any number from 0 to 95 (there are 96 rows with no text window in graphics mode 7). The new point will be picked each time the computer starts to draw a new design.

Lines 60-90 draw the design from the random point to the top and bottom edges of the screen. The number of points skipped between each line is determined by the value of S. To give the illusion of the design being drawn with one sweeping movement, the second line that draws the lines across the bottom of the screen subtracts the value of X from 159. In lines 70 and 80 the lines start with the random point, and end at the edge of the screen. The first number following DRAWTO is the column, the second is the row.

Lines 100-130 draw the design from the random point to the left and right edges of the screen. The lines are drawn from top to bottom along the right side of the screen, and from bottom to top along the left side. This completes the design on the screen.

Line 140 is a timing loop. Without it, there would not be enough time to see the design on the screen.

Line 150 completes the first For . . . Next loop. Another design will be drawn on the screen. This time there will be larger spaces between the lines.

Listing 16-5. Lines

```
10 REM LISTING XVI-5
20 REM LINES
30 REM BY L.M.SCHREIBER FOR TAB BOOKS
40 FOR S=2 TO 10
45 GRAPHICS 23:REM GRAPHICS 7 WITH NO TEX
T WINDOW
50 C=INT(RND(1)*16):SETCOLOR 0,C,4:COLOR
1:REM PICK A COLOR FOR EACH PATTERN
55 P=INT(RND(1)*160):P1=INT(RND(1)*96):RE
M START IN A DIFFERENT POSITION EACH TIME

60 FOR X=0 TO 159 STEP S:REM THE WIDTH OF
 THE SCREEN - STEP BY NUMBER IN 40
70 PLOT P,P1:DRAWTO X,0:REM DRAWTO ACROSS
 THE TOP
80 PLOT P,P1:DRAWTO 159-X,95:REM AND ACRO
SS THE BOTTOM
90 NEXT X
100 FOR X=0 TO 95 STEP S
110 PLOT P,P1:DRAWTO 159,X:REM DRAWTO THE
 RIGHT EDGE
120 PLOT P,P1:DRAWTO 0,95-X:REM AND UP TH
E LEFT
130 NEXT X
140 FOR ZZ=1 TO 500:NEXT ZZ:REM VIEWING T
IME
150 NEXT S:REM MAKE THE LINES FURTHER APA
RT
160 GOTO 40:REM KEEP AT IT UNTIL SOMEONE
PRESSES THE BREAK KEY
```

Line 160 makes this program an endless loop. By sending the computer back to line 40, the program will continue until someone presses the break key.

This program uses only one color. The color was randomly chosen in line 50. By adding one more line to this program, you can have the design drawn in two colors.

95   C=INT(RND(1)*16):SETCOLOR 1, C, 4:COLOR 2

XIO (FILL)

The plot and DRAWTO commands are fine for single lines, but it could be very time-consuming if you want an entire area filled with one color. The XIO command will fill an area with

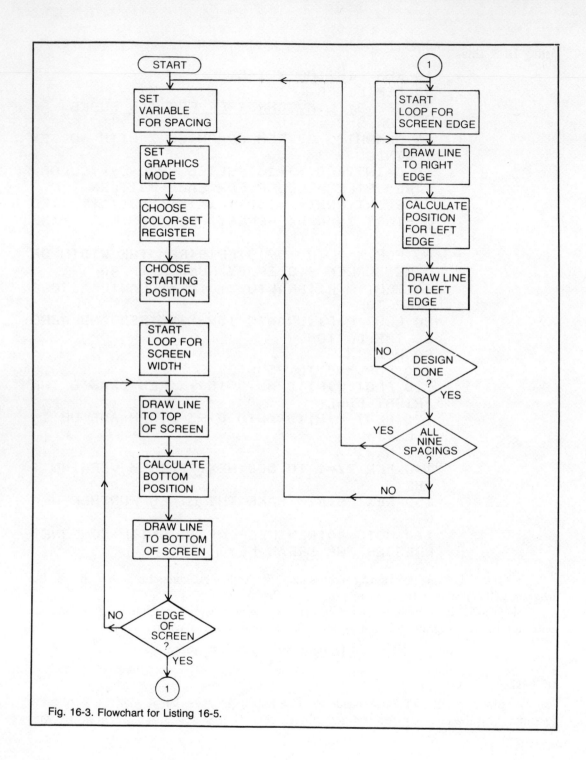

Fig. 16-3. Flowchart for Listing 16-5.

158

one color if you give it the outline of the area you want filled. The following procedure must be followed for the command to work properly.

1. Plot the bottom right corner.
2. DRAWTO the upper right corner.
3. DRAWTO the upper left corner.
4. Position the pointer (cursor) to the bottom left corner.
5.   POKE 765   with the color register number you want used.
6.   XIO 18, #6,0,0,"S:"

Let's use this in Listing 16-6.

Line 50 changes the color in color register 0 to dark blue.   COLOR 1   tells the computer to use this color with the plot statements.

Line 60 follows the first step. The point in the bottom right corner is plotted.

Line 70 is the second step. A line is drawn from the first point to the point indicated in this line.

Line 80 is the third step. Another line is drawn from the last point to the new one. When a DRAWTO follows another DRAWTO command, the computer does not need another plot command. The point indicated in DRAWTO will be the starting point for this line.

Line 90 is step 4. The position command places the cursor at the twentieth column in row 30. Nothing will appear on the screen at this point.

Line 100 is step 5. This command places 1 at memory location 765. The computer checks this location to determine which color register to use. A different color register can be used to outline the shape and to fill in the shape.

Line 110 is step 6 and completes the shape.   XIO 18   tells the computer to fill in a shape.   #6   indicates the graphics display, the two zeroes are dummy values, and   S: is the device the computer will fill.

As you can see, the computer filled the screen within the area defined with our selected color. To be used properly, the command can only color an area that has not been colored. The computer starts on the left and continues to place the selected color in each pixel until it reaches a

Listing 16-6. Fill

```
10 REM LISTING XVI-6
20 REM FILL
30 REM BY L.M.SCHREIBER FOR TAB BOOKS
40 GRAPHICS 7
50 SETCOLOR 0,8,4:COLOR 1
60 PLOT 50,30
70 DRAWTO 60,15
80 DRAWTO 20,15
90 POSITION 20,30
100 POKE 765,1
110 XIO 18,#6,0,0,"S:"
```

pixel containing a color. It returns to the left and starts again. It will continue until it reaches the row the cursor was positioned in. The computer will stop filling the area at this point. If no points have been colored on a line, the program will loop continuously. Press the break key or system reset button if you suspect this has happened.

POSITION

The position command places the cursor at a location on the screen. In the graphics modes this command works just as it does in the text mode, however, there is no visible cursor. As we saw earlier, the print command can be used with the position command in modes 1 and 2 to print text onto the screen. In other modes, it will only print colored squares.

SOUND

The ATARI is equipped with four separate and distinct sound generators. Each voice or sound generator requires its own sound statement. The format for producing sound is:

SOUND 0, 150, 10, 12

The first number is the voice, register, or channel used in producing the sound. It can be any number from 0-3. The second number is the pitch of the sound. Any number from 0-255 can be used. The smaller the number, the higher the sound. The ATARI is capable of producing tones from lower C to high C, over three octaves. The third number is the distortion of the tone. Any even number from 0-14 can be used. A 10 gives the purest tone and is usually used for music.

Other numbers produce buzzing, crackling, and explosion sounds. Of course, if the tone or pitch is set very high, the buzz may sound more like a ring. The fourth number sets the volume. One is the softest and 15 is the loudest. Zero will turn the sound generator off. If you are using more than one sound generator, it is not recommended that the total of the volumes used exceed 32.

This sound system gives you the ability to have the computer play four-part harmony as well as produce several unrelated sounds simultaneously. Listing 16-7 plays a prelude by J.S. Bach.

Line 40 sets the graphics mode to 0 and erases the cursor. The graphics mode is set in this program because it will be using the plot and DRAWTO commands. The graphics command opens the screen for these commands. Without it, we would receive an error 133 message.

Line 50 dimensions the four strings that hold notes for this prelude. Although the sound command needs numbers, it is much easier to store the music in a string.

Lines 60-70 put the title page on the screen. In line 70 the color is 42. This is the ASCII value of the asterisk. The plot and DRAWTO commands make a frame of asterisks on the screen.

Line 90 places 35 in the TL variable. TL is used as the duration or length of time the note will be held. To shorten the time, make the value of TL less. Increasing its value lengthens the duration of the notes.

Lines 100-107 place characters in the four strings. Each character represents a note. These characters must be entered exactly, or the music will not sound right.

Line 108 directs the computer twice to the subroutine at line 1000. This subroutine plays the notes stored in the four strings. Executing this subroutine twice will play the strings twice.

Lines 120-165 repeat the last procedure. The strings are filled with the notes, and the

Listing 16-7. Prelude

```
10 REM LISTING XVI.7
20 REM MUSIC
30 REM BY L.M.SCHREIBER FOR TAB BOOKS
40 GRAPHICS 0
50 DIM S0$(192),S1$(192),S2$(192),S3$(192
)
60 POSITION 5,10:? "1.PRELUDE AND FUGUE I
N C MAJOR"
70 COLOR (42):PLOT 2,2:DRAWTO 38,2:DRAWTO
 38,21:DRAWTO 2,21:DRAWTO 2,2
90 TL=35
100 S0$="<@<Q<@<`````<@<Q<@<H[`[y[`[
15<5H5<5@QUQ1QUQ`/5/@/5/<HLH`HLH<U`U<U`U@
QUQ@QUQ@`1`@`1`HU`UHU`U"
101 S0$(97,192)="H1y1H1y1Q`1`Q`1`QrrQrr
U1r1U1r1QUQ1HQH1@H@1<@<15555555/(5(<(@(H
HHH@@<5@<HHHQQQQQ"
102 S1$="yy"yy""""yyyyy
11111`````11111
111yyyyyyyy"
103 S1$(97,192)="
""""1`UQyy""1
1111111111111"
104 S2$="},,,,,,,,,,,,,,,,,,,,,,,,,,,,,,
,,,,,,,,,,,,,,,,,,,,,,,,,,,,,,,,,,,,,,,,,
,,,,,,,,,,,,,,,,,,,,,,,}"
105 S2$(97,192)="
UQH@QQQQQQQQQ
QU`UUQQHHQQ"
106 S3$="AAAA""
----yyyy
....."
107 S3$(97,192)="----"""AAAA
----."""----."""
""--""YYYY"-"Y"-""6"A"Y""
108 GOSUB 1000:GOSUB 1000
110 S0$="<@<Q<@<HHHH@H[@H@LLLL
H`1`H`1`L1y1L1y1H`1`H`1`@LUL@LUL<<@@<<55@
@HH@@<<HHLLHH@@LL``<<<<"
111 S0$(97,192)="@@HHLLLLHHHHH/5/@/5/
```

Listing 16-7. Prelude. (Continued from page 161.)

```
<<<<<(-(5(-(/<@<Q<@<````<@<Q<@<H
[`[H[`[5<5H5<5@QUQ@QUQ/5/@/5/"
112 S1$="},,,,,,,,,}[[[[},,,,,,,,,,,,,,,,,
,,,,,,,,,,,,,,,,,,,,,,,,,,,,,,,,,,,,,,,,,
,,,,,,,,,,,,,,,,,,,,,,,}HH"
113 S1$(97,192)="[[`````````````
`````yyyyy
yyy111111111```````"
114 S2$=""""""6A6s6A66666AYAAYA
yyyyyyyyA`1`A`1`````-1"
1-1"1Ay6yAy6yY```"
115 S2$(97,192)="11yyyyy
Alll1yyyyy"yy""""""
"
116 S3$="AAAA},,,,,,,,,,,,,}YYYY},,,,,,,,,
,,,,,,,,,,,,,,,,,,,,,,,,,,,,,,,,,,,,,,,,,
,,,,,,,,,,,,,,,,,,,}AAAA},,,,,}"
117 S3$(97,192)="A
A""""
"
120 GOSUB 1000:IF TP=1 THEN 130
121 S0$="<HLH<HLH}}(-(5(-(/(/(-#-#5-5-/(
/(</</5-5-@QH@<<<<<<<@@@@<<<<},,,,,}"
122 S1$="}.,,,,,,,}QQQQ},,,}QQ},,,,,,,,,,,
,,,,,,,,,,,,,,}1111QQQQQQQQQQ[[QQQQ},,,,,}"

123 S2$="y},}y},}y},,}y},,}1111},,,}11y}.}y}
.}y[y[},}1},}1},,.,.P}y}P}y}P}1}P}1"""""""
"""""""""sy},}y"yA""
124 S3$="},,,,,,,,,,,,,,,,,,,,,,,,,,,,,,,,,
,,,,,,,,,,,,,,,,.}1y111111111}...,,,,,}"
125 GOSUB 1000:TP=1:GOTO 110
130 S0$="<HLH<HLH},}(-(5(-(/(/(-#-#5-5-/(
/(</</5-5-@QH@<<<<<<<@@@@<<<<<<<<"
131 S1$="}.,,,,,,,}QQQQ},,,}QQ},,,,,,,,,,,
,,,,,,,,,,,,,,}1111QQQQQQQQQQ[[QQQQQQQQ"
132 S2$="y},}y},}y},,}y},,}1111},,,}11y}.}y}
.}y[y[},}1},}1},,.,.P}y}P}y}P}1}P}1"""""""
""""""""""ssssssss"
133 S3$="},,,,,,,,,,,,,,,,,,,,,,,,,,,,,,,,,
```
```

```
,,,,,,,,,,,,,,,.}1y11111111}........}"
135 GOSUB 1000
140 S0$="<<<<<<<<<<<<<////55<<<<@<
5555<<@@@@H@<5<5//////HH55<5@<@<55555

5QQ<<@<H@H@<<<<<<<<@@@@"
141 S0$(97,192)="<</5</5<@<@<5555////////
H@H@<<<<55555555<<<<<DDHHHHHHH@@@@@HHQ
QQQQQHHHHQQQQ"
142 S1$="QQQQQQQQ
QQQHHHHQQCCCC`CQQQQCC`
```1`CCy1`HQHCC`1QQCC"
143 S1$(97,192)="```QC`QC`QHQH@@@@@``HHQH
UQUQHHHHHH@HQHQC`C`CQQQQ1`1`CCCC
y1y1````1`1`CCCC`U`U11`1"
144 S2$="ssssssss},,,,,,,,,,,,,,,,,,,,,
,,,,,,,,,,,,,,,,,,,,,,,,,,,,,,,,,,,,,
,,,,,,,,,,,,,,,,,,,,,,}"
145 S2$(97,192)="yyy````11yyyyy
1111yyy1y1```````11y1yy11111
1""yyyyyyyy1111y1yyy"
146 S3$="}...........,,,,,,,,,,,,,,,,,,,
,,,,,,,,,,,,,,,,,,,,,,,,,,,,,,,,,,,,,
,,,,,,,,,,,,,,,,,,,,}"
147 S3$(97,192)="

"
148 GOSUB 1000
150 S0$="QQHQUUUQQQ555////55<<<<@<
5555<<@@@@H@<<QQ<<<<<<5<@@@@<</5</5<@
<@<5555//////5/H@H@<<<<"
151 S0$(97,192)="555555<5QHQH@@@H@H@<<<<
@<@<5/5/<<55@@@HHHHH
<<<////55<<<<@<5555<<"
152 S1$="111111yy1111QQQQHHHHQQ
CCCC`CQQQQCC````1`1111QQCC``QQQQ
QCCCC````UU`````"
153 S1$(97,192)="1111``11``UU``UU
LL@@```````````HHH@@@HHQ
Q`CQHQC```````````HHHHQH"
154 S2$="
```

163
```

Listing 16-7. Prelude. (Continued from page 163.)

```
yyy"
"AA-"-""
155 S2$(97,192)="YY""""A-A-"""-"-"
""yy```[[[[``1111yl`
`yl`[`lyyyyyy``1111``"
156 S3$="YYYYYYYY""""
sssA
AAAYY"
157 S3$(97,192)="


 "
159 GOSUB 1000
160 S0$="@},}@},}@@H@<<<<},,}@@HH@@<<<<<<
<<@@@@<<<<<<<<"
161 S1$="QQQQ},,}11Q},}Q},}QQ[Q[[[[QQQ},}
QQQQQQ},}QQQQQQQQ"
162 S2$="1111},,}11yyyy},,}11yy11}....}11
1111[[}........}"
163 S3$="},,,,,,,,,,,,,,,,,,,,,,,,,,,,,,
,}ssssssss"
165 GOSUB 1000
170 END
1000 FOR T=1 TO LEN(S0$):SOUND 0,ASC(S0$(
T)),10,10:SOUND 1,ASC(S1$(T)),10,8:SOUND
2,ASC(S2$(T)),10,6
1001 SOUND 3,ASC(S3$(T)),10,6:FOR W=1 TO
TL:NEXT W:NEXT T
1002 RETURN
1050 REM THE FOLLOWING LINES REPEAT THE D
ATA LINE LISTED ABOVE - CHARACTERS OR LET
TERS THAT APPEAR BETWEEN } }
1051 REM ARE GRAPHIC CHARACTERS. USE THE
CONTROL KEY TO ENTER THOSE CHARACTERS OR
LETTERS
1100 REM LINE 100 },}<@<Q<@<}....,,,,,}<@
<Q<@<H[}.}[[}.}[15<5H5<5@QUQ1QUQ}.}/5/@/5
/<HLH}.}HLH<UU<U}.}U@QUQ@
1101 REM LINE 100 con't QUQ@}.}1}.}@}.}1}
.}HU}.}UHU}.}U
1102 REM LINE 101 H1y1H1y1Q}.}1}.}Q}.}1}.
```

```
}Qr},,}rQr},,}rU1r1U1r1QUQ1HQH1@H@1<@<15555
5},}55/(5(<(@(HHHH},,,}@@<
1103 REM LINE 101 con't 5@<HHHQQQQQ},,,,,,
,,,,,,,,}
1104 REM LINE 102 },,,,,,,,,,}у},,}"y},,}у""
""},,,}y},,}yyyy},,,,,PPPP,,}1},,}1111},,,,,,,,
,,,,,.,....,,,,}1},,}1},,}1
1105 REM LINE 102 con't },,}1},,}1},,}1},,}1}
,,}1},,}y},,}y},,}y},,}y},,}y},,}y},,}y},,}y},,}
1106 REM LINE 103 },,,,,,,,,,,,,,,,P,P,P,
P,P,P,P,P,,,,,PPPP}"""}PPPP,}1}.}UQ},,,,}
yy},,,PP}""1111},,,}1},,}1},,}1
1107 REM LINE 103 con't },,}111},,}1111},,,,
,,,,,,,,,}
1108 REM LINE 105 },,,,,,,,,,,,,,,,,,,,,,,
,,,,,,,,,,,,,,,,,,,,,,,,,,,,}UQH@},,}Q},,}QQ
QQQQQQQU}.}UUQQHHQQ
1109 REM LINE 105 con't },,,,,,,,,,,,,,,,,
,,,,}
1110 REM LINE 106 },,,,,,,,,,,,,,,,,,}AAAA}
,,,}""}PPPP,,,,,}----},,,PP,,,,,,,,,YYYY,,,,}
yyyy},,,,,P,P,P,P,,,,,,,,,,}
1111 REM LINE 106 con't "},,}"},,}"},,}"},,P,
P,P,P,}
1112 REM LINE 107 _},,}-},,}-},,}-},,}"},,}"},
}"},,}"},,}A},,}A},,}A},,}A},,}-},,}-},,}-},,}-},,}
""""----},,,,,}----""""
1113 REM LINE 107 con't },,,,,,,,,,,,,,,,,
,,}""--""YYYY},,}"-"Y"-"},,}"6"A"Y""
1114 REM LINE 110 },,}<@<Q<@<HHHH},,,,,,}@H
@[@H@LLLL},,,,,}H}.}1}.}H}.}1}.}L1y1L1y1H}
.}1}.}H}.}1}.}@LUL@LUL<<@
1115 REM LINE 110 cont @<<55@@HH@@<<HHLLH
H@@LL}..}<<<<
1116 REM LINE 111 @@HHLLLHHHHH},,,,,,}/5/@
/5/<<<<},,,,,,}(-(5(-(/<@<Q<@<}....,,,,,,}<
@<Q<@<H[}.}[H[}.}[},,}
1117 REM LINE 111 con't 5<5H5<5@QUQ@QUQ},
}/5/@/5/
1118 REM LINE 113 [[},,..,,..,,,,,,,,,,,,
.,,..,,,,,,,,,,,,,,,,,,,,,,,,}yyyy},
```

Listing 16-7. Prelude. (Continued from page 165.)

```
,}y},,}y},,}y},,}y},,}y},,}
1119 REM LINE 113 con't 1111},,,}1,}1},,}1}
,}1},,}1},,....,,..
1120 REM LINE 114 """"},,,,,,}6A6s6a66666}
,,,,,,}AYA},,}AYA},,}y},}y},,}y},}y},,,P,,,P,,
}y},,}y},,}y},,}yA}.}1}.}A}.}1
1121 REM LINE 114 con't }.P.Y.P.}=1"1-1"1
Ay6yAy6yY},,,,,,,,,..}
1122 REM LINE 115 11yy},,,,,}yyyy},,,,,,,,,
,,,,,PYPAPYP}1},,}1},,}1},,}1},,}yyyyy},,,,,,}y
},,}y"y},,}y""""},,,}""
1123 REM LINE 115 con't }P,P,P,P,PPPP,,PP
,,,,,,,,,,,,,,,}
1124 REM LINE 117 },,,,,,,,,,PYP}A}PYPY,,Y,
Y,Y,,PYP}A}PYP,,,,,,,,}""""},,,,,,,,,,,,,
,,,,,,,,,,,,,,,,,,,,,,,}
1125 REM LINE 117 con't },,,,,,,,,,,,,,,}
1126 REM LINE 140 <<<<<<<<},,}<}<},}<>,}<}<},
}////},,,}55<},}<},,}<<@<5555},,,}<<@},}@},}
@@H@<5<5//////HH55<5@<@<
1127 REM LINE 140 con't 555555QQ<<@<H@H@<
<<<<<<@@@@
1128 REM LINE 141 <</5</5<@<@<5555///////
/H@H@<<<<55555555<<<<<<DDHHH},}HHHH@@@@@@
HHQQ},}QQQQHHHH
1129 REM LINE 141 con't },,,,,,,,,,,,,,,,,
}QQQQ"
1130 REM LINE 142 QQQQQQQQ},,,,,,,,,,,,,,,
,,,,,,,,,,,,,,,,,,,,,,,}Q},,}Q},,}Q},,}HHHH},,,}
QQ[},}[},}[[}.}[QQQQ
1131 REM LINE 142 con't },,,}[[}.,,.,..}1}.
}[[y1}.}HQH[[}.}1QQ[["
1132 REM LINE 143 }...}Q[}.}Q[}.}QHQH@@@@@
@}..}HHQHUQUQHHHHHHH@HQHQ[}.}[}.}[QQQQ},,,
,,,,,,}1}.}1
1133 REM LINE 143 con't }.}[[[[},,,,,,,,,}
y1y1}....}1}.}1}.}[[[[}.}U}.}U11}.}1"
1134 REM LINE 145 },,,}y},,}y},}y},,....,,}1
1y},}y},,}yy},}y11111},,,}yy},,,,,,,,,}y1y1}.
```

```
.....PP}11y1},)y},)
1135 REM LINE 145 con't y111111**yy},)y}p
,P,)yyyy},)y},)y1111y1yy},,)y},)
1136 REM LINE 147 },,,,,,,,,,,,,,,,,,,,,
,,,,,,,,,,,,,,,,,,,,,,,,,,,,,,,,,}
1137 REM LINE 147 con't },,,,,,,,,,,,,,,,
,,,,,,,,,,,,,,,,,,,,}
1138 REM LINE 150 QQHQUUUQQQ5},)5},)5},)/
///},,,)55<},)<},)<<@<5555},,)<<@},)@},)@@
H@<<QQ<<<<<<5<@@@@<</
1139 REM LINE 150 con't 5</5<@<@<5555////
//5/H@H@<<<<
1140 REM LINE 151 555555<5QHQH@@@@H@H@<<<
<@<@<5/5/<<55@@HHHHH},,,,,,,,,,,,,,,,,}
1141 REM LINE 152 111111yy1111},,,,,,,)Q},
Q},)QQHHHH},,,)QQ[},)[},)[[},)[QQQQ},,,)[[}
.,,.,,.)1}.)1111QQ[[}..)Q
1142 REM LINE 152 con't },,)Q},)Q},)Q},)Q}
,)[[[[}.,,.,,,,)U},)U},,,...}
1143 REM LINE 153 1111},,,,,.,,)11}..)U},
)U},..)UUL},)L},,,,)@@}...,.,....,..,,,,,)
H},)H},)H},)@@@
1144 REM LINE 153 con't @},,,)HHQQ}.)[QHQ[
},.,,.,,.,.,.,,..)H},)H},)HHQH"
1145 REM LINE 154 )PPPPPPPP,,,,,,,,,,,,,
,,,,,,,,,,,,,,,,,,,,,,,,,,,,,,,,,,,,,,,,,
,,,)y
1146 REM LINE 154 },,)y},)y},,)*)P}*)P,,,,,
,)AA)PPPP}-"-")PPPP}
1147 REM LINE 155 )PP)YY****A-A-****-"-")
PPPPYPYP,,)*")PPPPYYYY)yy},,,,,,)[[[[},,.
.)1},)1
1148 REM LINE 155 con't },)11y1}..)y1}.)[
}.)1yy},,,,,,,)yyyy},,,..)1111},,,..}
1149 REM LINE 156 YYYYYYYY****},,,,,,,,,,
,,,,,,,,,,,,,,,,,,,,,,,,,,,,,,,,,,,,,,,,,
,,,
1150 REM LINE 156 con't )s},)s},)s},)AAAA
},,)YY},,,,,,,,,,,,,,,,,,}
1151 REM LINE 157 },,,,,,,,,,,,,,,,,,,,,,
,,,,,,,,,,,,,,,,,,,,,,,,,,,,,,,,,,,,,,,}
```

Listing 16-7. Prelude. (Continued from page 167.)

```
1152 REM LINE 157 con't },,,,,,,,,,,,,,,,,,
,,,,,,,,,,,,,,,,,,,,,,}
```

computer plays the notes. One of the sections has two endings. The first time the computer plays lines 100-117, it plays the notes in lines 121-124. The second time it plays the notes in 130-133. The value of TP indicates which time the computer is playing the section. After the entire piece has been played, the four sound generators are shut off by the end statement in line 170.

Lines 1000-1002 are the subroutine lines that play the music. The For . . . Next loop begins with 1 and continues for the length of S0$. The computer takes the ASCII value of each character in the four strings for the second value in each sound statement. Sound 0 uses S0$, sound 1 uses S1$, sound 2 uses S2$, and sound 3 uses S3$. The nested For . . . Next loop holds the tone played for the length of time specified by TL. After the entire string has been played, the computer returns to the main program for the next set of characters.

As you can see, the entire piece can be packed into strings. Each element of the string corresponds to one unit of the beat. A quarter note would be written four times, since the shortest note is a sixteenth. Numbers are not used to produce the notes. Each note played has a corresponding character. The Table 16-2 shows you the corresponding character for each note the ATARI is capable of generating.

Sound effects can be produced in a similar manner. The tones can be placed in a string and a sound routine can be called whenever you want the program to make a particular sound.

MIXING SOUND AND GRAPHICS

Once you start to add sound to your programs, any other silent program will seem dull in comparison. Sound can be used to prompt the person using the program, or it can be used in response to an answer. Most programs will give a bell sound to signal you to respond to a question on the screen. Many programs play a short tune when the correct answer is entered, and another tune for the wrong answer. The ultimate use of sound, however, is to combine it with animation. The early pong games made a sound each time the ball was struck with the paddle, adding realism to the program.

ACCESSORIES

Built into ATARI BASIC are commands for reading the positions of the joysticks and paddles. The keyboard is a good way to enter information, but a joystick or paddle can make a program easier to use. If you have ever played an arcade-type game that used the keyboard to move characters, you will understand why the joystick is a better choice. The user has no chance to press the wrong key and then wonder why the character isn't moving in the direction expected. Also, because there are fewer directions than keys, you do not have as many inputs to check for. A joystick can even be used to select a routine from a menu.

STICK

To determine which direction the joystick is pointing, let a variable equal the stick number,

Note	Decimal Value	Character	
A #	33	!	
A	35	#	
G#	37	%	
G	40	(	
F#	42	*	
F	45	-	
E	47	/	
D#	50	2	
D	53	5	
C#	57	9	
C	60	<	
B	64	@	
A#	68	D	
A	72	H	
G#	76	L	
G	81	Q	
F#	85	U	
F	91		left bracket
E	96		diamond (control period)
D#	102	f	
D	108	l	
C#	114	r	
C	121	y	
B	128		heart reverse video
A#	136		control H reverse video
A	144		club (control P) reverse video
G#	153		control Y reverse video
G	162	"	reverse video
F#	173	—	reverse video
F	182	6	reverse video
E	193	A	reverse video
D#	204	L	reverse video
D	217	Y	reverse video
C#	230	f	reverse video
C	243	s	reverse video

Table 16-2. Decimal Values and Characters for Notes.

e.g.,   X=STICK(0)   . The number in the parentheses corresponds to the joystick being checked minus one.

If you look at the front of your computer, you will see four plugs or *ports* the joystick can be plugged into. Subtract one from the number of the port you are plugging your joystick into. This is the number you would place into the parentheses.

When the stick on the joystick is not being moved, the value of the variable will equal 15. Figure 16-4 shows the value of each direction.

STRIG

When the red button on the joystick is pressed, the value of STRIG# will change. The value of STICK# does not reflect whether or not the red button has been pressed. STICK# only checks the direction, STRIG# checks the red button. Again, a variable must equal STRIG#. The

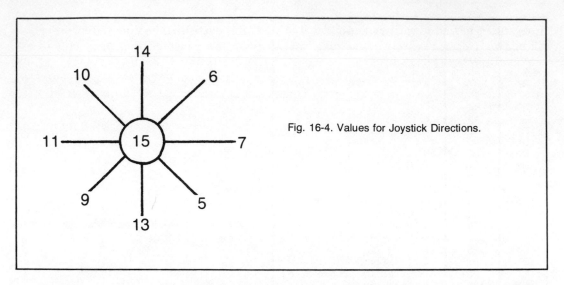

Fig. 16-4. Values for Joystick Directions.

number in parentheses is the same number you are using in STICK#. When the variable that equals STRIG# is one, the button has not been pressed. When the variable equals zero, you know the button is pressed. The variable will equal the condition of the button when the computer checked it.

Listing 16-8 illustrates using the joystick to make a selection from a menu (see Fig. 16-5). As you can see, there is no possibility the user can enter the wrong number. The arrow can only move up and down becuase it is under program control—it can only point to the numbers on the screen.

Line 40 dimensions P$ for two characters. The arrow will be stored in this string.

Lines 45-50 erase the cursor and place an arrow into P$.

Lines 60-110 clear the screen and place the menu on the screen. There are five units the user can choose from.

Line 120 begins the routine that moves the arrow up or down on the screen. The SP variable will contain the row the arrow will be printed in. Each item on the menu is four rows from the other. This makes it easy to move the arrow from one to another.

Line 130 prints the arrow in the tenth column of the specified row. When the program is first run, the arrow will be pointing to the first unit. The timing loop is necessary to slow the computer down. If it were not there, the arrow would move too fast up and down on the screen making it almost impossible to make a selection.

Line 135 checks to see if the red button has been pressed on the first joystick. This program will work only if the joystick is plugged into the first port of the computer. If the reading from the trigger is zero, the computer will go to the part of the program specified by that unit number. Instead of going to another routine, you could have the computer compute the line number of the routine based on the unit it is pointing to.

Line 140 records the direction the stick has been moved in. Since the difference between the values indicating up and down is only one, the program subtracts 12 from the value it received. If the joystick is moved down, the value of X will be one; if the joystick has been moved up, the value will be two. By using selective branching, we can direct the computer to the correct lines.

Line 145 checks the value of X. If the joystick was moved in any direction other than up or down, the value of X would be negative. The computer cannot go to a negative line number, and the program would crash. This line sends the computer back to line 140 if the value of X is negative or zero.

Line 150 uses selective branching to send the computer to the correct line. The value of X can only be 1, 2, or 3 at this time.

Listing 16-8. Menu

```
10 REM LISTING XVI.8
20 REM MENU
30 REM BY L.M.SCHREIBER FOR TAB BOOKS
40 DIM P$(2)
45 POKE 752,1
50 P$="->"
60 ? "}clear}"
70 POSITION 15,4:? "1. NUMBERS"

80 POSITION 15,8:? "2. LETTERS"
90 POSITION 15,12:? "3. COLORS"
100 POSITION 15,16:? "4. SHAPES"
110 POSITION 15,20:? "5. SIZES"
120 SP=4:REM ROW OF THE POINTER
130 POSITION 10,SP:? P$:FOR ZZ=1 TO 100:N
EXT ZZ:REM PAUSE BETWEEN MOVES
135 IF STRIG(0)=0 THEN 200:REM SELECTION
HAS BEEN MADE
140 X=STICK(0):X=X-12:REM SUBTRACT 12 FOR
 SELECTIVE BRANCHING
145 IF X<1 THEN 140:REM DON'T LET IT CRAS
H ON A NEGATIVE NUMBER
150 ON X GOTO 180,160
155 GOTO 135
160 POSITION 10,SP:? "   ":SP=SP-4:IF SP<4
 THEN SP=4:REM DON'T ALLOW IT ABOVE #1
170 GOTO 130
180 POSITION 10,SP:? "   ":SP=SP+4:IF SP>2
0 THEN SP=20:REM DON'T ALLOW BELOW #5
190 GOTO 130
200 REM GO NOW TO THE UNIT SELECTED
210 END
```

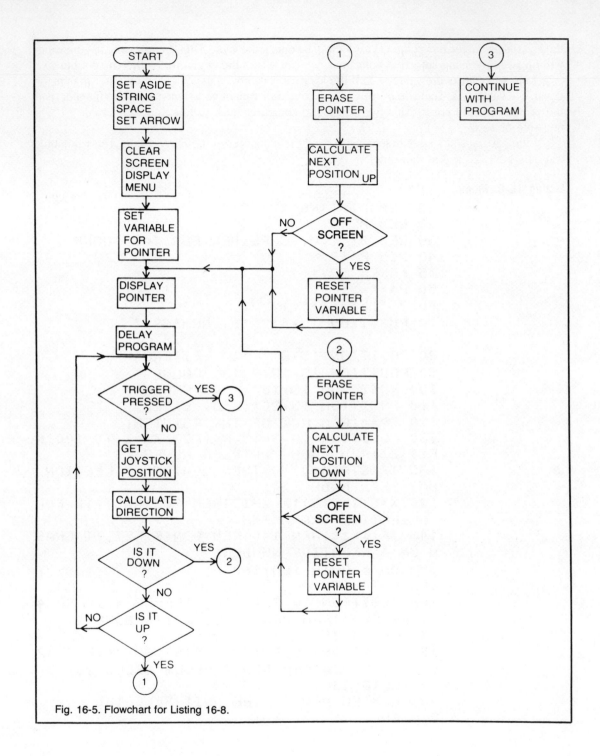

Fig. 16-5. Flowchart for Listing 16-8.

172

Line 155 sends the computer back to line 135 to check the red button if the value of X is 3.

Lines 160-170 move the arrow up. First the arrow is erased from the position it is currently placed, and four is subtracted from SP because the next unit is four rows above this location. The value of SP is checked for a number less than four. If it is less than four, SP is reset to four, keeping the arrow on the screen. The computer goes back to the line that prints the arrow on the screen.

Lines 180-190 move the arrow down. Since the rows increase as you go down the screen, four will be added to the value in SP. This value is checked for a number larger than 20. Twenty is the last row a unit number is on. If SP is greater than 20, it will be reset to 20. Now the arrow can't go off the screen. The computer goes back to the line that prints the arrow on the screen.

Line 200 contains the routine that sends the computer to the unit selected. In this example, the program ends here.

PADDLE

Sometimes a joystick is not the best choice for a program. You may want the character on the screen to move in two directions, but where it moves needs to be calibrated in some way. The paddle sends a number from 1 to 228 to the computer. This means you can divide the screen into 228 different locations, and, depending on the number received by the computer, place the character in the desired position. Getting the number from the paddle is similar to using the joystick: V=PADDLE(#). The number in the parentheses can be any number from zero to seven depending on which port you are using.

PTRIG

The red button on the paddle operates exactly like the red button on the joystick. A variable equals PTRG#,e.g., X=PTRIG(#). Again, the number within the parentheses can be any number from zero to seven depending on the paddle the program is using. If the button is pressed, the value of X will be zero, otherwise it will be one.

For both joystick and paddle, the value of the variable will be set when the computer executes that line. Therefore, if you press the button on the paddle or joystick and the computer is not watching for the trigger, it will not register. If you want to use the button, be sure your program continues to loop until the button has been pressed. Also, the joystick will send a 15 if it is not moved in a direction when the computer checks the joystick. The program receives that value from the joystick at the time it checks directions.

If the entire game is played using the joystick or paddle, be sure any subroutines used to update the score and/or sounds are short. Otherwise, you will see a time-delay as the program executes each subroutine.

Chapter 17

Special Functions

Only a few of the programs we wrote in previous chapters took into account any values the computer, itself, may have stored in various memory locations. When you turn the computer on, the video screen is blue. This color value is set by the computer's operating system. In Chapter 16, you learned how to change the color values stored in the computer's memory to suit your needs. Table 17-1 contains decimal locations or addresses for other values you can change.

Every memory location in your computer, whether it is RAM or ROM, has its own address. The first address is 0 and the last is 65535. If you have 40K RAM and the BASIC cartridge plugged in, every address will have some type of information in it. RAM addresses 0 to 1792 are reserved by the operating system, and store values for the screen width, the amount of RAM available to the system, buffer addresses, memory available for the program, the position of the cursor, routines for floating point arithmetic, etc. Most programs do not use any of the memory locations the operating system uses, but there are times when you may need to know the value the computer has stored, or place your own value there to make the computer do something.

PEEK

To find out what value the computer has stored in a particular location, we need to be able to ask the computer what is being stored. We can do this by PEEKing at a location. The format is:

40 X=PEEK(106)

X will now be equal to the number stored in location 106. If you multiply the value of X by 256, you will know how much RAM your system has. PEEK at location 82:

X=PEEK(82):? X

and you will see the left margin of the screen is set to two. You can use the PEEK command as a line statement or a direct command.

Since the number stored in one location cannot exceed 255, we need a way to store or locate addresses or numbers larger than 256. The display list the computer uses to place information on the screen usually starts in RAM located just before the screen area. This will obviously have an address greater than 255.

174

Decimal Location	Comment/Explanation
14,15	Highest byte in RAM used by BASIC.
18, 19, 20	Use these locations as a clock.
65	POKE a zero to quiet data being sent to cassette.
77	When this register is 128, screen begins to change colors.
82, 83	Left and right margins. Value POKEd here will limit number of characters printed on the screen line (BASIC sets to 2,39).
106	Value in this register is the amount of RAM in machine. Multiply by 256 for actual bytes.
694	Value is 0 in normal text, 128 for reverse video.
752	Cursor control: POKE 0 to turn cursor on; 1 to turn cursor off.
764	PEEK at this location for the last key pressed.
53279	Console keys. PEEK at this location to see which key (yellow) has been pressed.

Table 17-1. Decimal Locations of RAM that can be Changed under Program Control.

The computer stores numbers larger than 255 in two consecutive memory locations. The first location is called the low-order address and the second is called the high-order address. When you multiply the number stored in the second location by 256 and add the contents of the first address, you will get the address or number larger than 255. In the direct mode, try this:

$$? \text{ PEEK}(741) + \text{PEEK}(742) * 256$$

The number printed on the screen is the last memory location your program can use. If you try to use memory past this location you will be writing into the computer's display list and the area of memory used to display information onto the screen.

POKE

To give the operating system a different value, POKE that value into a memory location. If you type:

POKE 82,5

into the computer as a direct command, you would change the left-hand margin on your screen. When you use a POKE command, the first number after POKE is the address or location where you want to store the new value. The number after the comma is the value you want placed in that location.

POKE 751,1 turns the cursor off, a nice feature when your program is printing instructions on the screen, or any time a cursor would be a distraction.

POKE 755,4 turns the characters in each line of the screen upside down.

Do *not* POKE values into unknown locations. The wrong value in an address can cause the system to crash.

Listing 17-1 will show you how to use POKE and PEEK to find out how much memory your system has, and use this information to move the character set stored in ROM into RAM. By

Listing 17-1. ROM-to-RAM

```
10 REM LISTING XVII-1
20 REM ROM-TO-RAM
30 REM BY L.M.SCHREIBER FOR TAB BOOKS
35 GRAPHICS 2
40 CHBAS=756:RAMTOP=106
50 ROMSET=PEEK(756)*256:REM THIS IS THE T
OP OF THE CHARACTER SET IN ROM
60 TOP=PEEK(RAMTOP):REM THE END OF RAM
70 TOP=TOP-8:REM START THE NEW CHARACTER
SET HERE
80 RAMSET=TOP*256:REM HERE'S THE NEW BASE

120 RMCHR=768:REM 'a' BEGINS HERE IN ROM
140 FOR X=0 TO 511:REM THERE ARE 512 BYTE
S TO BE TRANSFERRED
150 C=PEEK(ROMSET+X):POKE RAMSET+X,C:REM
GET THE BYTE AND TRANSFER IT
160 NEXT X
170 FOR X=8 TO 216:REM THERE ARE 208 BYTE
S TO BE TRANSFERRED
180 C=PEEK(ROMSET+RMCHR+X):POKE RAMSET+X,
C:REM GET THE BYTE AND TRANSFER IT
190 NEXT X
200 POKE CHBAS,TOP
210 POSITION 2,5:? #6;"UPPER AND ,/7%2
  #13%"
220 END
```

storing the lowercase characters in the area normally used by the numbers and symbols, both upper- and lowercase letters can be displayed in modes 1 and 2.

Line 35 sets the graphics to mode 2. Always set the graphics mode first. The computer's operating system sometimes changes values in memory locations after the mode has been set.

Line 40 sets the variable CHBAS to 756 and RAMTOP to 106. These numbers are the memory locations for the address of the character set the computer will use, and the address for the amount of RAM in the system.

Line 50 takes the number stored in memory location 756 and multiplies it by 256. The variable ROMSET now holds the address for the beginning of the character set the computer is using. This number should be 57344.

Line 60 finds the end of available RAM by PEEKing at RAMTOP. We will not multiply this number by 256 because it will be much easier to work with this number.

Line 70 subtracts 8 from the value stored in TOP. We know the operating system needs about 1K, or 1024 bytes, of memory for the screen display and its display list. This is the last 1024 bytes of RAM. We want to move the character set just in front of this RAM. The character set is another 1K of memory. If we had multiplied TOP by 256, we would have to subtract 2048 from this value to arrive at the memory location the character set should be moved to: eight times 256 is 2048. Since we did not multiply TOP by 256, simply subtract eight from its value. Whenever possible, we do not multiply a value by 256, because it can result in needless converting and reconverting.

Line 80 multiplies the new value in TOP by 256. This is the value BASIC will use when it is moving the character set. The new value is stored in RAMSET.

Line 120 stores the value 769 in RMCHR. Each character in the character set needs eight bytes of memory. After moving the numbers and capital letters to RAM, the computer needs to know how far into the character set the lowercase a is. There are 97 characters before the a in the character set. The first character is considered location zero, so we can subtract one. Since there are eight bits for each character, 8 times 96 equals 768.

Lines 140-160 move the first 512 bytes of the character set into RAM. We can move only 512 bytes because modes 1 and 2 can display only 64 characters. In line 150, C holds the number the computer gets from the location stored in ROMSET plus X. Remember: the value of ROMSET is the first byte of the character set. By adding the value of X to it, we can get every byte in the character set. That byte is then placed into RAM by POKEing it into the memory location computed by adding X to the value of RAMSET. Again, the value of RAMSET will remain constant. By changing the value of X, the entire first 512 bytes of the character set will be placed in the correct positions.

Lines 170-190 move the lowercase character set from ROM into RAM. If the program were to stop before these lines, the new character set would only contain numbers and uppercase letters. We want to replace the numbers with lowercase letters. The first eight memory locations in the character set (0-7) are correct. They are used for the space. The next 26 characters are the lowercase letters. We will start moving the bytes from the ROMSET location plus RMCHR plus the value of X. By adding the values stored in these variables, we obtain the first byte for the lowercase letters. As in the prior routine the value is POKEd into RAM. The memory location for the new character is computed by adding the value of X to the value of RAMSET. When this routine is completed, the numbers and symbols will be replaced by lowercase letters.

Line 200 stores the value of TOP in memory location CHBAS. If we had multiplied TOP by 256 earlier in the program, we would have to divide by 256 here because you cannot POKE a number greater than 255. The computer no longer looks at the character set in ROM. It considers the character set we just moved into RAM as the correct character set.

Line 210 prints a message on the screen. Enter the line just as it is shown here. The computer will interpret the numbers and symbols as letters with the new character set. When you run this program, the message will appear in both upper- and lowercase letters in two different colors. Press system reset to return to the normal character set.

CONSOLE KEYS

The three yellow keys on the ATARI are called the console keys. The computer does not check these keys as it does the keyboard keys. PEEK at location 53279:

$$? \text{ PEEK } (53279)$$

It should be 7. Run Listing 17-2. Press the console keys one at a time. You will see the keys correspond to the following values:

Start = 6

Select = 5

Option = 3

Start and Option = 2

Select and Option = 1

Start and Select = 4

Press the break key or system reset to stop the program. Use these keys when you want to be able to continue the program, as when there are directions or instructions, or some other message on the screen. You can direct the player to press start to begin, press option for a different level, select for one of several programs, or two players instead of one. Each key can be used to set up a game level, or as part of the program.

In the last chapter we used an arrow and the joystick to make sure the person using the program made the correct entry by eliminating the keyboard. Listing 17-3 shows you how to use the console keys to give the player choices, but not allow the player to enter incorrect answers. These keys can also eliminate the many questions programs often start with (how many players, which level, etc.).

Lines 40-50 set graphics mode 2, make the CONSOL variable equal to 53279, P equal to one, L equal to one and B equal to zero. P indicates how many players will be playing, L indicates which level will be played. B indicates which console key has been pressed.

Lines 60-110 print a welcome message on the screen. Notice that line 90 prints the level held in the variable L. Line 100 prints the correct variation of player. If there are two, line 110 will be printed.

Line 120 checks to see if one of the console keys has been pressed. B contains a value from 1-7 depending on which key has been pressed.

Line 130 sends the computer to line 200. The main program starts here.

Line 140 changes the level if the option key has been pressed. By subtracting the value stored in L from three, the variable L will fluctuate between one and two.

Line 150 changes the number of players when the select key is pressed. The same formula is used to compute how many persons will play.

Line 160 is a timing loop. If it were not there, the computer would get the key pressed too fast, and you might never set the game up properly.

Listing 17-2. Console Keys

```
10 REM LISTING XVII-2
20 REM CONSOLE KEYS
30 REM BY L.M.SCHREIBER FOR TAB BOOKS
40 CONSOL=53279
50 ? PEEK(CONSOL)
60 GOTO 50
```

Listing 17-3. Console Keys, Version 2

```
10 REM LISTING XVII-3
20 REM CONSOLE KEYS
30 REM BY L.M.SCHREIBER FOR TAB BOOKS
40 GRAPHICS 2
50 CONSOL=53279:P=1:L=1:B=0
60 POSITION 7,1:? #6;"welcome"
70 POSITION 9,2:? #6;"to"
80 POSITION 7,3:? #6;"CIRCUS"
90 POSITION 7,5:? #6;"LEVEL ";L
100 POSITION 6,7:IF P=1 THEN ? #6;P;" PLA
YER ":GOTO 120
110 ? #6;P;" PLAYERS"
120 B=PEEK(CONSOL)
130 IF B=6 THEN 200
140 IF B=3 THEN L=3-L
150 IF B=5 THEN P=3-P
160 FOR X=1 TO 75:NEXT X:GOTO 90
200 REM MAIN PROGRAM STARTS HERE
210 STOP
```

ELIMINATING THE RETURN KEY

In Listing 17-3 the player was given choices, but possible answers were limited by changing the choices each time a console key was pressed. When the correct combination was on the screen, the player pressed start and the program began. There are times you want the player to use the keyboard, but you do not want the answers on the screen, or you may want to check the entry before it is printed on the screen. Using the input command places any letters or characters typed by the user on the screen as soon as the key is pressed. The program cannot check the answer until the return key is pressed.

GET

You can get the value of any key pressed before the computer prints it on the screen. The get command takes the information requested from the device we request it from—in this case the keyboard—and stores it in a variable. It is used with the open command. Before we can check which key is pressed, we must open the keyboard.

OPEN #2,4,0, "K:"

This tells the computer to open a buffer (or area of memory where information can be stored) and call it #2. The 4 means it will receive the information (read it), the 0 is a dummy value, and the "K:" means the computer will receive the information from the keyboard. A buffer is opened once in a program. Do not open the same buffer again unless it has been closed. Once a buffer has been opened for the keyboard:

80 GET #2,A

The get command tells the computer the program should wait until it receives some information or values. In this case it is waiting for a key to be pressed. When a key is pressed, the computer will store it in the variable A. The contents of A can be checked. If it is correct, the computer can continue with the program. If not, the program loops back and gets another entry. The pressed key does not have to be displayed on the screen. Since every key is converted to a value, it doesn't matter if numbers or letters are pressed. The program will check each key as it is pressed.

Listing 17-4 uses the number keys 1-8 to play tones.

Line 40 dimensions KEY$ to eight. This program will play eight notes.

Line 50 places the characters that represent the notes into the string.

Line 60 opens the keyboard.

Line 70 gets the value of the key pressed and stores it in A. The program will not advance until a key has been pressed.

Lines 75-90 test the value of A. If it is 48, then a 0 has been pressed and the computer is directed to line 140. If A is less than 49, the computer is told to ignore the key and go back to line 70. If the value is greater than 56 the computer will also ignore the key. The computer will only continue with the program if the correct key has been pressed.

Line 100 turns the last note off and subtracts 48 from A. This tells the computer which key has been pressed.

Line 110 finds the ASCII value of the character in KEY$. A determines which character in KEY$ will be chosen. T contains the ASCII value of that character.

Line 120 plays the sound, which will continue until another key or 0 has been pressed.

Listing 17-4. Music Keys

```
10 REM LISTING XVII-4
20 REM MUSIC KEYS
30 REM BY L.M.SCHREIBER FOR TAB BOOKS
40 DIM KEYS$(8)
50 KEYS$="y1}.}[QH@<"
60 OPEN #2,4,0,"K:"
70 GET #2,A:REM GET A VALUE FOR THE KEY P
RESSED
75 IF A=48 THEN 140
80 IF A<49 THEN 70
90 IF A>56 THEN 70
100 SOUND 0,0,0,0:A=A-48
110 T=ASC(KEYS$(A,A))
120 SOUND 0,T,10,10
130 GOTO 70
140 END
```

Line 130 sends the computer back to line 70 to get another note.

Line 140 ends the program. The end command also turns off the sound.

PUT

The put command is the opposite of the get command. This command sends data to a device. Most commonly it is used to send data to a cassette or disk, but it can also be used to put characters on the screen. Used with the position command, you can direct the cursor to a row and column, and put a value at that position. The computer will print the character corresponding to the value in that position; e.g., in the direct mode, type:

GR. 2
POSITION 5,2: PUT #6,65

A yellow A should appear on the screen.

LOCATE

This command lets you examine the location on the screen under program control. It can be used when you need to know what is in a particular location on the screen. For example, in an arcade-type game, a laser is fired and moves across the screen. Your program can check the next location to be plotted to see if the object that was fired upon is there. Use the following format for the locate command:

50 LOCATE 40,50,X

The two numbers after locate indicate the column and row you are examining. It is similar to the plot or position command. The variable will hold the value of the location. This value can be checked to see if it is a hit or a miss. Listing 17-5 relies on the locate command to determine whether to move to the next location.

Lines 50-60 set the graphics mode and the color. By typing   COLOR 1   ,the color stored in SETCOLOR 0 will be used to draw lines.

Lines 70-90 draw a square spiral on the screen. The first point is plotted on the screen. Each DRAWTO command following draws a straight line from the last point drawn to the point indicated in the command.

Lines 100-120 change the color to be plotted, set the variables X and Y to the column and row the point will be plotted in, and plot a point. The user will move this point.

Line 130 gets the direction of the stick. The variable S holds one of nine different numbers.

Lines 140-210 check the value of S. If it is 15, the stick has not been moved and the program directs the computer to check again in line 130. If it is 14, the user wants to move up. Subtract one from the old row to arrive at the new one. A 13 means the user wants the point to move down. Add one to the row to move down. A 7 indicates a move to the right. This time 1 is added to the column. An 11 is a move to the left. One is subtracted from the column to move it. The program directs the computer to line 240 after the row or column has been adjusted.

Line 230 sends the computer back to line 130 for another value. The joystick must have been moved on a diagonal and the program does not handle diagonal moves.

Listing 17-5. Paths

```
10 REM LISTING XVII-5
20 REM PATHS
30 REM BY L.M.SCHREIBER FOR TAB BOOKS
40 REM USES PORT #1
50 GRAPHICS 7
60 SETCOLOR 0,5,8:COLOR 1
70 PLOT 0,0:DRAWTO 159,0:DRAWTO 159,79:DR
AWTO 39,79:DRAWTO 39,19:DRAWTO 119,19:DRA
WTO 119,59:DRAWTO 59,59
80 DRAWTO 59,29:DRAWTO 99,29:DRAWTO 99,49
:DRAWTO 69,49:DRAWTO 69,34:DRAWTO 89,34:D
RAWTO 89,44
90 DRAWTO 74,44:DRAWTO 74,39:DRAWTO 84,39
:DRAWTO 84,40
100 COLOR 2
110 X=19:Y=70
120 PLOT X,Y
130 S=STICK(0):REM GET THE DIRECTION
140 IF S=15 THEN 130:REM NOT BEING MOVED
150 IF S=14 THEN Y=Y-1:GOTO 240
170 IF S=13 THEN Y=Y+1:GOTO 240
190 IF S=7 THEN X=X+1:GOTO 240
210 IF S=11 THEN X=X-1:GOTO 240
230 GOTO 130:REM STICK IS DIAGONAL
240 LOCATE X,Y,B:IF B=1 THEN 300
250 IF X>0 AND Y<79 THEN 120
260 IF X=0 THEN X=1
270 IF Y=79 THEN Y=78
280 GOTO 130
300 C=7:FOR ZZ=1 TO 6:SOUND 0,C*10,10,10:
SETCOLOR 4,C,8:FOR Z=1 TO 100:NEXT Z:C=10
-C:NEXT ZZ:SOUND 0,0,0,0
310 GOTO 50
```

Line 240 uses the locate command to find out what is on the screen in the new location. If B contains a one, the wall has been hit. The computer is sent to line 300.

Lines 250-280 check the values of X and Y. If both X and Y are on the screen, the program will send the computer to line 120 so the new point can be plotted. The values the program checks are the left edge of the screen and the bottom. If X is a 0, the point is too close to the left edge. By resetting X to 1, the point can't go off the screen. Again, if the value of Y is 79, the point is too close to the bottom of the screen, and is reset to 78. The program goes back to line 130 for another input from the joystick.

Lines 300-310 flash the screen and make a sound when the wall is hit. The program resets itself for another game by going to line 50.

USING THE CLOCK

The ATARI has a clock built in its operating system. This clock is used to set the attract mode and start changing the colors on the screen whenever a key has not been pressed for about eight minutes. It can also be used by a program to limit the amount of time a user has to play, or to keep track of how long it takes a user to answer a question. The clock is in locations 18, 19, and 20. PEEK at location 20. This address is updated 60 times a second. Each time this memory location is reset to 0, the contents of location 19 are increased by 1. The contents of address 18 are increased by one each time location 19 is reset to 0.

Sometimes it is easier to PEEK at the values in one of these memory locations when you need a timing loop rather than using a For . . . Next loop.

To start the clock for your own purposes, POKE a 0 into any or all of the memory locations starting with 20 and ending with 18. Listing 17-6 gives you five seconds to answer each problem.

Line 35 opens the keyboard. The program will check which key has been pressed before it is displayed.

Line 40 sets the graphics to mode 2 without the text window.

Line 50 sets N1 to a random number between zero and nine. This will be the first number displayed on the screen.

Line 60 subtracts the random number the computer has just chosen from 10. The largest answer this program will accept is a nine, by subtracting the first number from 10, we know the upper limit for the second number.

Line 70 chooses the second number for the equation. It will be stored in N2.

Line 80 computes the answer by adding the value of N1 to N2.

Line 90 prints both numbers on the screen with the plus sign between them.

Line 100 clears two of the clock locations. Always clear the more frequently updated location first.

Line 120 checks memory location 764. If a key has been pressed, the location will not contain 255. The computer must go to line 150 to find out which key has been pressed.

Line 130 checks location 19. If it is a one, about five seconds have passed and the program will send the computer to line 170.

Line 140 sends the computer back to line 110 to check for a key if no key has been pressed and the time is not up.

Line 150 gets the value of the pressed key. This value must have 48 subtracted from it for the true number of the key. 255 is POKEd into location 764 to reset that memory location. Memory location 764 can only change when it is reset, or another key has been pressed.

Line 160 compares the pressed key with Answer. If both are the same, a message will be printed on the screen, and a tone will sound. The computer is directed to line 180.

Line 170 prints the answer if the incorrect key was pressed, or time ran out. Another tone will sound when the correct answer is printed on the screen.

Listing 17-6. Timer

```
10 REM LISTING XVII-6
20 REM TIMER
30 REM BY L.M.SCHREIBER FOR TAB BOOKS
35 OPEN #2,4,0,"K:":REM OPEN THE KEYBOARD
 FOR INPUT
40 GRAPHICS 18:REM SET GRAPHICS MODE
50 N1=INT(RND(1)*10):REM FIRST NUMBER IS
BETWEEN 0 AND 9
60 N=10-N1:REM GET LARGEST NUMBER THAT SE
COND NUMBER CAN BE
70 N2=INT(RND(1)*N):REM GET THE SECOND NU
MBER
80 ANSWER=N1+N2
90 POSITION 8,5:? #6;N1;" + ";N2:REM PRIN
T THE PROBLEM ON THE SCREEN
100 POKE 20,0:POKE 19,0:REM CLEAR TWO CLO
CK REGISTERS
110 A=PEEK(764):REM CHECK FOR KEY
120 IF A<>255 THEN 150:REM KEY HAS BEEN P
RESSED
125 IF PEEK(19)=1 THEN 160:REM TIME'S UP
130 IF PEEK(19)=1 THEN 160:REM TIME'S UP
140 GOTO 110
150 GET #2,A:POKE 764,255:REM CLEAR THE K
EY
160 IF A-48=ANSWER THEN POSITION 5,7:? #6
;"VERY GOOD":SOUND 0,20,10,10:GOTO 180
170 POSITION 9,7:? #6;ANSWER:SOUND 0,128,
10,10
180 FOR ZZ=1 TO 200:NEXT ZZ:SOUND 0,0,0,0
190 GOTO 40
```

Line 180 is a timing loop to give the user time to read the message or the answer on the screen. It can be adjusted for any length.

Line 190 sends the computer back to the beginning of the program for another problem.

The routine to change the colors on the screen when the computer is left unattended is also dependent on the clock. The value in location 77 is increased by one every time location 20 is reset. When location 77 reaches 128, the attract mode begins and the screen changes colors. This can be very annoying in a game that does not use the keyboard. To stop the computer from going to the attract mode, POKE 77 with 0 regularly during the course of a game. When you do disable the attract mode, be sure to POKE the 0 after a move has been made rather than in the main loop.

Listings 17-7A and 17-7B are two examples of turning off the attract mode.

Lines 40-90 represent the main part of the program.

Lines 100-250 contain the subroutine that checks the joystick. The value in location 77 is changed to a 0. This disables the attract mode. Line 120 determines the direction the joystick has been moved. Lines 130 and 140 direct the computer to the correct lines if the joystick has been moved up or down. Line 150 sends the computer back to line 110 if the joystick has not been moved. Lines 190-250 are the routines for moving a character up and down on the screen.

The computer will always start at line 110 and disable the attract mode. If the program were left unattended, the attract mode could never begin and the screen could be damaged.

Listing 17-7B is nearly identical to Listing 17-7A with one exception: line 110 has been removed. The attract mode will still be disabled, but only after the joystick has been moved. Line 130 and 140 POKE location 77 only after the joystick has been moved. This is the correct way to disable the attract mode. If the computer were left unattended the computer would be able to begin the color cycle. However, once a joystick has been moved, the color cycle would stop.

LIGHT PENS

The light pen is another peripheral device that can be attached to the ATARI. The pen is pointed at the screen and the location it is pointing to is stored in memory locations 564 and 565.

Listing 17-7A. Attract, Version 1

```
10 REM LISTING XVII-7A
20 REM ATTRACT
30 REM BY L.M.SCHREIBER FOR TAB BOOKS
40 REM USES PORT #0
50 REM THIS IS THE MAIN PART OF THE PROGR
AM
60 REM USE THIS AREA TO SET THE VARIABLES
   AND
70 REM THE DISPLAY ON THE SCREEN
80 REM
90 REM
100 REM THIS IS THE ROUTINE TO CHECK THE
JOYSTICK
110 POKE 77,0
120 S=STICK(0)
130 IF S=14 THEN 200
140 IF S=13 THEN 250
150 GOTO 110
190 REM ROUTINE TO MOVE UP
200 GOTO 110
240 REM ROUTINE TO MOVE DOWN
250 GOTO 110
```

Listing 17-7B. Attract, Version 2

```
10 REM LISTING XVII-7B
20 REM ATTRACT
30 REM BY L.M.SCHREIBER FOR TAB BOOKS
40 REM USES PORT #0
50 REM THIS IS THE MAIN PART OF THE PROGR
AM
60 REM USE THIS AREA TO SET THE VARIABLES
 AND
70 REM THE DISPLAY ON THE SCREEN
80 REM

90 REM
100 REM THIS IS THE ROUTINE TO CHECK THE
JOYSTICK
120 S=STICK(0)
130 IF S=14 THEN POKE 77,0:GOTO 200
140 IF S=13 THEN POKE 77,0:GOTO 250
150 GOTO 110
190 REM ROUTINE TO MOVE UP
200 GOTO 120
240 REM ROUTINE TO MOVE DOWN
250 GOTO 120
```

Listing 17-8. Paddle Draw

```
10 REM LISTING XVII.8
20 REM BY L.M.SCHREIBER FOR TAB BOOKS
30 REM PADDLE DRAW
40 DIM A$(1)
50 ? ">THIS PROGRAM WILL DRAW A PICTURE
IN   GRAPHICS 7 USING TWO PADDLES.   ONE"
60 ? "PADDLE WILL DRAW THE LINES UP AND D
OWNTHE OTHER PADDLE WILL DRAW RIGHT TO
LEFT."
70 ? :? "USE THE NUMBERS 1, 2, AND 3 TO C
HANGE THE COLOR."
80 ? :? "PRESS RETURN TO BEGIN";
90 INPUT A$
100 GRAPHICS 23:OPEN #2,4,0,"K:":REM OPEN
 KEYBOARD FOR READ
```

```
110 A=1:REM START WITH COLOR 1
120 R=PADDLE(0)/2:REM GET STARTING POINT
OF ROW
130 C=PADDLE(1):IF C>159 THEN C=159:REM G
ET STARTING POINT OF COLUMN
140 R1=R:R=PADDLE(0):REM THE ROW IS READ
FROM THE FIRST PADDLE
150 C1=C:C=PADDLE(1):REM THE COLUMN IS RE
AD FROM THE SECOND PADDLE
160 R=INT(R/2):IF R>95 THEN R=95:REM KEEP
 LINE ON SCREEN
170 IF C>159 THEN C=159:REM CHECK FOR RIG
HT MARGIN
180 IF PEEK(764)=255 THEN 210:REM NO KEY
PRESSED
190 GET #2,A:IF A<49 OR A>51 THEN 210:REM
 CHECK FOR GOOD ENTRY
200 A=A-48:REM GET NUMBER PRESSED
210 COLOR (A):PLOT C,R:DRAWTO C1,R1:REM P
LOT THE DOT
220 GOTO 140:REM DRAW SOME MORE
```

Listing 17-9. Paddle Music

```
10 REM LISTING XVII.9
20 REM BY L.M.SCHREBIER FOR TAB BOOKS
30 REM PADDLE MUSIC
40 ? ">This prosam will produce music ba
sed  on the values of two paddles.  The"
50 ? "paddles must be in the first port."

60 ? "Press START to besin."
70 IF PEEK(53279)<>6 THEN 70
80 GRAPHICS 23:REM GRAPHICS 7 WITH NO TEX
T WINDOW
90 COLOR 3:REM BLUE
100 PLOT 0,48:DRAWTO 159,48:REM DRAW THE
CENTER LINE
110 PL=0:REM START AT THE LEFT OF THE SCR
EEN
```

Listing 17-9. Paddle Music. (Continued from page 187.)

```
120 S=PADDLE(0):S1=PADDLE(1):REM GET THE
VALUES TO BE SOUNDED OF BOTH PADDLES
130 P=PADDLE(0)/5:P1=PADDLE(1)/5:REM GET
THE VALUES TO BE PLOTTED
140 SOUND 0,S,10,10:SOUND 1,S1,10,10:REM
MAKE BOTH SOUNDS
150 COLOR 1:REM YELLOW
160 PLOT PL,48:DRAWTO PL+2,48-P:DRAWTO PL
+6,48+P:DRAWTO PL+8,48
170 COLOR 2:REM GREEN
180 PLOT PL,48:DRAWTO PL+2,48+P1:DRAWTO P
L+7,48-P1:DRAWTO PL+8,48
190 PL=PL+8:IF PL<151 THEN 120
200 GOTO 80
```

The value stored would be equivalent to the row and column for the print or position commands. By checking these values when the trigger on the pen is pressed, the program can determine whether the person playing the game was pointing to the right location.

At the time of this writing, light pens from ATARI are not available. Light pens are available, however, from other hardware manufacturers and are compatible with the ATARI microcomputer.

JUST FOR FUN

Listings 17-8 and 17-9 combine graphics with the paddles. Listing 17-8 uses the paddle in port 1 as a drawing tool. Change the color on the screen by pressing keys 1, 2, or 3. Listing 17-9 uses the values of the paddles to produce tones. These tones are interpreted and drawn on the screen. To end either program, press the break key. To stop the sound in Listing 17-9, type   END

Chapter 18

Advanced Programming Skills

Now that you are confidently programming on your ATARI, you may want to give your programs a more professional look. Routines may be taking too long; other programs could use more color or graphics. By working directly with the 6502 microprocessor through a BASIC program, you can have the best of two worlds. BASIC can access small machine-language programs that will enhance or speed up your program. You can still write the main part of your program in BASIC.

Before writing a machine language subroutine you must have knowledge of the instructions the microprocessor follows. Figure 18-1 lists the entire 6502 instruction set with a brief explanation of each code.

Each instruction can be used by itself or with addresses or numbers. For example—LDA means to load the accumulator with a number. We can enter computer   LDA $56
This tells the computer to load the accumulator with the hex number 56. The pound sign tells the computer to use this number, the dollar sign stands for a hexadecimal number. We could enter   LDA $7A   which means the number to place in the accumulator is found in memory location hex 7A.   LDA $E002   tells the computer to load the accumulator with the contents of memory location hex E002. Each of these operations has a different code or number to differentiate one from the other. Figure 18-2 lists the codes for these commands.

It would be tedious to write large programs with these codes. When you are ready to work in machine code, you will use an editor/assembler to help you. The editor understands the mnemonic or instruction code, and the assembler converts these instructions into machine code.

It *is* possible to write short machine language subroutines directly in machine code and POKE these instructions into memory with your BASIC program. Your program would access the machine language subroutine through a BASIC statement, execute it, then return to the BASIC program.

USR

In Chapter 17 we moved the character set normally in ROM into RAM. Using BASIC, we PEEKed at a location, then POKEd that value into RAM. This can be accomplished much faster with a machine-language subroutine.

The machine-language subroutine must be placed in an area of RAM where it will not be touched by BASIC or the operating system. There are 256 bytes of memory, beginning with memory location 1536, set aside for this purpose. You can place a short machine-language subroutine there and know it will not be touched unless you POKE another value into that location. All the machine language subroutines in this chapter will be located in this area of RAM. Listing 18-1 moves the character set from ROM into RAM by using a machine-language subroutine.

Line 40 PEEKs at location 106. The amount of available memory is stored here. Eight is subtracted from this amount. This will be the starting location of the RAM-based character set. We need to save this value, so POKE it into location 204. We also store the beginning location of the ROM character set in location 206.

Line 50 begins the For . . . Next loop that moves the machine language subroutine into memory. The decimal equivalents to the instructions the computer will follow are in line 200. Location 1536 is the first memory location where this routine will start. The program will read the data, then:

Line 60 POKEs it into memory and continues until the entire routine has been moved.

Line 80 uses the USR instruction. Q is a dummy variable. The number in the parentheses is the first location of the machine language subroutine. The program sends the computer to this address to complete the routine. If there is no routine at this location, the system could crash.

Line 90 POKEs the new character-base address into location 756. Now the computer will use this character base.

Line 200 contains the machine-language subroutine the program is using.

Figure 18-3 lists the assembly-language version of the machine-language subroutine used in this program. When you are using a machine-language subroutine accessed from BASIC, the routine must first pull a number off the stack. This number was placed there when the computer went to the routine. If it is not removed, the routine will not return to BASIC properly.

The next command tells the computer to load its X index with the number 4. Then it will load the Y index with a 0. This resets the index. We will use this to count with when we move the character base.

The 6502 can add a number stored in one of its indexes to an address to obtain a new address. LDA 205,Y tells the computer to add the value stored in Y to the address stored in memory locations 205-206. Location 205 stores the low order address, location 206 contains the high order address. We POKEd the beginning address of the ROM character base to this location in the BASIC program. Once the computer adds the contents of Y to this address, it will get the value stored at this new address and place it into the accumulator.

The computer has to store this number somewhere. 204 is the location of the new character base. The computer adds the value stored in Y to the address stored in memory locations 203-204 and stores the number in its accumulator in the new location.

INY tells the computer to add 1 to the value of the Y index and store it in index Y. Both the X and Y index registers can count up to 255. If they are incremented past 255, they will reset to zero. When this happens, a *flag* or bit will be set in another register indicating the index has been zeroed.

ADC	Add memory to Accumulator with Carry
AND	'AND' Memory with Accumulator
ASL	Shift Left one bit in memory or Accumulator
BCC	Branch on Carry Clear
BCS	Branch on Carry Set
BEQ	Branch on Result Zero
BIT	Test Bits in Memory with Accumulator
BMI	Branch on Result Minus
BNE	Branch on Result not Equal to Zero
BPL	Branch on Result Plus
BRK	Force Break
BVC	Branch on Overflow Clear
BVS	Branch on Overflow Set
CLC	Clear Carry Flag
CLD	Clear Decimal Mode
CLI	Clear Interrupt Disable Bit
CLV	Clear Overflow Flag
CMP	Compare Memory and Accumulator
CPX	Compare Memory and Index X
CPY	Compare Memory and Index Y
DEC	Decrement Memory by One
DEX	Decrement Index X by One
DEY	Decrement Index Y by One
EOR	'Exclusive-Or' Memory with Accumulator
INC	Increment Memory by One
INX	Increment Index X by One
INY	Increment Index Y by One
JMP	Jump to New Location
JSR	Jump to New Location but save return address
LDA	Load Accumulator with Memory
LDX	Load Index X with Memory
LDY	Load Index Y with Memory
LSR	Shift Right One BIt in Memory or Accumulator
NOP	No Operation
ORA	'OR' Memory with Accumulator
PHA	Push Accumulator on Stack
PHP	Push Processor Status on Stack
PLA	Pull Accumulator from Stack
PLP	Pull Processor Status from Stack
ROL	Rotate One Bit Left in memory or Accumulator
ROR	Rotate One Bit Right in memory or Accumulator
RTI	Return from Interrupt
RTS	Return from Subroutine
SBC	Subtracts Memory from Accumulator with Borrow
SEC	Set Carry Flag
SED	Set Decimal Mode
SEI	Set Interrupt Disable Status
STA	Store Accumulator in Memory
STX	Store Index X in Memory
STY	Store Index Y in Memory
TAX	Transfer Accumulator to Index X
TAY	Transfer Accumulator to Index Y
TSX	Transfer Stack Pointer to Index X
TXA	Transfer Index X to Accumulator
TXS	Transfer Index S to Stack Pointer
TYA	Transfer Index Y to Accumulator

Fig. 18-1. 6502 microprocessor instructions.

Instruction	Assembly Language Form	Hex Code	Decimal Code	Instruction	Assembly Language Form	Hex Code	Decimal Code
ADC	ADC #nn	69	105		CMP aaaa	CD	205
	ADC aa	65	101		CMP aaaa,X	DD	221
	ADC aa,X	75	117		CMP aaaa,Y	D9	217
	ADC aaaa	6D	109		CMP (aa,X)	C1	193
	ADC aaaa,X	7D	125		CMP (aa),Y	D1	209
	ADC aaaa,Y	79	121	CPX	CPX #nn	E0	224
	ADC (aa,X)	61	97		CPX aa	E4	228
	ADC (aa),Y	71	113		CPX aaaa	EC	236
AND	AND #nn	29	41	CPY	CPY #nn	C0	192
	AND aa	25	37		CPY aa	C4	196
	AND aa,X	35	53		CPY aaaa	CC	204
	AND aaaa	2D	45	DEC	DEC aa	C6	198
	AND aaaa,X	3D	61		DEC aa,X	D6	214
	AND aaaa,Y	39	57		DEC aaaa	CE	206
	AND (aa,X)	21	33		DEC aaaa,X	DE	222
	AND (aa),Y	31	49	DEX	DEX	CA	202
ASL	ASL A	0A	10	DEY	DEY	88	136
	ASL aa	06	6	EOR	EOR #nn	49	73
	ASL aa,Y	16	22		EOR aa	45	69
	ASL aaaa	0E	14		EOR aa,X	55	85
	ASL aaaa,X	1E	30		EOR aaaa	4D	77
BCC	BCC aa	90	144		EOR aaaa,X	5D	93
BCS	BCS aa	B0	176		EOR aaaa,Y	59	89
BEQ	BEQ aa	F0	240		EOR (aa,X)	41	65
BIT	BIT aa	24	36		EOR (aa),Y	51	81
	BIT aaaa	2C	44	INC	INC aa	E6	230
BMI	BMI aa	30	48		INC aa,X	F6	246
BNE	BNE aa	D0	208		INC aaaa	EE	238
BLP	BLP aa	10	16		INC aaaa,X	FE	254
BRK	BRK	00	0	INX	INX	E8	232
BVC	BVC aa	50	80	INY	INY	C8	200
BVS	BVS aa	70	112	JMP	JMP aaaa	4C	76
CLC	CLC	18	24		JMP (aaaa)	6C	108
CLD	CLD	D8	216	JSR	JSR aaaa	20	32
CLI	CLI	58	88	LDA	LDA #nn	A9	169
CLV	CLV	B8	184		LDA aa	A5	165
CMP	CMP #nn	C9	201		LDA aa,X	B5	181
	CMP aa	C5	197		LDA aaaa	AD	173
	CMP aa,X	D5	213				

Fig. 18-2. Decimal and hex codes for instruction set.

BNE means branch not equal. If the Y index has not been reset to 0, the computer will go back to the **LDA 205,Y** . The number following the BNE instruction tells the computer how many bytes to branch and whether to go backwards or forwards. If the number is less than 128, the computer branches forward; if the number is greater than 128 the computer branches backward. Subtract the number following BNE (249) from 255 to find out how many bytes backward the computer will branch.

Instruction	Assembly Language Form		Hex Code	Decimal Code	Instruction	Assembly Language Form		Hex Code	Decimal Code
	LDA	aaaa,X	BD	189	ROR	ROR	A	6A	106
	LDA	aaaa,Y	B9	185		ROR	aa	66	102
	LDA	(aa,X)	A1	161		ROR	aa,X	76	118
	LDA	(aa),Y	B1	177		ROR	aaaa	6E	110
LDX	LDX	#nn	A2	162		ROR	aaaa,X	7E	126
	LDX	aa	A6	166	RTI	RTI		40	64
	LDX	aa,Y	B6	182	RTS	RTS		60	96
	LDX	aaaa	AE	174	SBC	SBC	#nn	E9	233
	LDX	aaaa,Y	BE	190		SBC	aa	E5	229
LDY	LDY	#nn	A0	160		SBC	aa,X	F5	245
	LDY	aa	A4	164		SBC	aaaa	ED	237
	LDY	aa,X	B4	180		SBC	aaaa,X	FD	253
	LDY	aaaa	AC	172		SBC	aaaa,Y	F9	249
	LDY	aaaa,X	BC	188		SBC	(aa,X)	E1	225
LSR	LSR	A	4A	74		SBC	(aa),Y	F1	241
	LSR	aa	46	70	SEC	SEC		38	56
	LSR	aa, X	56	86	SED	SED		F8	248
	LSR	aaaa	4E	78	SEI	SEI		78	120
	LSR	aaaa,X	5E	94	STA	STA	aa	85	133
NOP	NOP	#	EA	234		STA	aa,X	95	149
ORA	ORA	#nn	09	9		STA	aaaa	8D	141
	ORA	aa	05	5		STA	aaaa,X	9D	157
	ORA	aa,X	15	21		STA	aaaa,Y	99	153
	ORA	aaaa	0D	13		STA	(aa,X)	81	129
	ORA	aaaa,X	1D	29		STA	(aa),Y	91	145
	ORA	aaaa,Y	19	25	STX	STX	aa	86	134
	ORA	(aa,X)	01	1		STA	aa,Y	96	150
	ORA	(aa),Y	11	17		STA	aaaa	8E	142
PHA	PHA		48	72	STY	STY	aa	84	132
PHP	PHP		08	8		STY	aa,X	94	148
PLA	PLA		68	104		STY	aaaa	8C	140
PLP	PLP		28	40	TAX	TAX		AA	170
ROL	ROL	A	2A	42	TAY	TAY		A8	168
	ROL	aa	26	38	TSX	TSX		BA	186
	ROL	aa,X	36	54	TXA	TXA		8A	138
	ROL	aaaa	2E	46	TXS	TXS		9A	154
	ROL	aaaa,X	3E	62	TYA	TYA		98	152

If the Y index has been reset to zero, the computer will continue with the program. First it will add one to the number in memory location 206. It will then add one to the number in memory location 204. The computer accesses the next 256 bytes of ROM, then subtracts one from the number stored in index X. If X has not been reset to zero, the program will cycle back to the LDA 205,Y command. Each time this routine is completed, the computer moves 256 bytes from the character set in ROM to the new location in RAM. Completing this routine four times will move

Listing 18-1. Move Character Base

```
10 REM LISTING XVIII.1
20 REM MOVE CHARACTER BASE
30 REM BY L.M.SCHREIBER FOR TAB BOOKS
40 A=PEEK(106)-8:POKE 204,A:POKE 206,224
50 FOR X=1536 TO 1555:READ V:REM GET THE
MACHINE CODE IN DECIMAL
60 POKE X,V:REM PUT IT INTO MEMORY
70 NEXT X:REM MOVE THE ENTIRE ROUTINE INT
O MEMORY
80 Q=USR(1536):REM NOW RUN IT
90 POKE 756,A:REM TELL THE COMPUTER WHERE
 THE CHARACTER SET IS
100 ? "}clear}NOW WE ARE USING THE CHAR
ACTER BASE   IN RAM":REM PRINT 2 ESCAPE-C
NTRL-DOWNARROW AFTER CLEAR
110 END
200 DATA 104,162,4,160,0,177,205,145,203,
200,208,249,230,206,230,204,202,208,242,9
6
```

the entire character set. Once the X index reaches zero, the routine returns to BASIC (see Fig. 18-4).

ANTIC AND THE SCREEN

Most microcomputers on the market today use the same CPU to handle instructions and commands and also display information on the screen. Some systems offer choice of text, text with limited graphics, or high-resolution graphics. The ATARI microcomputer has a video microprocessor called Antic which handles the screen display. It has its own set of instructions that are different from the 6502 instructions, its own program, and data. This makes it possible to display several different modes on the screen at the same time. By using interrupts, you can display more colors than BASIC normally allows.

To understand the graphic capabilities of the Antic chip, you must first understand how a television screen works. An image is drawn on the screen by means of a *raster scan*: A beam starts at the upper left corner of the screen, and moves across the top of the screen. When it reaches the right side of the screen, it is turned off and returns to the left side of the screen. It is also lowered one line below the line just traced. It continues this pattern until it reaches the bottom of the screen. The beam will shut off and return to the upper left corner of the screen. The period of time it takes the beam to return to the left side of the screen is called the *horizontal blank*. The time needed to return to the upper left corner is the *vertical blank*.

The ATARI displays information using 192 scan lines. Each mode uses from 16 to 1 scan line(s). In mode 0 there are 24 rows on the screen. Each character stands eight scan lines high (8×24=192 scane lines).

The Antic chip must be able to determine which modes are used in a program. To do this, it uses a display list. In direct command, type: ? PEEK(560)+PEEK(561)*256   . This location (560-561) is a two-byte address that stores the beginning address of the display list. Run Listing 18-2.

The numbers printed vertically on your screen are instructions for the Antic chip. The numbers should read:

112
112
112
66
64* may vary
156* may vary
2
2
2
2
2
2
2
2
2
2
2
2
2
2
2
2
2
2
2
2
2
2
2
2
65
32* may vary
156* may vary

Decimal Code		Assembly Language Listing
104	PLA	;Pull the accumulator off the stack
162 4	LDX #4	;Load the index X with 4
160 0	LDY #0	;Load the index Y with 0.
177 205	LDA (205),Y	;Load the accumulator with the contents of the memory location that is arrived at by adding the contents of index Y to the memory location contains in location 205-206
145 203	STA (203),Y	;Store the number in the accumulator in the address arrived at by adding the contents of the index Y with the contents of locations 203-204
200	INY	;Increment the index Y
208 249	BNE	;Branch if the index Y is not 0 backwards 6 bytes.
230 206	INC 206	;Add one to the number in location 206.
230 204	INC 204	;Add one to the number in location 204
202	DEX	;Decrement the index X
208 242	BNE	;Branch if the index X is not 0 backwards 13 bytes.
96	RTS	;Return to BASIC

Fig. 16-3. Assembly Language Listing for Moving Character Set from ROM to RAM.

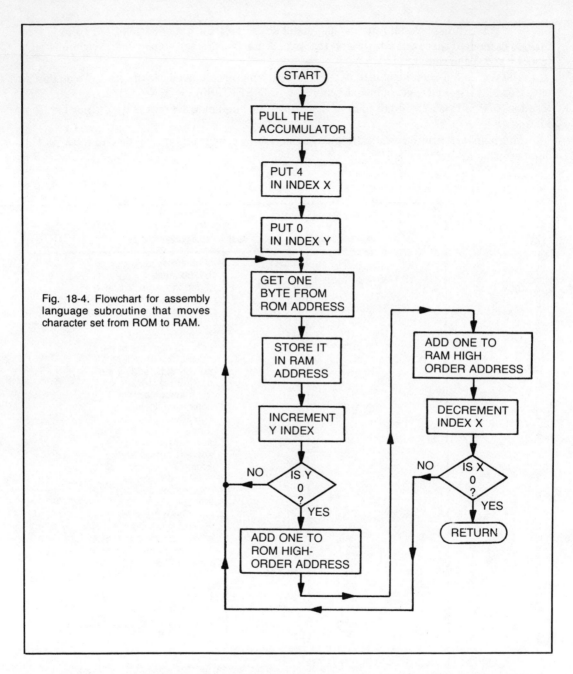

Fig. 18-4. Flowchart for assembly language subroutine that moves character set from ROM to RAM.

This display list contains 32 bytes. The first three numbers (112) are blank lines. Because there is an overscan on most television sets, the first 24 scan lines are blanked out. The next

Decimal Code	Assembly Language Listing	
72	PHA	;Push the contents of the accumulator on the stack.
169	LDA #88	;Load the accumulator with
88		88.
141	STA 54282	;Store the contents of the
10		accumulator in this location
212		- wait for horizontal sync.
141	STA 53272	;Store the contents of the
24		accumulator in the color
208		register.
104	PLA	;Put the number that was stored on the stack back into the accumulator.
64	RTS	;Return

Fig. 18-5. Assembly Language Subroutine that adds more colors to screen.

number, 66, is a combination of two numbers. 64 tells the Antic chip to load its memory scan counter with the following two numbers. By adding two to it, we tell it to use graphics mode 0. The next two numbers may vary, and contain the starting location of the screen. The first number is the low order address, the second number is the high order address. This address should be followed by 23 twos. Each two represents one row on the screen in mode 0. The 65 is another combination instruction. 64 means to jump to the location in the next two bytes when there is a vertical blank. Add one for a jump address. The next two numbers are the address the Antic chip will jump to—the beginning of the display list. Antic will continue with this display list until it is changed.

There are two important features about this display list. Because you can POKE numbers into it, you can change your screen display for any area of memory. You can even alternate between two screen display areas for animation or special effects. Also you can change the mode of one display line or several display lines and create multi-mode displays.

If you have less than 192 scan lines, your screen display will be shortened by that number of lines. Display lists must not cross a 1K boundary. If you have no choice but to cross a boundary, you must use a jump instruction or the Antic chip could get confused and never access the last part of your display list. One other problem arises with BASIC. If you try to print on the screen in a

Listing 18-2. Display List

```
10 REM LISTING XVIII.2
20 REM DISPLAY LIST
30 REM BY L.M.SCHREIBER FOR TAB BOOKS
40 DISPLAY=PEEK(560)+PEEK(561)*256:REM FI
ND THE BEGINNING OF THE DISPLAY LIST
50 FOR X=DISPLAY TO DISPLAY+31:? PEEK(X):
NEXT X:REM PRINT THE DISPLAY LIST
```

position that would normally be out of range for the cursor, BASIC will refuse to print there. Mixing 20 column modes with 40 column modes will move the position locations also.

Listing 18-3 mixes three modes to give you a varied print in the display message.

Line 40 finds the beginning of the display list. The display list address, a two-byte address, is stored in locations 560 and 561. Multiply the second byte by 256 and add it to the first byte to arrive at the address.

Line 50 saves the screen address. Since we will be using mode 0 for most of the screen display, we do not have to recalculate the screen area. The fifth and sixth numbers in the display list are the screen address.

Line 60 shuts off the Antic chip (since the Antic chip is constantly accessing the display list, we cannot change values in it while the chip is on). Memory location 559 tells Antic whether it should be working or not.

Lines 70-190 change the display list. We want to display one line in mode 1 and one line in mode 2. First decide which lines to change. The numbers in the display list must reflect this change.

Line 70 POKEs 112 into the first three memory locations of the display list. (Remember, the display list address is the first memory location, so the first three locations are 0 to 2.)

Line 80 POKEs the command that tells Antic the next two bytes contain the screen address and the mode the first line on the screen is in.

Line 90 POKEs the screen address. This program will reuse the address previously stored there.

Lines 100-110 POKE a 2 into the next six locations. This tells Antic to use mode 0 for these lines of the display.

Line 120 POKEs a 6 into the next location. The eighth line on the screen is now in graphics mode 1.

Lines 130-140 POKE a 2 into the display list for seven more lines in mode 0.

Line 150 POKEs a 7 into the next location. This makes the sixteenth line on the screen mode 2.

Lines 160-170 POKE a 2 into the remaining locations in the display list. The rest of the screen will be in mode 0.

Line 180 POKEs a 65 into the next location. This instruction tells Antic to jump to the address contained in the next two memory locations and start the display list instructions again after a vertical blank.

Line 190 POKEs the display list address into the next two memory locations. Since we did not move the display list, we can reuse the address in locations 560 and 561.

Line 200 turns the Antic chip on by POKEing a 34 into location 559.

Line 210 turns the cursor off and sets the background color for mode 0 to black.

Lines 220-230 clear the screen and print a message in the two lines in modes 1 and 2.

Line 240 loops until the break key or system reset is pressed.

If you press the break key and list the program without pressing the system reset key, the screen display will be the same as it is for the program. Your listing will appear in three different modes and the sections of the screen between mode 1 and mode 2 will appear off. Instead of the lines starting at the left side of the screen, they will begin in the middle of the screen, because the

Listing 18-3. Changing the Display Listing

```
10 REM LISTING XVIII.3
20 REM CHANGING THE DISPLAY LIST
30 REM BY L.M.SCHREIBER FOR TAB BOOKS
40 DISPLAY=PEEK(560)+PEEK(561)*256:REM FI
ND THE BEGINNING OF THE DISPLAY LIST
50 SCL=PEEK(DISPLAY+4):SCH=PEEK(DISPLAY+5
):REM SAVE THE SCREEN ADDRESS
60 POKE 559,0:REM SHUT OFF THE ANTIC CHIP

70 FOR X=DISPLAY TO DISPLAY+2:POKE X,112:
NEXT X:REM BLANK LINES
80 POKE DISPLAY+3,66:REM MODE 0 AND SCREE
N ADDRESS FOLLOWS
90 POKE DISPLAY+4,SCL:POKE DISPLAY+5,SCH
100 FOR X=DISPLAY+6 TO DISPLAY+11:REM THE
RE ARE 6 MORE MODES 0 LINES
110 POKE X,2:NEXT X
120 POKE DISPLAY+12,6:REM THIS LINE IS MO
DE 1
130 FOR X=DISPLAY+13 TO DISPLAY+19:REM 7
LINES OF MODE 0
140 POKE X,2:NEXT X
150 POKE DISPLAY+20,7:REM MODE 2
160 FOR X=DISPLAY+21 TO 27:REM THE REST I
S MODE 0
170 POKE X,2:NEXT X
180 POKE DISPLAY+28,65:REM JUMP AND WAIT
FOR VERTICAL BLANK
190 POKE DISPLAY+29,PEEK(560):POKE DISPLA
Y+30,PEEK(561)
200 POKE 559,34:REM TURN ANTIC BACK ON
210 POKE 752,1:POKE 710,0:REM TURN OFF CU
RSOR AND SET COLUR TO BLACK
220 ? "}clear}":POSITION 2,7:? "CHANGING"
230 POSITION 29,14:? "modes"
240 GOTO 240
```

computer thinks the entire screen is displayed in mode 0. The lines in mode 0 are 40 characters
long. When we changed the eighth line to mode 1, the computer will still count to 40 when
displaying that line. This causes a wrap-around to the next line. Every line following is off by 20
characters. The situation rights itself when we change the sixteenth display line to mode 2. Also,

because of this wrap-around effect, the first position in line 16 is not 0, but 20. BASIC will also produce the display on that line as if it was row 14 rather than 15.

Once you have a good idea of how the screen will be displayed when the modes are mixed, you can develop some interesting effects.

GETTING MORE COLOR

Changing the graphics modes in the display list is just one of the features of the display list. Since the Antic is a true microprocessor, the display list instructions can be interrupted, another routine can be performed, and the list can be continued. The trick is to do it without disturbing the screen display.

Let's say the program you are writing requires five colors in large letters. Graphics mode 2 can display only four colors at once. Solution—interrupt the display list, use a machine language subroutine to change the color in one of the color registers, then continue the program. This subroutine would have to be accessed each time the screen is updated, which is about 60 times a second. It must also be very short and to the point. The computer must read and execute in line in the time it takes for the scan to come back to the left side of the screen.

Listing 18-4 displays a message in mode 2 with the standard colors on the top part of the screen. The message on the lower half of the screen, however, is in a fifth color.

Line 50 sets the graphics mode. The mode you are going to use must be set before you change the display list, because the computer changes the display list each time the mode changes.

Line 80 finds the beginning of the display list and adds 10 to it. This will give us the seventh line of the screen.

Line 90 POKEs this location with 128 plus the number already there. This will not change the mode. By adding 128 to the mode code, the Antic chip will know there is an interrupt routine it must complete after it completes this line.

Line 100 reads the data in line 120 and POKEs it into memory. This data is the machine-language subroutine that will add another color to this graphics mode.

Line 110 POKEs the address of the machine-language subroutine into locations 512 and 513. Location 512 contains the low-order address and 513 contains the high-order address. This subroutine is POKEd into locations 1526-1551. By dividing 1536 by 256 we arrive at the high-order address. Since there is no remainder, POKE 0 into the low-order address. By POKEing 192 into 54286 the computer knows there will be an interrupt during the display list.

Lines 150-190 display a message on the screen. The second color and the fifth color look the same in the listing. Both use reverse video—uppercase. However, when the program is run, the second color appears blue on the screen while the fifth color is pink.

Line 200 loops until the break key or system reset is pressed.

To understand why we can change the color in a color register without affecting the color the first time it is displayed, we should look at the assembly-language program (Fig. 18-5).

Because we are not using the USR function from BASIC to access this subroutine, we do not have to do a PLA. Instead, since we are changing the value in the accumulator, we will first save the value in the accumulator by pushing it on the stack. Next we will load the accumulator with 88. This number produces pink. Store this number in the hardware register that waits for the

Listing 18-4. Adding Colors

```
10 REM LISTING XVIII-4
20 REM ADDING MORE COLORS
30 REM BY L.M.SCHREIBER FOR TAB BOOKS
50 GRAPHICS 18
80 DL=PEEK(560)+PEEK(561)*256:DL=DL+10:RE
M FIND THE MIDDLE OF THE SCREEN
90 POKE DL,PEEK(DL)+128:REM ADD THE INTER
RUPT CODE TO THE MODE CODE
100 FOR DL=1536 TO 1546:READ Q:POKE DL,Q:
NEXT DL:REM POKE THE MACHINE LANGUAGE PRO
GRAM
110 POKE 512,0:POKE 513,6:POKE 54286,192:
REM POKE THE ADDRESS OF THE MACHINE LANGU
AGE SUBROUTINE
120 DATA 72,169,88,141,10,212,141,24,208,
104,64
150 POSITION 2,1:? #6;"FIRST COLOR":REM C
APITAL LETTERS
160 POSITION 2,3:? #6;"SECOND COLOR":REM
CAPITAL LETTERS/REVERSE VIDEO
170 POSITION 2,5:? #6;"third color":REM L
OWER CASE LETTERS
180 POSITION 2,7:? #6;"fourth color":REM
LOWER CASE/REVERSE VIDEO
190 POSITION 2,9:? #6;"FIFTH COLOR":REM C
APITAL LETTERS/REVERSE VIDEO
200 GOTO 200
```

horizontal sync. We do not want to change the color until the beam is turned off and returning to the left side of the screen. Certain hardware addresses can have values stored in them when we work in machine language. You could not do this in BASIC because it is too slow. By the time BASIC POKEd a value into a hardware location, the operating system would write over it and it would not register on the screen. The operating system replaces this number with the original color number (blue) during the vertical blank. That is why the second color never changes to pink.

When the Antic chip starts from the top of the display list, it has blue in that location. When it gets to the seventh line, and the horizontal sync occurs, the interrupt program will put pink into that location. Once the horizontal sync occurs, 88 can be placed into location 53272. This is the equivalent of the SETCOLOR register 2 command in BASIC. After the new color has been placed into the correct register, the routine will pull the value off the stack and place it into the accumulator and return to the display list. Everytime Antic comes to this line in the display list, it will wait until this routine has been completed.

When the beam reaches the bottom of the screen and the vertical blank occurs, the original color (blue) will replace the new color (pink). One note of caution: the way this routine is written, the color in this register will not cycle when the rest of the screen does. This could cause damage to the screen if it is left on for a period of time and defeats the attract mode. This can be changed by using the following data line and changing 1546 in line 100 to 1550. The 69 exclusive ors the value in location 79 with the 88 and ANDs it with the value in 78. Now all the colors on the screen can cycle.

120 DATA 72,169,88,69,79,88,78,141,10,212,141,24,208,104,64

PLAYER/MISSILE GRAPHICS

In addition to the five color registers for the background and characters, the ATARI also has four color registers for its players and missiles. If you want to draw a character with any other microcomputer, then move the character across the screen, you would have to erase the old character and redraw the new one. The players in the ATARI computer are characters you can create and move instantaneously anywhere on the screen. The character is eight bits or points wide, but it can be in one of three sizes. It can also be only one line tall or as tall as the screen. You may imagine it as a band that fits over the screen from top to bottom. This band can be moved from left to right and back again. The character is within the band and can be moved up or down.

CREATING A PLAYER

Since a player can only be eight bits or points wide, it's a good idea to draw the character on graph paper first. Maybe you're writing a space program and would like to design a ship. Figure 18-6 is an example of a space ship that can be used as a player. It is eight points wide and seven lines high. Using binary to compute the numbers, each line of the ship has the following values (from top to bottom): 15,2,226,66,66,255

Now we have a player, we have to be able to tell the computer we want to use player/missile graphics in this program and draw the player in memory to use and reuse. The area of memory the characters for the player/missile graphics occupy must be in a single 1K (1024 bytes) or 2K (2048 bytes) of continuous memory. The beginning address of the character block must be divisible by 1024 with no remainder.

For Listing 18-5 we will use the single line players that use 2K of memory. In the second program we will use the same players in 1K of memory. Each number will display two lines on the screen.

Line 50 POKEs values into the color register for the first player (address 704) and changes the background color to black.

Line 60 finds out how much memory is available and subtracts 16. This value will be more than 2048 bytes above the display list. We need 2K of memory for the player/missile graphics, but if we simply subtract 2048 from the display list, we could cross a boundary line somewhere in memory. This would confuse Antic, so instead, subtract an even 4K from the amount of memory in the system. This leaves 2K for the screen display and display list and 2K for the player/missiles.

Line 70 POKEs the address the player/missiles will begin at into location 54279. This is a hardware register. Now Antic knows where the characters will be located. By multiplying that number by 256 we have the decimal location of the beginning of the player/missile display.

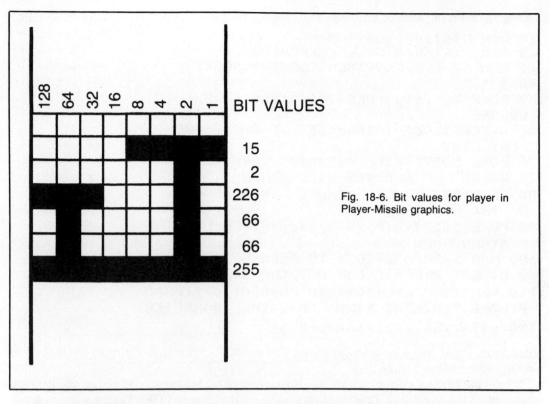

BIT VALUES

15
2
226
66
66
255

Fig. 18-6. Bit values for player in Player-Missile graphics.

Line 80 POKEs location 559 with a 62. In a previous program we POKEd that location with 0 to turn Antic off, then POKEd it with a 34 to turn it back on. Now POKE it with 62 to tell it we will be using the player/missile with single-line resolution.

Line 90 POKEs memory location 53277 with a 3. The player/missile graphics are now enabled. If we told Antic to use player/missile graphics (previous line), but never enabled them, they would not be displayed on the screen. POKEing 75 into location 53248 moves the player onto the screen. This number can be changed to any number from 0 to 255. Numbers less than 50 or greater than 200 will place the character off the screen.

Line 100 clears the memory the player will occupy. The first player starts 1024 bytes below the address we calculated. It uses 256 bytes of memory. We are clearing enough memory for two different players.

Line 110 places the character we created into the memory set aside for the player. Placing it 70 bytes from the top of that player's area is just one area the character could occupy. The character can be placed in any area from 1024 to 1274. Again, if you place your character too close to the top or bottom of the area, it will not be displayed on the screen.

When you run this program, the screen should clear and after a few seconds, a small ship will appear in the upper left corner of the screen. If you list your program, the space ship will not move. It will not scroll up with the program listing nor will it disappear if you press the shift and

Listing 18-5. Player/Missile Graphics.

```
10 REM LISTING XVIII-5
20 REM PLAYER/MISSILE GRAPHICS
30 REM BY L.M.SCREIBER FOR TAB BOOKS
40 ? "}"
50 POKE 704,124:POKE 710,0:REM CHANGE THE
   COLORS
60 A=PEEK(106)-16:REM GET 2K ABOVE THE DI
SPLAY LIST
70 POKE 54279,A:PMBASE=A*256:REM TELL ANT
IC WHERE THE PLAYERS WILL BEGIN
80 POKE 559,62:REM SINGLE LINE RESOLUTION
   ON THE PLAYERS
90 POKE 53277,3:POKE 53248,75:REM LET THE
   PLAYERS SHOW
100 FOR X=PMBASE+1024 TO PMBASE+1536:POKE
    X,0:NEXT X:REM CLEAR OUT THE GARBAGE
110 FOR X=PMBASE+1094 TO PMBASE+1099:READ
    P:POKE X,P:NEXT X:REM DRAW THE CHARACTER
120 DATA 15,2,226,66,66,255
```

clear keys. Player/missiles act independently of the other characters on the screen. Let's add another character to Listing 18-6.

Line 140 POKEs a color (yellow) into the color register for the second player. 53249 is the register for the second player's position on the screen. If a 75 were POKEd into this location, the second ship would appear under the first ship.

Line 150 reads the numbers that create the second ship and POKEs them into the memory set aside for the second ship.

Now we have defined the two players we must be able to move them around and fire at each other. Moving them horizontally is very easy. Changing the value in register 53248 moves the first ship, changing the value in register 53249 moves the second ship. Moving the ships vertically requires some planning; each ship occupies seven continuous memory locations. To move the ship up, each byte would have to be moved up one memory location and the last byte erased. To move the ship down, each byte would have to be moved down one location and again, the first one erased. This can be done slowly in BASIC, or quickly with a machine language subroutine.

Figure 18-7 shows the machine-language subroutine needed to move the space ship in Listing 18-7.

Line 210 reads the data from line 220 and POKEs it into memory locations 1536-1548. This is the routine to move the ship up.

Line 230 sets the up variable to the beginning of this routine.

Line 240 reads the data from line 250 and POKEs it into memory locations 1552-1564. This is the routine that moves the ship down.

Line 260 stores the beginning location of this routine in the down variable.

Line 270 stores the positions of the ships in four variables. RKT1H is the horizontal position of the first ship. RKT1V is the vertical position of the first ship. RKT2H is the horizontal position of the second ship and RKT2V is the vertical position of the second ship. These variables will change as we move the ships around the screen.

Lines 280-330 check the joystick for the first ship. The joystick must be plugged into port 1 on the front of the keyboard. If the stick has not moved, the computer will go to line 330 to check the fire button. If the stick has moved to the right or left, RKT1V will be increased or decreased accordingly. If the stick has moved up or down, RKT1H will be increased or decreased.

In any event, the trigger or red button on the joystick will also be checked. If it has been pressed, a missile will be placed into the area set aside for player/missile graphics. The missile area begins 768 bytes below the area set aside for player/missile graphics. The beginning location of the ship is added to this number and 11 more bytes, so the missile will appear at the lower edge of the ship. A 3 is POKEd into this memory location. The 3 sets the last two bytes, the only two that are allowed for missile 0. The program now GOSUBs to line 600.

Listing 18-6. Player/Missile Graphics, Version 2

```
10 REM LISTING XVIII-6
20 REM PLAYER/MISSILE GRAPHICS
30 REM BY L.M.SCREIBER FOR TAB BOOKS
40 POKE 752,1:? ">clear>"
50 POKE 704,124:POKE 710,0:REM CHANGE THE
   COLORS
60 A=PEEK(106)-16:REM GET 2K ABOVE THE DI
   SPLAY LIST
70 POKE 54279,A:PMBASE=A*256:REM TELL ANT
   IC WHERE THE PLAYERS WILL BEGIN
80 POKE 559,62:REM SINGLE LINE RESOLUTION
   ON THE PLAYERS
90 POKE 53277,3:POKE 53248,75:REM LET THE
   PLAYERS SHOW
100 FOR X=PMBASE+1024 TO PMBASE+1536:POKE
    X,0:NEXT X:REM CLEAR OUT THE GARBAGE
110 FOR X=PMBASE+1094 TO PMBASE+1099:READ
    P:POKE X,P:NEXT X:REM DRAW A CHARACTER
120 DATA 15,2,226,66,66,255
130 REM ADD ANOTHER SPACE SHIP
140 POKE 705,30:POKE 53249,154:REM GIVE T
HE 2nd SHIP COLOR AND A PLACE
150 FOR X=PMBASE+1380 TO PMBASE+1386:READ
    P:POKE X,P:NEXT X:REM DRAW THE SECOND CH
ARACTER
160 DATA 130,146,186,254,186,146,130
```

Decimal Code	Assembly Language Listing	
104	PLA	;Pull the accumulator off the stack
160 0	LDY #0	;Load the index Y with zero
200	INY	;Increment the index Y
177 205	LDA (205),Y	;Load the accumulator with the value of the address in location 205-206 offset by Y
136	DEY	;Decrement the index Y
145 205	STA (205),Y	;Store the value in the accumulator in the memory locations pointed to by 205-206 offset by Y
200	INY	;Increment Y
208 247	BNE	;If the index Y is not zero, go back 8 bytes
96	RTS	;Return to BASIC

Routine to move character up

104	PLA	;Pull the accumulator off the stack
160 255	LDY #255	;Load the index Y with 255
136	DEY	;Decrement index Y
177 205	LDA (205),Y	;Load the accumulator with the value of the address in location 205-206 offset by Y
200	INY	;Increment Y
145 205	STA (205),Y	;Store the value in the accumulator in the memory location pointed to by 205-206 offset by Y.
136	DEY	;Decrement Y
208 247	BNE	;If the index Y is not zero, go back 8 bytes
96	RTS	;Return to BASIC

Routine to move character down

Fig. 18-7. Assembly language listings to move players up and/or down.

Lines 350-400 operate the same way, but for the second ship. This time port number 4 must be used for the joystick. If the fire button is pressed (line 400), the beginning of the second rocket ship is added to the lcoation for the player/missile graphics.

Lines 410-470 move the rocket ships. In line 410, the variable is checked for the edge of the screen for the first ship. If it would go off the left or right edge of the screen, the computer is directed to a subroutine that corrects the situation. Line 420 checks the second ship. Line 430 checks how high or low the ship is on the screen. Again, if the ship would go off the screen, the computer is sent to a routine that will correct the variable. Line 440 checks the second ship. When all the variables have been checked, the vertical values are POKEd into the locations that move the ships to the left or right. If these variables have changed, the ship will move in that direction. Lines 460 and 470 check the variables DIR1 and DIR2 to see if the ship should move up or down. If

Listing 18-7. Player/Missile Graphics, Version 3

```
10 REM LISTING XVIII-7
20 REM PLAYER/MISSILE GRAPHICS
30 REM BY L.M.SCREIBER FOR TAB BOOKS
40 POKE 752,1:? "}clear}"
50 POKE 704,124:POKE 710,0:REM CHANGE THE
   COLORS
60 A=PEEK(106)-16:REM GET 2K ABOVE THE DI
SPLAY LIST
70 POKE 54279,A:PMBASE=A*256:REM TELL ANT
IC WHERE THE PLAYERS WILL BEGIN
80 POKE 559,62:REM SINGLE LINE RESOLUTION
   ON THE PLAYERS
90 POKE 53277,3:POKE 53248,75:REM LET THE
   PLAYERS SHOW
100 FOR X=PMBASE+768 TO PMBASE+1536:POKE
X,0:NEXT X:REM CLEAR OUT THE GARBAGE
110 FOR X=PMBASE+1094 TO PMBASE+1099:READ
 P:POKE X,P:NEXT X
120 DATA 15,2,226,66,66,255
130 REM ADD ANOTHER SPACE SHIP
140 POKE 705,30:POKE 53249,154:REM GIVE T
HE 2nd SHIP COLOR AND A PLACE
150 FOR X=PMBASE+1380 TO PMBASE+1386:READ
 P:POKE X,P:NEXT X
160 DATA 130,146,186,254,186,146,130
200 REM MOVE THE SHIPS
210 FOR X=1536 TO 1548:READ P:POKE X,P:NE
XT X:REM ROUTINE TO MOVE UP
220 DATA 104,160,0,200,177,205,136,145,20
5,200,208,247,96
230 UP=1536
240 FOR X=1552 TO 1564:READ P:POKE X,P:NE
XT X:REM ROUTINE TO MOVE DOWN
250 DATA 104,160,255,136,177,205,200,145,
205,136,208,247,96
260 DOWN=1552
270 RKT1H=60:RKT1V=75:RKT2H=100:RKT2V=154

280 IF STICK(0)=15 THEN 330:REM JOYSTICK
NOT MOVED
290 IF STICK(0)=7 THEN RKT1V=RKT1V+1:GOTO
```

Listing 18-7. Player/Missile Graphics, Version 3. (Continued from page 207.)

```
330:REM MOVED TO THE RIGHT
300 IF STICK(0)=11 THEN RKT1V=RKT1V-1:GOT
O 330:REM MOVED TO THE LEFT
310 IF STICK(0)=14 THEN RKT1H=RKT1H-1:DIR
1=UP:GOTO 330:REM MOVED UP
320 IF STICK(0)=13 THEN RKT1H=RKT1H+1:DIR
1=DOWN:GOTO 330:REM MOVED DOWN
330 IF STRIG(0)=0 THEN POKE PMBASE+768+RK
T1H+11,3:GOSUB 600:REM FIRE BUTTON PRESSE
D
340 REM NOW CHECK PLAYER 2
350 IF STICK(3)=15 THEN 400:REM JOYSTICK
HAS NOT MOVED
360 IF STICK(3)=7 THEN RKT2V=RKT2V+1:GOTO
 400:REM MOVED TO THE RIGHT
370 IF STICK(3)=11 THEN RKT2V=RKT2V-1:GOT
O 400:REM MOVED TO THE LEFT
380 IF STICK(3)=14 THEN RKT2H=RKT2H-1:DIR
2=UP:GOTO 400:REM MOVED UP
390 IF STICK(3)=13 THEN RKT2H=RKT2H+1:DIR
2=DOWN:GOTO 400:REM MOVED RIGHT
400 IF STRIG(3)=0 THEN POKE PMBASE+768+RK
T2H+5,12:GOSUB 650:REM FIRE BUTTON PRESSE
D
410 IF RKT1V<50 OR RKT1V>200 THEN GOSUB 5
00:REM IT'S OFF THE SCREEN
420 IF RKT2V<50 OR RKT2V>200 THEN GOSUB 5
20
430 IF RKT1H<40 OR RKT1H>200 THEN GOSUB 5
40:REM TOO HIGH OR TOO LOW
440 IF RKT2H<40 OR RKT2H>200 THEN GOSUB 5
60
450 POKE 53248,RKT1V:POKE 53249,RKT2V:REM
 MOVE THE SHIPS LEFT OR RIGHT
460 IF DIR1<>0 THEN POKE 206,A+4:Q=USR(DI
R1):DIR1=0:REM MOVE SHIP 1 UP OR DOWN
470 IF DIR2<>0 THEN POKE 206,A+5:Q=USR(DI
R2):DIR2=0:REM MOVE SHIP 2 UP OR DOWN
480 GOTO 280:REM GET NEW DIRECTION
500 IF RKT1V<50 THEN RKT1V=50:RETURN
510 IF RKT1V>200 THEN RKT1V=200:RETURN
```

```
520 IF RKT2V<50 THEN RKT2V=50:RETURN
530 IF RKT2V>200 THEN RKT2V=200:RETURN
540 IF RKT1H<40 THEN RKT1H=40:DIR1=0:RETU
RN
550 IF RKT1H>200 THEN RKT1H=200:DIR1=0:RE
TURN
560 IF RKT2H<40 THEN RKT2H=40:DIR2=0:RETU
RN
570 IF RKT2H>200 THEN RKT2H=200:DIR2=0:RE
TURN
580 RETURN
600 POKE 53252,RKT1V+10:M1=RKT1V+10
610 FOR X=M1 TO 250:POKE 53252,X:SOUND 0,
X,6,10:IF PEEK(53256)<>0 THEN 700
620 NEXT X:SOUND 0,0,0,0:POKE PMBASE+768+
RKT1H+11,0
630 RETURN
650 POKE 53253,RKT2V-10:M2=RKT2V-10
660 FOR X=M2 TO 10 STEP -1:POKE 53253,X:S
OUND 0,X,6,10:IF PEEK(53257)<>0 THEN 700
670 NEXT X:SOUND 0,0,0,0:POKE PMBASE+768+
RKT2H+5,0
680 RETURN
700 S=100:C=50:FOR ZZ=1 TO 6:SOUND 0,S,10
,10:POKE 710,C:FOR TL=1 TO 50:NEXT TL:S=1
50-S:C=75-C:NEXT ZZ
710 SOUND 0,0,0,0:POKE 710,0
720 POKE 53252,0:POKE 53253,0:POKE 53278,
0
730 POKE PMBASE+768+RKT2H+5,0:POKE PMBASE
+768+RKT1H+11,0:RETURN
```

these variables have been set, the program will POKE the starting location of the memory area that contains that ship into location 206 (the high order byte). Then it executes the machine language subroutine and resets DIR1 or DIR2 to 0. If the first ship is to move, the high order byte is POKEd with a 4 because the first ship starts 1024 bytes below the area set aside. A contains the beginning of the area set aside for the player/missile graphics. If the second ship is to move, 5 is added to the value in A because the second ship is located 1280 bytes below the beginning of the area set aside for player/missile graphics.

Line 480—once the ships have moved, the program directs the computer to line 280 and checks the joysticks once more. The break key or system reset must be pressed to stop this program.

Lines 500-580 reset the variables when they are beyond the value set for the edge of the screen. Once the variable has been reset, the program returns to the main routine.

Lines 600-680 move the missile across the screen.

Lines 600-630 move the missile for the first ship. Location 53252 is POKEd with the vertical location of the ship plus 10. This moves the missile out from under the ship. This value is then stored in M1. Lines 610-620 move the missile from the ship towards the right edge of the screen. Each time it moves the missile, it checks location 53256 for a value other than 0. This is a hit location for this missile. Rather than check if the vertical and horizontal location of the missile is the same as the location of the ship it is trying to hit, a very long and time consuming project, ATARI BASIC can check one memory location to see if the missile that has been fired has hit anything. If it has, the value in that location changes. If the missile has hit the ship, the computer is directed to line 700. If it has not, the missile will continue to move across the screen until it goes out of sight. Lines 660-680 move the missile for the second ship to the left across the screen. It checks location 53257 after each movement to see if the other ship has been hit. In both routines the missile is removed from the player/missile area by POKEing the location that contained the missile with a 0.

Lines 700-730 contain the routine that flashes the screen when the missile hits the ship. Line 720 moves the missiles off the screen. By POKEing 53278 with 0, we clear the hit register. Now we can return to the program and check for hits again. If this register is not cleared after each hit, it will continue to show a hit whether or not one has been made. Line 700 erases the missiles in the player/missile area and returns to the part of the program that called it.

In addition to checking for missiles hitting players, the ATARI has registers that can check players hitting players, players hitting the playfield and missiles hitting the playfield. The playfield characters are the characters placed on the screen with print or plot and draw to commands. Players refer to the characters created and stored in the player/missile area. The two ships in the preceding program are players. The missiles (characters that are two bits wide) are referred to as missiles.

The size of the characters in the player/missile graphics area can be changed two different ways. In line 120, each number represented one line on the screen. Line 80 set the resolution for the player/missile graphics to one line. This mode uses 2K of memory. By making a few changes in the program, each number in lines 120 and 160 can be represented in two lines on the screen.

Listing 18-8 is nearly identical to Listing 18-7. Line 80 POKEs 46 into location 559. So each number in the data lines will be displayed as two lines on the screen. Because this mode uses only 1K of memory, the player/missile area starts nearer to the area set aside for it.

Line 60 subtracts 8 from the amount of memory available. This sets aside 1K for the screen and display list and 1K for the player/missile.

Line 100 is changed to reflect the area the characters will occupy. The missiles begin 384 bytes from the area set aside instead of 768 in the single resolution mode.

Line 110 starts placing the character into the 547th byte of the area. Since the players use two lines on the screen for every number entered, the area set aside for their display is half as long as when they use one line for every number.

Line 150 changes the second ship's location to 690.

Line 210 adds two numbers to the area where the machine language subroutine will be stored.

210

Listing 18-8. Player/Missile Graphics, Version 4

```
10 REM LISTING XVIII-8
20 REM PLAYER/MISSILE GRAPHICS
30 REM BY L.M.SCREIBER FOR TAB BOOKS
40 POKE 752,1:? ")clear}"
50 POKE 704,124:POKE 710,0
60 A=PEEK(106)-8:REM GET 1K ABOVE THE DIS
PLAY LIST
70 POKE 54279,A:PMBASE=A*256:REM TELL ANT
IC WHERE THE PLAYERS WILL BEGIN
80 POKE 559,46:REM TWO LINE RESOLUTION ON
 THE PLAYERS
90 POKE 53277,3:POKE 53248,75:REM LET THE
 PLAYERS SHOW
100 FOR X=PMBASE+384 TO PMBASE+768:POKE X
,0:NEXT X:REM CLEAR OUT THE GARBAGE
110 FOR X=PMBASE+547 TO PMBASE+552:READ P
:POKE X,P:NEXT X
120 DATA 15,2,226,66,66,255
130 REM ADD ANOTHER SPACE SHIP
140 POKE 705,30:POKE 53249,154:REM GIVE T
HE 2nd SHIP COLOR AND A PLACE
150 FOR X=PMBASE+690 TO PMBASE+696:READ P
:POKE X,P:NEXT X
160 DATA 130,146,186,254,186,146,130
200 REM MOVE THE SHIPS
210 FOR X=1536 TO 1550:READ P:POKE X,P:NE
XT X:REM ROUTINE TO MOVE UP
220 DATA 104,160,0,200,177,205,136,145,20
5,200,192,128,208,245,96
230 UP=1536
240 FOR X=1552 TO 1564:READ P:POKE X,P:NE
XT X:REM ROUTINE TO MOVE DOWN
250 DATA 104,160,128,136,177,205,200,145,
205,136,208,247,96
260 DOWN=1552
270 RKT1H=35:RKT1V=75:RKT2H=50:RKT2V=154
280 IF STICK(0)=15 THEN 330:REM JOYSTICK
NOT MOVED
290 IF STICK(0)=7 THEN RKT1V=RKT1V+1:GOTO
 330:REM MOVED TO THE RIGHT
300 IF STICK(0)=11 THEN RKT1V=RKT1V-1:GOT
```

```
0 330:REM MOVED TO THE LEFT
310 IF STICK(0)=14 THEN RKT1H=RKT1H-1:DIR
1=UP:GOTO 330:REM MOVED UP
320 IF STICK(0)=13 THEN RKT1H=RKT1H+1:DIR
1=DOWN:GOTO 330:REM MOVED DOWN
330 IF STRIG(0)=0 THEN POKE PMBASE+384+RK
T1H+5,3:GOSUB 600:REM FIRE BUTTON PRESSED

340 REM NOW CHECK PLAYER 2
350 IF STICK(3)=15 THEN 400:REM JOYSTICK
NOT MOVED
360 IF STICK(3)=7 THEN RKT2V=RKT2V+1:GOTO
 400:REM MOVED TO THE RIGHT
370 IF STICK(3)=11 THEN RKT2V=RKT2V-1:GOT
O 400:REM MOVED TO THE LEFT
380 IF STICK(3)=14 THEN RKT2H=RKT2H-1:DIR
2=UP:GOTO 400:REM MOVED UP
390 IF STICK(3)=13 THEN RKT2H=RKT2H+1:DIR
2=DOWN:GOTO 400:REM MOVED DOWN
400 IF STRIG(3)=0 THEN POKE PMBASE+384+RK
T2H+2,12:GOSUB 650:REM FIRE BUTTON PRESSE
D
410 IF RKT1V<50 OR RKT1V>200 THEN GOSUB 5
00:REM IT'S OFF THE SCREEN
420 IF RKT2V<50 OR RKT2V>200 THEN GOSUB 5
20
430 IF RKT1H<15 OR RKT1H>100 THEN GOSUB 5
40:REM TOO HIGH OR TOO LOW
440 IF RKT2H<15 OR RKT2H>100 THEN GOSUB 5
60
450 POKE 53248,RKT1V:POKE 53249,RKT2V:REM
 MOVE THE SHIPS LEFT OR RIGHT
460 IF DIR1<>0 THEN POKE 206,A+2:POKE 205
,0:Q=USR(DIR1):DIR1=0:REM MOVE SHIP 1 UP
OR DOWN
470 IF DIR2<>0 THEN POKE 206,A+2:POKE 205
,125:Q=USR(DIR2):DIR2=0:REM MOVE SHIP 2 U
P OR DOWN

480 GOTO 280
500 IF RKT1V<50 THEN RKT1V=50:RETURN
```

```
510 IF RKT1V>200 THEN RKT1V=200:RETURN
520 IF RKT2V<50 THEN RKT2V=50:RETURN
530 IF RKT2V>200 THEN RKT2V=200:RETURN
540 IF RKT1H<15 THEN RKT1H=15:DIR1=0:RETU
RN
550 IF RKT1H>100 THEN RKT1H=100:DIR1=0:RE
TURN
560 IF RKT2H<15 THEN RKT2H=15:DIR2=0:RETU
RN
570 IF RKT2H>100 THEN RKT2H=100:DIR2=0:RE
TURN
580 RETURN
600 POKE 53252,RKT1V+10:M1=RKT1V+10
610 FOR X=M1 TO 250:POKE 53252,X:SOUND 0,
X,6,10:IF PEEK(53256)=2 THEN 700
620 NEXT X:SOUND 0,0,0,0:POKE PMBASE+384+
RKT1H+5,0
630 RETURN
650 POKE 53253,RKT2V-10:M2=RKT2V-10
660 FOR X=M2 TO 10 STEP -1:POKE 53253,X:S
OUND 0,X,6,10:IF PEEK(53257)=1 THEN 700
670 NEXT X:SOUND 0,0,0,0:POKE PMBASE+384+
RKT2H+2,0
680 RETURN
700 S=100:C=50:FOR ZZ=1 TO 6:SOUND 0,S,10
,10:POKE 710,C:FOR TL=1 TO 50:NEXT TL:S=1
50-S:C=75-C:NEXT ZZ
710 SOUND 0,0,0,0:POKE 710,0
720 POKE 53252,0:POKE 53253,0:POKE 53278,
0
730 POKE PMBASE+384+RKT2H+2,0:POKE PMBASE
+384+RKT1H+5,0:RETURN
```

Line 220 adds two numbers to the list of instructions. Since there are only 128 bytes to be moved, the computer must check the value of index Y against 128. If it moves 256 bytes, both ships will move on the screen when you want only the first ship to move. Add 192 and 128 after the second 200.

Line 270 changes the horizontal position of the ships. Again, this number is less because these characters are occupying less room.

Lines 330 and 400 are changed so the missiles will appear in the correct locations.

Address	Poke Value	Result	Address	Poke Value	Result
560	low order	Low order address of the display list		53260	0	normal size missile 0
561	high order	High order address of the display list			1	twice normal size - missile 0
704	color	Color register player 0			3	four times normal size - missile 0
705	color	Color register player 1		add	4	twice normal size - missile 1
706	color	Color register player 2			12	four times normal size - missile 1
707	color	Color register player 3			16	twice normal size - missile 2
708	color	Color register playfield 0			48	four times normal size - missile 2
709	color	Color register playfield 1		54272	64	twice normal size - missile 3
710	color	Color register playfield 2			192	four times normal size - missile 3
711	color	Color register playfield 3			32	ANTIC can now use player/missile graphics
712	color	Color register playfield 4		add	16	1 line resolution
756	high order	High order address of the character set being used.		or	0	2 line resolution
53248	position	Horizontal position player 0		53277	add 8	players enabled
53249	position	Horizontal position player 1			add 4	missiles enabled
53250	position	Horizontal position player 2		53278	add 1	narrow playfield
53251	position	Horizontal position player 3		54279	or 2	standard playfield
53252	position	Horizontal position missile 0			or 4	wide playfield
53253	position	Horizontal position missile 1			3	Player/missiles can now appear on screen
53254	position	Horizontal position missile 2			0	clear hits
53255	position	Horizontal position missile 3		high order		High order address of the player/missile graphics display area
53256	0	Player 0 normal size				
	1	Player 0 twice normal size				
	3	Player 0 four times normal size				
53257	0	Player 1 normal size				
	1	Player 1 twice normal size				
	3	Player 1 four times normal size				
53258	0	Player 2 normal size				
	1	Player 2 twice normal size				
	3	Player 2 four times normal size				
53259	0	Player 3 normal size				
	1	Player 3 twice normal size				
	3	Player 3 four times normal size				

Fig. 18-8. Addresses to POKE or READ values for display list and player/missile graphics.

Address	Read Value	Result	Address	Read Value	Result
53248	1	Missile 0 hit playfield 0	53260	2	Player 0 hit player 1
	2	Missile 0 hit playfield 1		4	Player 0 hit player 2
	4	Missile 0 hit playfield 2		8	Player 0 hit player 3
	8	Missile 0 hit playfield 3	53261	1	Player 1 hit player 0
53249	1	Missile 1 hit playfield 0		4	Player 1 hit player 2
	2	Missile 1 hit playfield 1		8	Player 1 hit player 3
	4	Missile 1 hit playfield 2	53262	1	Player 2 hit player 0
	8	Missile 1 hit playfield 3		2	Player 2 hit player 1
53250	1	Missile 2 hit playfield 0		8	Player 2 hit player 3
	2	Missile 2 hit playfield 1	53263	1	Player 3 hit player 0
	4	Missile 2 hit playfield 2		2	Player 3 hit player 1
	8	Missile 2 hit playfield 3		4	Player 3 hit player 2
53251	1	Missile 3 hit playfield 0			
	2	Missile 3 hit playfield 1			
	4	Missile 3 hit playfield 2			
	8	Missile 3 hit playfield 3			
53252	1	Player 0 hit playfield 0			
	2	Player 0 hit playfield 1			
	4	Player 0 hit playfield 2			
	8	Player 0 hit playfield 3			
53253	1	Player 1 hit playfield 0			
	2	Player 1 hit playfield 1			
	4	Player 1 hit playfield 2			
	8	Player 1 hit playfield 3			
53254	1	Player 2 hit playfield 0			
	2	Player 2 hit playfield 1			
	4	Player 2 hit playfield 2			
	8	Player 2 hit playfield 3			
53255	1	Player 3 hit playfield 0			
	2	Player 3 hit playfield 1			
	4	Player 3 hit playfield 2			
	8	Player 3 hit playfield 3			
53256	1	Missile 0 hit player 0			
	2	Missile 0 hit player 1			
	4	Missile 0 hit player 2			
	8	Missile 0 hit player 3			
53257	1	Missile 1 hit player 0			
	2	Missile 1 hit player 1			
	4	Missile 1 hit player 2			
	8	Missile 1 hit player 3			
53258	1	Missile 2 hit player 0			
	2	Missile 2 hit player 1			
	4	Missile 2 hit player 2			
	8	Missile 2 hit player 3			
53259	1	Missile 3 hit player 0			
	2	Missile 3 hit player 1			
	4	Missile 3 hit player 2			
	8	Missile 3 hit player 3			

Note: playfield refers to the graphics or characters on the screen displayed with a print or plot and draw to command.

Lines 430 and 440 change the upper and lower screen limits.

Lines 460 and 470 change the values POKEd into 206 and 205. Since the characters begin 512 bytes below the area set aside, a 2 is added to the beginning value. In the low-order address, a 0 is POKEd for the first player (512/256=2). The second player begins 128 bytes lower—640 bytes after the beginning address. 128 must be POKEd into the low-order address (205) because 640 divided by 256 equals 2.5. 128 is half of 256. Now the computer can figure out where the two players are.

Lines 540-570 reset the upper and lower limits if the player moves past them.

Lines 620, 670 and 730 erase the missile from the player/missile area.

There is another way to make the characters larger and smaller. Each player has a size register. This register is set to the normal size. You can make the player on the screen twice as wide or four times as wide as it would normally be under program control. Add this line to the program:

85 POKE 53246,3:POKE 53247,1

Run the program. The first ship appears very elongated, the second ship is also larger. Because each player has a size register, you can control the size of each player individually. One can get larger while the other gets smaller.

Figure 18-8 contains the locations that have been used in this chapter and the values that must be POKEd into them, or the information that can be read from them.

Chapter 19
Using
Disks

Sooner or later you'll find the cassette is too slow for you, or your programs need the random-access capabilities of the disk. The programs and directions listed in this chapter use DOS II, currently available from ATARI. Some of the applications may not work with DOS I.

DOS

DOS is the *Disk Operating System*. It is a program that makes disk operations available to the user with easy instructions and minimal configurations. To boot or load DOS from disk, you must first turn the disk on before you turn on your computer. The disk contains its own microcomputer chip and has a small routine that initializes the drive. If you have an interface, turn it on after the drive. Place your disk into the drive and turn on the computer. The busy light will go on and you will hear the drive making noises. You will also hear sounds coming from the speaker on the television set. The sounds are similar to the sounds of a cassette loading, only faster. This is the operating system being loaded into the computer. If you have DOS II, the videoscreen should say **READY**. You are in BASIC and the computer is ready for the next command. If you type DOS, the screen will go blank and you will hear another program being loaded. A menu will appear on the screen.

If you had a program in your computer, you just lost it. When you initialize your disks for the first time, there is a way to save your program automatically:

1. Place your master disk into the drive.
2. Turn on the computer.
3. Type **DOS**.
4. When the menu appears on the screen, remove the master disk.
5. Insert a new disk.
6. Press **I -** to format the new disk.
7. Press **H -** to write DOS to the new disk.
8. Now Press **N** and a file called MEM.SAV will be created on the disk.
9. Place the master disk into the drive and copy the AUTORUN.SYS program to the new disk.

(The AUTORUN.SYS program is available on DOS II and automatically initializes the interface.)

Now, because you have the MEM.SAV file on the disk, the program you are working on will be saved to disk every time you type DOS, and reloaded when you return to BASIC.

USING DISKS WITH BASIC

The commands to save and load programs to and from the disk are similar to cassette operations. To save a program, type: SAVE   "D:PROGRAM"
     D: must precede the program name. This tells the operating system the program should go to the disk. The same holds true for loading a program: LOAD "D:PRO-GRAM"   . A program can also be listed to the disk with   LIST "D:PRO-GRAM"   and re-entered with   ENTER "D:PROGRAM"

Some of the DOS operations can also be accomplished from BASIC. These include getting the directory, deleting files, renaming files, locking and unlocking files, and formatting disks. Listing 19-1 can be saved on disk with the save or list commands. If you use the save command you will have to run the program and it will erase any program you have in memory. If you list the program to disk, you can merge it with any program you have in memory with the enter command, use it, and then delete it if you want. Your original program will remain intact provided you do not reuse these lines. It is placed above the line numbers used in most programs.

Lines 30040-30070 print a menu on the screen and wait for the letter to be entered.

Line 30080 checks for a valid letter. If the letter entered is not correct, the menu will repeat itself.

Line 30090 subtracts 64 from the ASCII value of the letter entered. This value will be used later in the program.

Line 30100 checks for the value of 2. This would be BASIC and the program ends, returning you to BASIC.

Line 30120 opens the disk files for reading the directory. The open command is similar to the one used when we opened the keyboard to read the pressed keys. The number 2 buffer is opened. The 6 indicates a read directory. Since we want to be able to read the entire directory, use   "D:*.*"   . D with no number following it defaults to drive 1. If we wanted to read the directory on another drive, we would have to insert the drive number after D and before the colon. The asterisks are wild cards. They tell the computer not to match the program name with one on the disk, but to show us every program listed in the directory. We use the asterisk before and after the period because we are not interested in searching for a particular program name or extender.

Lines 30130-30140 use the input statement to get the directory from the disk. The program name and sectors are printed on the screen, and the first character in the string is checked for a number. If it is a number, the end of the directory has been reached. Two lines are used so the directory can be placed in two columns.

Line 30150 closes the buffer and directs the computer to a line number dependent on what was chosen from the menu.

Line 30160 waits for the return key to be pressed. It will return the program to the menu.

Listing 19-1. DOS from BASIC

```
30000 REM LISTINGXIX.1
30010 REM DOS FROM BASIC
30020 REM BY L.M.SCHREIBER FOR TAB BOOKS
30030 DIM FILE$(30),FUNC$(1),FIL1$(12)
30040 ? ">clear}    DOS FUNCTIONS":? :? "
A. DIRECTORY":? "B. BASIC"
30050 ? "D. DELETE FILE(S)":? "E. RENAME
FILE(S)":? "F. LOCK FILE(S)"
30060 ? "G. UNLOCK FILE(S)":? "I. FORMAT
DISK"
30070 ? :? "ENTER THE LETTER";:INPUT FUNC
$
30080 IF FUNC$<"A" OR FUNC$>"I" OR FUNC$=
"" OR FUNC$="H" OR FUNC$="C" THEN 30040
30090 KEY=ASC(FUNC$)-64
30100 IF KEY=2 THEN END
30110 ? ">clear}PROGRAM ON FILE ARE:":TR
AP 30900:REM SET TRAP FOR EMPTY DISK-ESC-
CNTRL-DOWNARROW AFTER CLEAR
30120 OPEN #2,6,0,"D:*.*":REM OPEN THE DI
SK TO READ THE DIRECTORY
30130 INPUT #2,FILE$:? FILE$;:IF ASC(FILE
$(1,1))>47 THEN 30150:REM CHECK FOR NUMBE
R
30140 INPUT #2,FILE$:? "   ";FILE$:IF ASC(
FILE$(1,1))<47 THEN 30130
30150 CLOSE #2:ON KEY GOTO 30160,30160,30
160,30170,30230,30340,30400,30160,30460
30160 ? :? "PRESS RETURN FOR MENU";:INPU
T FUNC$:GOTO 30040:REM RETURN TO THE MENU
-ESC-CNTRL-DOWNARROW AFTER ?
30170 ? :? "ENTER THE FILE TO BE DELETED
":INPUT FIL1$:REM GET THE FILE NAME-ESC-C
NTRL-DOWNARROW AFTER PRINT
30180 IF FIL1$="" THEN 30040:REM NOTHING
30190 ? :? "VERIFY - DELETE FILE -";FIL1$
;" Y/N";:INPUT FUNC$:REM DELETE IT?
30200 IF FUNC$="N" THEN 30040:REM DON'T D
O IT
30210 L=LEN(FIL1$):FILE$(3,L+2)=FIL1$(1,L
):FILE$(1,2)="D:":FILE$=FILE$(1,L+2):REM
```

219

Listing 19-1. DOS from BASIC. (Continued from page 219.)

```
ADD DEVICE NAME
30220 XIO 33,#2,0,0,FILE$:GOTO 30040:REM
DELETE THE FILE
30230 ? :? "ENTER THE FILE TO BE RENAMED
":INPUT FIL1$:REM GET THE OLD NAME
30240 IF FIL1$="" THEN 30040:REM NO NAME
ENTERED
30250 ? "VERIFY - RENAME FILE -";FIL1$;"
 Y/N";:INPUT FUNC$:REM VERIFY THE NAME-ES
C-CNTRL-DOWNARROW AFTER PRINT
30260 IF FUNC$="N" THEN 30040:REM WRONG N
AME
30270 L=LEN(FIL1$):FILE$(3,L+2)=FIL1$(1,L
):FILE$(1,2)="D:":L=L+2:REM ADD DEVICE
30280 ? :? "ENTER THE NEW FILE NAME":INP
UT FIL1$:REM GET THE NEW NAME-ESC-CNTRL-D
OWNARROW AFTER PRINT
30290 IF FIL1$="" THEN 30040:REM NO NAME
30300 ? "VERIFY - RENAME FILE -";FIL1$;"
 Y/N";:INPUT FUNC$:REM CHECK THE NEW NAME
-ESC-CNTRL-DOWNARROW AFTER PRINT
30310 IF FUNC$="N" THEN 30280:REEM WRONG i
AME
30320 FILE$(L+1)=" ":FILE$(L+2)=FIL1$:REM
 ADD NEW NAME TO OLD NAME
30330 XIO 32,#2,0,0,FILE$:GOTO 30040:REM
CHANGE THE NAME
30340 ? "ENTER THE NAME OF THE FILE TO L
OCK":INPUT FIL1$:REM GET THE FILE NAME-ES
C-CNTRL-DOWNARROW AFTER PRINT
30350 IF FIL1$="" THEN 30040
30360 ? "VERIFY - RENAME FILE -";FIL1$;"
 Y/N";:INPUT FUNC$:REM ESC-CNTRL-DOWNARRO
W AFTER PRINT
30370 IF FUNC$="N" THEN 30040
30380 L=LEN(FIL1$):FILE$(3,L+2)=FIL1$(1,L
):FILE$(1,2)="D:":REM ADD DEVICE TO NAME
30390 XIO 35,#2,0,0,FILE$:GOTO 30040:REM
LOCK THE FILE
30400 ? "ENTER THE NAME OF THE FILE TO U
NLOCK":INPUT FIL1$:REM ESC-CNTRL-DOWNARRO
```

```
W AFTER PRINT
30410 IF FIL1$="" THEN 30040
30420 ? "VERIFY - RENAME FILE -";FIL1$;"
 Y/N";:INPUT FUNC$:REM ESC-CNTRL-DOWNARRO
W AFTER PRINT
30430 IF FUNC$="N" THEN 30040
30440 L=LEN(FIL1$):FILE$(3,L+2)=FIL1$(1,L
):FILE$(1,2)="D:"
30450 XIO 36,#2,0,0,FILE$:GOTO 30040:REM
UNLOCK THE FILE
30460 ? "PLACE A NEW DISK INTO THE DRIVE
 AND   PRESS RETURN ":INPUT FUNC$:REM ESC
-CNTRL-DOWNARROW AFTER PRINT
30470 TRAP 30510:OPEN #2,6,0,"D:*.*":REM
CHECK FOR PROGRAMS ON DISK
30480 CLOSE #2:? "THERE IS SOMETHING ON T
HIS DISK       FORMAT ANYWAY (Y/N)"
30485 INPUT FUNC$
30490 IF FUNC$="N" THEN 30040:REM DON'T F
ORMAT IT
30500 IF FUNC$<>"Y" THEN 30480
30510 XIO 254,#1,0,0,"D1:":GOTO 30040:REM
 FORMAT THE DISK
30900 ? "NO PROGRAMS ON FILE":GOTO 30040
```

Line 30170 asks for the name of the file to be deleted.

Line 30180 returns you to the menu if only a return key was pressed.

Lines 30190-30200 ask you to verify the name of the file you want deleted. This gives you a chance to correct an error in case you mistyped the name of the program.

Line 30210 places the name of the file to be deleted into FILE$. The first two characters of FILE$ must be   D: . This tells the computer the file is located on the first drive.

Line 30220 deletes the file specified in FILE$. Through the XIO command. The 33 tells the computer to delete a program. Number 2 is the buffer number. Once the file has been deleted, the program will return to the menu.

Lines 30230-30250 begin the routine to rename a file. The file name is stored in FIL1$. You will be asked again to verify that this is the name of the file to be renamed.

Line 30270 places the file name in FILE$. The string must begin with   D: . Two is added to the length of FILE$ to indicate the last location of a letter in the string.

Lines 30280-30310 ask you for the name of this file. You are asked to verify this name also.

Line 30320 places the new name into FILE$. One space is placed between the old name and the new name.

Line 30330 replaces the old program name with the new one.

One note of caution here: whether you use the rename command from BASIC or DOS, do not rename a file with a name already on the disk. The DOS does not check the directory to see if that name is already in existence. The old file will be changed to the new name. When you try to load the program, the computer will load the first program it finds with that name. When you try to delete it, both programs will be deleted.

Lines 30340-30390 lock the files on the disk. You are asked for the name of the file to be locked and to verify the file name. The file name is stored in FILE$. Using a 35 after XIO will lock the file named in FILE$. These files will be displayed with an asterisk in front of their name.

Lines 30400-30450 unlock the files on the disk. Again enter and verify the name of the file you want unlocked. A 36 after the XIO will unlock the file name stored in FILE$.

Lines 30460-30510 format a new disk. Line 30470 opens the directory. If there is a directory, the program asks you if you want to format the disk anyway. This is a safeguard so you won't destroy information on a disk you thought was blank. The 254 after the XIO tells the computer to format the disk. D1 indicates the first drive. This number can be changed for any drive.

Line 30900 is the trap line for trying to read a directory on a disk that has not been formatted and therefore has no directory.

OPEN

The open command opens a buffer to the disk. It can be opened for input, output, input/ output, or for the disk directory. In the last program we opened a buffer for the disk directory. The format for an open statement is:

OPEN buffer number, operation, auxiliary code, file e.g.,   OPEN #2,4,0,"D:name"

This statement would open buffer number 2 to input from the file specified by name. The zero is a dummy variable. It is used with certain devices (like a printer) for specific applications. The operation number tells the computer how to open the file. The operation numbers are as follows:

> 4   input operation
> 6   disk directory
> 8   output operation
> 9   end-of-file
> 12 input/output operation

Opening a file opens an area where information can be passed to and/or from the disk. It will not, however, pass the information.

PRINT

The print command works the same with disk as it does in graphics mode. The print command must be followed by the buffer number to send the information to the disk. The information can be a string, variable, or within quotation marks. The format for print is:

PRINT #2;A$ or
PRINT #2;A   or

PRINT #2;"HELLO"

The #2 is the buffer number that has been opened for disk operations.

INPUT

The input command gets information from the disk and places it in a variable or string variable. If a buffer number is not specified, the computer assumes the information will be entered from the keyboard. By stating the buffer number after the input, the computer will look to the disk for the information, e.g., INPUT #2,A$. The computer will take the next piece of information available from the disk. With a For ... Next loop an entire file can be brought into the computer.

PUT

The put command places one byte of information onto the disk at a time. If you are storing numbers or variables on the disk, it will place each number on the disk one at a time. To put a string on the disk, you must convert each letter or character to its ASCII value first: PUT #2;A or PUT #2;ASC(A$(1,1))

GET

The information put on the disk can be retrieved with the get command. Again, only numbers will be brought into the computer from the disk, so a variable is used with the get command. To convert a number to a string, you must use CHR$.

Listing 19-2 sets up an address list that stores information on the disk.

Line 40 dimensions two strings. NAME$ will be the string that stores all the information and places it on the disk, or has the information placed on the disk. NA$ is used to get the entries that make up NAME$. NAME$ will contain six fields, each of a specific length or containing a certain number of bytes. The length of NAME$ will not exceed 91 bytes.

Lines 50-80 contain the menu. On this menu there are only two routines to choose from: enter names, or print names. If a number other than 1 or 2 is entered, the computer will be directed to line 50. If a letter or character is entered, the trap set in line 60 will send the computer to line 50.

Line 90 begins the routine to enter names. The string for the names is cleared.

Line 100 sets up the screen. All the information to be requested is set on the screen at the same time.

Lines 110-160 set the cursor to the correct position of the entry. The variable B is the position in the string where the entered information will be stored. C is the column for that entry. R is the row and L is the maximum length for the entry. Once the variables have been set, the computer can go to the line requesting the information.

Line 170 sets W to 0. This variable is used as a flag. If it is 0, no corrections have been made. When it is −1 the program is in the correction mode. The program asks if the information entered is correct. Any program that gets information from the keyboard should give the user an option to correct any entry. If the information was not entered correctly, you would want a way to correct it

Listing 19-2. Mailing List

```
10 REM LISTINGXIX.2
20 REM MAILING LIST
30 REM BY L.M.SCHREIBER FOR TAB BOOKS
40 DIM NAME$(92),NA$(30)
50 ? "}clear}1. ENTER NAMES":? "2. P
RINT NAMES":REM 3 ESC-CNTRL-DOWNARROWS AF
TER CLEAR-ESC-TAB BEFORE NUMBERS
60 TRAP 50:? "PLEASE ENTER A NUMBER";:I
NPUT N:REM ESC-CNTRL-DOWNARROW/ESC-TAB AF
TER PRINT
70 IF N<0 OR N>2 THEN 50
80 ON N GOTO 90,400
90 NAME$(1)=" ":NAME$(92)=" ":NAME$(2)=NA
ME$
100 ? "}clear}1.NAME:":? "2.ADDRESS:":?
 "3.CITY:":? "4.STATE:":? "5.ZIP:":? "6.P
HONE:":REM 2 ESC-CNTRL-DARROW
110 B=1:C=10:R=2:L=25:GOSUB 250:REM SET T
HE BEGINNING OF FIELD,LENGTH,ROW AND COLU
MN
120 B=26:C=13:R=3:GOSUB 250
130 B=51:L=15:C=10:R=4:GOSUB 250
140 B=66:L=2:C=11:R=5:GOSUB 250
150 B=68:L=9:C=9:R=6:GOSUB 250
160 B=77:L=15:C=12:R=7:GOSUB 250
170 W=0:POSITION 5,10:? "ARE ALL ENTRIES
CORRECT (Y/N)   ";:INPUT NA$:IF NA$(1,
1)="Y" THEN 200
180 IF NA$(1,1)<>"N" THEN 170
190 TRAP 190:POSITION 2,12
195 ? "ENTER THE NUMBER OF THE INCORRECT
    ENTRY";:INPUT N:W=-1:GOTO 100+10*N
200 NAME$(92)=" ":OPEN #1,9,0,"D:DIRECT":
PRINT #1;NAME$:CLOSE #1:REM PUT NAME AT E
ND OF FILE
210 POSITION 2,20:? "ANOTHER NAME (Y/N)"
;:INPUT NA$:REM CHECK FOR MORE ENTRIES-ES
C-SHIFT-DELETE AFTER PRINT
220 IF NA$="Y" THEN 90
230 IF NA$<>"N" THEN 210
240 GOTO 50
```

```
250 POSITION C,R:? "
       ":REM CLEAR THE LINE
260 POSITION C,R:INPUT NA$:REM GET THE EN
TRY
265 IF LEN(NA$)>L THEN POSITION 2,20:? "P
LEASE LIMIT LENGTH TO *";L;"* LETTERS":GO
TO 250
270 NAME$(B)=NA$:POSITION 2,20:? "":REM
ESC-SHIFT-DELETE
280 IF W=-1 THEN POP :GOTO 170
290 RETURN
400 TRAP 590:OPEN #1,4,0,"D:DIRECT":REM O
PEN THE FILE TO READ NAMES
410 INPUT #1,NAME$
420 ? "}clear}1.NAME:":? "2.ADDRESS:":?
 "3.CITY:":? "4.STATE:":? "5.ZIP:":? "6.P
HONE:":REM 2 ESC-CNTRL-DARROW
430 B=1:C=10:R=2:L=25:GOSUB 550
440 B=26:C=13:R=3:GOSUB 550
450 B=51:L=15:C=10:R=4:GOSUB 550
460 B=66:L=2:C=11:R=5:GOSUB 550
470 B=68:L=9:C=9:R=6:GOSUB 550
480 B=77:L=LEN(NAME$)-B+1:C=12:R=7:GOSUB
550
490 POSITION 2,12:? "PRESS RETURN FOR NEX
T NAME":INPUT NA$
500 GOTO 410
550 POSITION C,R:? NAME$(B,B+L-1):RETURN

590 ER=PEEK(195):CLOSE #1:IF ER=136 THEN
50
595 ? "ERROR -";ER:REM PRINT THE ERROR NU
MBER
```

without having to run the program again. If a Y is entered, the program directs the computer to line 200.

Line 180 checks for an N. If it was not entered, the program asks the question again. If it is an N, the program continues.

Line 190 sets a trap. The program asks for the number of the incorrect entry. If a letter or character is entered, the line will repeat. If a number is entered, the variable W is set to a − 1 and the program will direct the computer to the line asking for that entry. The correct line number is calculated by multiplying the number entered by 10 and adding it to 100.

Line 200 opens buffer 1 with a 9. This will place the information in NAME$ at the end of the direct file. If we opened with an 8, the information in that file would be written over. The contents of NAME$ is printed to the disk. Be sure to separate   **1**   from **NAME$** with a semicolon. Using a comma would have the same effect as using a comma with a print statement on the screen: a series of blank spaces would be printed before the contents of NAME$. Once the information has been printed, the buffer is closed.

Lines 210-240 ask if you want to enter another name. NA$ is checked for a Y, sending the program to line 90. If an N is not entered, line 210 will be repeated. Only if an N is entered will the program return to the menu.

Lines 250-290 contain the subroutine that places information into NAME$. First, the line the information will be placed on is cleared. Then the information is entered into NA$. If the entry is longer than the field allows (The maximum number of characters is stored in L), a message will appear near the bottom of the screen and the program will direct the computer back to line 250. If the entry does not exceed the field length the entry will be stored in NAME$ beginning with the first position of that field (value in B). The message line is then cleared. Line 280 checks the flag (variable W) to see if this is a correction routine. If it is, the stack will be POPped, and the program will go to line 170 to check if all the entries are correct. If this was not a correction, the program returns to the line that called it and procedes to get the rest of the information.

Line 400 begins the routine to print the names stored on the disk to the screen. A trap is set for line 590. The file is opened with a 4. It can then be read. If there is no file by this name the trap sends the program to line 590.

Line 410 inputs the name from the disk. This is the first file stored on the disk and the first file read back into the computer.

Lines 420-480 display the information contained in NAME$. Once again, the titles of the entries are printed on the screen. The same variables are used for the beginning of the information in the string, the column and row they will be printed in and the length of the field. In line 480, the length of the last field can change with each entry, so it is calculated by subtracting the position of the first character of that entry from the last position of the entry and adding 1.

Line 490 waits until the return key is pressed before going back to line 410 for another entry from the disk.

Line 550 is a one-line subroutine that prints the contents of NAME$ from the first character of that field to the last one.

Line 590-595 is the error-trapping routine. If an error occurs during the disk operation, the computer will be sent to this line. The ER variable stores the number of the error, and the buffer is closed. If the error is 136, the end-of-file has been reached and there are no more names to be read. The program will continue to line 50 and repeat the menu. If any other disk error occurs, the program will print the error number and end.

To use this program, the direct file must be placed on the disk. To do this, in the direct mode type:

```
OPEN #1,8,0,"D:DIRECT"
CLOSE #1
```

NOTE

Each name entered in Listing 19-2 was placed on the disk in the next available area. When the information was read back into the computer, the program started with the first name and continued until the last name was read. You do not know where this information is on the disk.

There is a way to find out with the note command. This command tells you where the next information will come from. The format is: NOTE #1,A,B.   #1 is the buffer that has been opened for disk read/write. The variables can be any variables. The first is the sector the information is stored in. The second is the byte to be read from or written to next.

POINT

The point command uses the information obtained in the note command to tell the disk where to write the information. By getting the sector and byte numbers with the note command you can read the information, change it, then write it back to the same place using point.

Another subroutine is added to the address program in Listing 19-3 so the information in the entries could be changed. Change lines 50-80 to include the new subroutine. Also add a way to end the program. Whenever possible, the programmer should provide a way for the user to end the program.

Line 700 asks the user to enter the name of the lisitng that should be changed. The entry must be typed in the way it was originally entered. If the name was misspelled when it was entered, you must enter the name with the misspelling.

Line 710 opens the file on the disk to read and/or write. By using 12, you can input from the disk or print to the disk. The trap is set to line 590 so the program will return to the menu when the end-of-file is reached.

Line 720 gets the sector and byte of the file before it is read into the computer. These numbers point to the file that will be read. If we got them after NAME$ was read, they would be pointing to the next file. After storing the sector and byte numbers in variables S and Y, input the file into NAME$.

Line 730 compares the name we are searching for with the name in the file just read. This is why the name entered must be exactly like the name in the file. If the names do not match, the program will return to line 720 and get the next file.

Lines 740-800 display the information when it finds a matching name. The variables are the same as those that have been used throughout this program for the fields.

Line 810 asks for the number of the incorrect entry. The trap is set so that if a letter or character is entered by mistake, the program will repeat the line.

Line 820 gets the number of the correction, checks to make sure the number is good and either goes to the line for the correction or back to get a valid number.

Lines 830-880 correct the entry that was incorrect.

Line 890 asks if the entries are now correct.

Line 900 gets the input. If the entries are correct, the computer is directed to line 930.

Line 910 sends the computer back to line 890 if an N was not entered.

Line 920 goes to line 810 to get the number of the incorrect entry.

Line 930 uses the values in S and Y to reset the disk head to the sector and byte this file was

Listing 19-3. Mailing List, Version 2

```
10 REM LISTINGXIX.3
20 REM MAILING LIST WITH CORRECT OPTION
30 REM BY L.M.SCHREIBER FOR TAB BOOKS
40 DIM NAME$(92),NA$(30)
50 ? ")clear}1. ENTER NAMES":? "2.
 PRINT NAMES":? "3. CORRECT NAMES":? "4
. END"
55 REM 5 ESC-CNTRL-DOWNARROWS AFTER CLEAR
/ESC-TAB BEFORE EACH NUMBER
60 TRAP 50:? "PLEASE ENTER A NUMBER";:I
NPUT N
70 IF N<0 OR N>4 THEN 50
80 ON N GOTO 90,400,700,1100
90 NAME$(1)=" ":NAME$(92)=" ":NAME$(2)=NA
ME$
100 ? ")clear}1.NAME:":? "2.ADDRESS:":?
 "3.CITY:":? "4.STATE:":? "5.ZIP:":? "6.P
HONE:":REM 2 ESC-CNRTL-DARROWS
110 B=1:C=10:R=2:L=25:GOSUB 250
120 B=26:C=13:R=3:GOSUB 250
130 B=51:L=15:C=10:R=4:GOSUB 250
140 B=66:L=2:C=11:R=5:GOSUB 250
150 B=68:L=9:C=9:R=6:GOSUB 250
160 B=77:L=15:C=12:R=7:GOSUB 250
170 W=0:POSITION 5,10:? "ARE ALL ENTRIES
CORRECT (Y/N)   ";:INPUT NA$:IF NA$(1,
1)="Y" THEN 200
180 IF NA$(1,1)<>"N" THEN 170
190 TRAP 190:POSITION 2,12:? "ENTER THE N
UMBER OF THE INCORRECT      ENTRY";:INPUT
N:W=-1
195 IF N>0 AND N<7 THEN GOTO 100+10*N
198 GOTO 90
200 NAME$(92)=" ":OPEN #1,9,0,"D:DIRECT":
PRINT #1;NAME$:CLOSE #1
210 POSITION 2,20:? "ANOTHER NAME (Y/N)"
;:INPUT NA$
220 IF NA$="Y" THEN 90
230 IF NA$<>"N" THEN 210
240 GOTO 50
250 POSITION C,R:? "
```

```
260 POSITION C,R:INPUT NA$
265 IF LEN(NA$)>L THEN POSITION 2,20:? "P
LEASE LIMIT LENGTH TO *";L;"* LETTERS":GO
TO 250
270 NAME$(B)=NA$:POSITION 2,20:? ""
280 IF W=-1 THEN POP :GOTO 170
290 RETURN
400 TRAP 590:OPEN #1,4,0,"D:DIRECT":REM O
PEN THE FILE TO READ NAMES
410 INPUT #1,NAME$
420 ? "}clear}1.NAME:":? "2.ADDRESS:":?
 "3.CITY:":? "4.STATE:":? "5.ZIP:":? "6.P
HONE:":REM 2 ESC-CNTRL-DARRWS
430 B=1:C=10:R=2:L=25:GOSUB 550
440 B=26:C=13:R=3:GOSUB 550
450 B=51:L=15:C=10:R=4:GOSUB 550
460 B=66:L=2:C=11:R=5:GOSUB 550
470 B=68:L=9:C=9:R=6:GOSUB 550
480 B=77:L=LEN(NAME$)-B+1:C=12:R=7:GOSUB
550
490 POSITION 2,12:? "PRESS RETURN FOR NEX
T NAME";:INPUT NA$
500 GOTO 410
550 POSITION C,R:? NAME$(B,B+L-1):RETURN
590 ER=PEEK(195):CLOSE #1:IF ER=136 THEN
50
595 ? "ERROR -";ER:END
700 ? "}clear}ENTER THE NAME THAT YOU W
ANT TO        CHANGE";:INPUT NA$:REM 2 ESC
-CNTRL-DOWNARROWS
710 TRAP 590:OPEN #1,12,0,"D:DIRECT":REM
OPEN FOR READ OR WRITE
720 NOTE #1,S,Y:INPUT #1,NAME$:REM SAVE T
HE SECTOR AND BYTE LOCATION
730 IF NA$<>NAME$(1,LEN(NA$)) THEN 720
740 ? "}clear}1.NAME:":? "2.ADDRESS:":?
 "3.CITY:":? "4.STATE:":? "5.ZIP:":? "6.P
HONE:":REM 2 ESC-CNTRL-DARRWS
750 B=1:C=10:R=2:L=25:GOSUB 550
760 B=26:C=13:R=3:GOSUB 550
```

Listing 19-3. Mailing List, Version 2. (Continued from page 229.)

```
770 B=51:L=15:C=10:R=4:GOSUB 550
780 B=66:L=2:C=11:R=5:GOSUB 550
790 B=68:L=9:C=9:R=6:GOSUB 550
800 B=77:L=LEN(NAME$)-B+1:C=12:R=7:GOSUB
550
810 TRAP 810:POSITION 2,12:? "ENTER THE N
UMBER OF THE INCORRECT       ENTRY ";
820 INPUT N:IF N>0 AND N<7 THEN GOTO 820+
10*N
825 GOTO 810
830 B=1:C=10:R=2:L=25:GOSUB 1050
840 B=26:C=13:R=3:GOSUB 1050
850 B=51:L=15:C=10:R=4:GOSUB 1050
860 B=66:L=2:C=11:R=5:GOSUB 1050
870 B=68:L=9:C=9:R=6:GOSUB 1050
880 B=77:L=15:C=12:R=7:GOSUB 1050
890 W=0:POSITION 2,15:? "ARE ALL ENTRIES
CORRECT (Y/N)    ";
900 INPUT NA$:IF NA$(1,1)="Y" THEN 930
910 IF NA$(1,1)<>"N" THEN 890
920 GOTO 810
930 POINT #1,S,Y:PRINT #1;NAME$:CLOSE #1:
GOTO 50:REM PUT IT BACK IN THE SAME PLACE

1050 POSITION C,R:? "
      ":FOR X=B TO B+L-1:NAME$(X,X)=" ":N
EXT X
1060 POSITION C,R:INPUT NA$
1065 IF LEN(NA$)>L THEN POSITION 2,20:? "
PLEASE LIMIT LENGTH TO *";L;"* LETTERS":G
OTO 1050
1070 NAME$(B)=NA$:POSITION 2,20:? "":NAM
E$(92)=" ":REM ESC-SHIFT-DELETE AFTER PRI
NT
1080 GOTO 890
1100 END
```

stored in. Now it can print the information onto the disk in the same space it was in originally. The file is closed and the program returns to the menu.

Lines 1050-1080 clear the incorrectly entered information and get the correct information. This new information is stored in NA$ and then transferred to the correct field in NAME$. B indicates the first location of the field in NAME$. The program then returns to line 890.

Line 1100 is the end of the program. When option 4 is entered from the menu, the program directs the computer to this line.

This program uses files set in strings. With the put and get commands the computer can set up files on the disk that can be used in other programs. For example, the disk can be used as an extension of memory for data and leave more memory free in the computer for the actual program. In the last chapter we used a machine-language subroutine in a few programs. This information for the subroutine was kept in a data line. It could just as easily be stored on disk, and the numbers read from the disk and POKEd into the memory locations when needed. Listing 19-4 stores the machine language subroutine on the disk under the file name MOVE. This program can be changed to store any data under any file name.

Line 40 opens the disk to write information to it. The information will be stored under the file name MOVE.

Lines 50-70 read the numbers from the data line. These numbers form the machine language subroutine that moves the character set from ROM to RAM. Each number is read from the data line and stored on the disk with the put command.

Line 80 closes the file and ends the program.

When you want to move the character set you do not have to include this data in your program. Listing 19-5 reads the subroutine from the disk and POKEs it into the correct memory locations. This routine can be added to any program.

Line 40 opens the disk to read the information from it. It opens the same file we just stored information in.

Lines 50-80 retrieve information from the disk with the get statement. Each byte or number will be stored in S. This value will be POKEd into the area of memory set aside for the machine language subroutine. Once the routine has been moved into memory the file is closed.

Line 90 finds the amount of RAM available and subtracts 8 to allow room for the screen display and the display list. This number is the beginning address of the area of RAM where the

Listing 19-4. PUT Demonstration

```
10 REM LISTING XIX.4
20 REM MOVE ON DISK
30 REM BY L.M.SCHREIBER FOR TAB BOOKS
40 OPEN #1,8,0,"D:MOVE":REM OPEN TO WRITE
50 FOR D=1 TO 20
60 READ S:PUT #1,S:REM GET THE INSTRUCTIO
N/PUT IT ON DISK
70 NEXT D
80 CLOSE #1
90 END
200 DATA 104,162,4,160,0,177,205,145,203,
200,208,249,230,206,230,204,202,208,242,9
6
```

Listing 19-5. READ Subroutine Demonstration.

```
10 REM LISTING XIX.5
20 REM READ SUBROUTINE FROM DISK
30 REM BY L.M.SCHREIBER FOR TAB BOOKS
40 OPEN #1,4,0,"D:MOVE":REM OPEN TO READ
FROM DISK
50 FOR D=1 TO 20
60 GET #1,S:POKE 1535+D,S:REM GET THE INS
TRUCTION/POKE IT INTO MEMORY
70 NEXT D
80 CLOSE #1
90 A=PEEK(106)-8:POKE 204,A:POKE 206,224:
REM SET UP THE NEW CHARACTER SET LOCATION
100 Q=USR(1536):REM RUN THE MACHINE LANGU
AGE SUBROUTINE
110 POKE 756,A
120 ? "{clear}  THIS MESSAGE IS MADE P
OSSIBLE WITH    THE NEW CHARACTER BASE.":
REM 3 ESC-CNTRL-DOWNARROWS
130 END
```

new character set will be moved. It is POKEd into location 204. Location 206 is POKEd with the beginning address of the ROM character base.

Line 100 calls the machine language subroutine.

Line 110 POKEs the new address of the character set into location 756.

Line 120 prints a message using the new character set.

Once you have moved the character set into RAM, you can change the character set by POKEing values into the characters' area.

Put and get can also be used to store the values of a numerical array, or the values used to draw characters on the screen. Any numbers that would normally be stored in data lines can be stored on the disk.

RUN "D:PROGRAM"

Several programs can be placed on one disk with a menu program. The menu lists the names of the programs on the disk. When the user enters the number of the program to be run, the computer can run that program with   RUN"D:name"   . The name of the program must follow the colon and be entered exactly the way it is stored on the disk.

Use RUN "D:name" format when one program is too large for the amount of memory available. The program can be broken into several smaller programs. Each mini-program can run the next program without having the user type in the command and the name of the program. Any variables needed for the next part of the program can be saved to the disk before the new part of the program is run. These variables can be re-entered from the disk by the new program.

In all, the disk expands the capabilities of the computer.

Chapter 20
Putting It All Together

Now that you can use multigraphic modes, move character sets and save data onto disk, you are ready to develop programs that use all these features. The entire character set uses 1K (1024 bytes) of memory. There are 128 different characters in the character set. Each character uses eight bytes of memory. When you move the character set into RAM, you can change any character by POKEing values into its area.

Figure 20-1 shows you how a character is constructed. The first character of the set is a space. Therefore, the first eight bytes of the character set are zeroes. If you were to POKE a value in the location set aside for the space, your entire screen would display dots in that location.

By knowing how to construct characters, you can replace an existing character with one that is more suitable for your program. This character set can be stored on disk and read into memory by another program. Listing 20-1 changes some of the characters in the character set and stores it on the disk under the name CHARS. It can be read back into memory and used by another program.

Line 40 opens the disk to read the MOVE file. This is the same subroutine used in Chapter 19 and stored on the disk.

Lines 50-70 POKE the machine language subroutine into the area of memory set aside for this purpose.

Line 90 places the new character set 2K above the end of available RAM and POKEs this value into location 204. It also POKEs the starting address of the ROM character set into location 206.

Line 100 tells the computer to use the machine language subroutine at location 1536.

Line 120 calculates the location of the exclamation point in the RAM character set. A contains the high-order address of the RAM character set. By multiplying this value by 256, we arrive at the decimal equivalent of the beginning of the character set. The first byte is a space. Add eight to the beginning address to find the first byte of the exclamation point. We will change this character and six other characters.

Line 130 POKEs 255 into the eight locations that made up the exclamation point. This will make a bar or cursor on the screen.

Line 140 POKEs 63 into the eight locations that made up the pound sign. This number will set the last six bits of every byte, making this bar three-fourths as long as the previous one. We

233

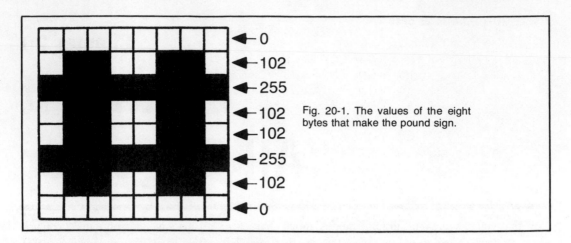

Fig. 20-1. The values of the eight bytes that make the pound sign.

did not replace the quotation marks because BASIC uses them for its string functions and you cannot have a quotation mark within a quotation mark.

Lines 150-190 continue to replace the dollar sign, percent sign, and sign, apostrophe, and open parenthesis with parts of a bar. These characters will be used in the next program.

Line 210 opens the disk for writing and calculates the beginning of the character set in RAM.

Line 270 writes the new character set to the disk. The entire set is stored on the disk even though we only changed eight characters. The next time we want to use this character set, we can read it in from the disk without having to move the set from ROM.

Now we have changed and stored our character set, we can write a program that uses it. This program can read in the character set and store it anywhere in RAM. This makes it easy to write a program on a machine with 32K or 40K RAM, but makes it inaccessible to persons with only 16K RAM.

Listing 20-2 is the Towers Puzzle. In it there are nine disks that must be moved from the first pole to the third. A smaller disk can always be placed on a larger one, but a larger one can never be placed on a smaller disk. This program uses player/missile graphics and a multi-mode display. Before we can write the program, the memory that will be used for the character set and the player/missile graphics must be considered. Figure 20-2 shows a memory map of how the character set and the player/missile graphics will be stored in BASIC.

We allow 1K (1024 bytes) for the display list and the screen display area. This is more memory than needed, but since the player/missile graphics must begin on an even 1K boundary, we will allow this much. The 1K of memory just above the screen and display list will be used for the player/missile graphics and the character set. We will be using two-line resolution for the player/missiles. Since we will not be using the missiles in this program, the first 512 bytes of this area will not be used. We will also be using mode 1. A character set in mode 1 uses half the standard character set, or 512 bytes of memory. We can, therefore, read the character set into this area of memory, conserving on the amount of memory needed in a program.

Listing 20-2 uses the joystick to lift the disk from the pole. Place the magnet above the disk you wanted lifted and press the red button on the joystick. Bring the magnet and disk over the pole

234

Listing 20-1. Character Base

```
10 REM LISTING XX.1
20 REM CHARACTER BASE
30 REM BY L.M.SCHREIBER FOR TAB BOOKS
40 OPEN #1,4,0,"D:MOVE":REM OPEN TO READ
FROM DISK
50 FOR D=1 TO 20
60 GET #1,S:POKE 1535+D,S:REM GET THE INS
TRUCTION/POKE IT INTO MEMORY
70 NEXT D:CLOSE #1
80 ? "}clear}"
90 A=PEEK(106)-8:POKE 204,A:POKE 206,224:
REM SET UP THE NEW CHARACTER SET LOCATION

100 Q=USR(1536):REM RUN THE MACHINE LANGU
AGE SUBROUTINE
110 REM CHANGE 8 CHARACTERS IN THE SET
120 B=A*256+8:REM LOCATION OF !
130 FOR X=0 TO 7:POKE B+X,255:NEXT X:REM
MAKE INTO A BAR
140 FOR X=16 TO 23:POKE B+X,63:NEXT X:REM
 3/4 BAR
150 FOR X=24 TO 31:POKE B+X,15:NEXT X:REM
 1/2 BAR
160 FOR X=32 TO 39:POKE B+X,3:NEXT X:REM
1/4 BAR
170 FOR X=40 TO 47:POKE B+X,192:NEXT X:RE
M LEFT 1/4 BAR
180 FOR X=48 TO 55:POKE B+X,240:NEXT X:RE
M LEFT 1/2 BAR
190 FOR X=56 TO 63:POKE B+X,252:NEXT X:RE
M LEFT 3/4 BAR
200 REM MAKE PSUEDO CHARACTER
210 POKE B+64,60:POKE B+65,192:POKE B+66,
153:POKE B+67,27:POKE B+68,28:POKE B+69,5
6:POKE B+70,204:POKE B+71,14
260 OPEN #1,8,0,"D:CHARS":B=A*256:REM SAV
E THE NEW CHARACTER SET
270 FOR X=0 TO 1024:PUT #1,PEEK(B+X):NEXT
 X
280 CLOSE #1
```

Listing 20-2. Towers Puzzle

```
10 REM LISTING XX.2
20 REM TOWERS
30 REM BY L.M.SCHREIBER FOR TAB BOOKS
40 DIM A$(45),P$(5),BL$(5),P(9,3)
50 GRAPHICS 17:A=PEEK(106)-8:REM SET UP T
HE NEW CHARACTER SET LOCATION
60 OPEN #1,4,0,"D:CHARS":B=A*256:REM GET
THE NEW CHARACTER
70 FOR X=0 TO 1024:GET #1,C:REM READ A CH
ARACTER BYTE
80 POKE B+X,C:REM STORE IT IN CHARACTER S
ET
90 NEXT X:CLOSE #1:POKE 756,A
100 A$=" !  %!&  )DAG}  #!(  !!! )EAAAF
)$!!!'#!!!()AAAAA)":P$="        ":BL$=P$:M=0

110 DL=PEEK(560)+PEEK(561)*256:REM GET TH
E DISPLAY LIST
120 POKE DL+6,7:REM CHANGE TO MODE 2
130 POKE 711,86:POKE 709,244:POSITION 4,1
:? #6;") towers )"
140 POKE 559,46:REM 2-LINE RESOLUTION
150 FOR X=B+512 TO B+1024:POKE X,0:NEXT X
:REM CLEAR PLAYER GRAPHICS AREA
160 POKE 53277,3:POKE 623,4:REM ENABLE PL
AYER/MISSILE GRAPHICS & SET PRIORITY
170 POKE 54279,A:REM TELL ANTIC WHERE P/M
 STARTS
180 FOR S=512 TO 768 STEP 128:FOR X=60 TO
 112:POKE B+S+X,30:NEXT X:NEXT S:REM DRAW
 STICKS
190 FOR S=571 TO 827 STEP 128:POKE B+S,12
:NEXT S
192 FOR X=B+935 TO B+940:READ S:POKE X,S:
NEXT X
195 DATA 28,54,99,99,99,99
200 FOR X=1 TO 19:POSITION X,23:? #6;"";
:NEXT X:REM DRAW BASE IN ORANGE
210 POKE 704,202:POKE 705,44:POKE 706,108
:POKE 707,9:REM COLOR THE POSTS
220 POKE 53248,71:POKE 53249,127:POKE 532
```

```
50,183:POKE 53251,71:PS=71
230 FOR X=1 TO 9:P(X,1)=X:P(X,2)=0:P(X,3)
=0:NEXT X:REM PUT DISKS VALUES IN STORAGE

250 FOR X=22 TO 14 STEP -1:POSITION 1,X:P
=(X-14)*5+1:? #6;A$(P,P+4):NEXT X:PL=1:R=
0:REM PUT DISKS ON POST
260 POSITION 2,3:? #6;"MOVES   ";M
280 IF STICK(0)=7 THEN GOSUB 400:POKE 77,
0:REM MOVE TO RIGHT
290 IF STICK(0)=11 THEN GOSUB 450:POKE 77
,0:REM MOVE TO LEFT
300 IF STRIG(0)=0 THEN GOSUB 500:POKE 77,
0:REM DROP OR PICK UP DISK
310 FOR X=1 TO 50:NEXT X:SOUND 0,0,0,0:GO
TO 260:REM TIMING LOOP/START AGAIN
400 IF PS<183 THEN PS=PS+56:POKE 53251,PS
:POSITION PL,R:? #6;BL$:PL=PL+7
410 POSITION PL,R:? #6;P$
420 RETURN
450 IF PS>71 THEN PS=PS-56:POKE 53251,PS:
POSITION PL,R:? #6;BL$:PL=PL-7:GOTO 410
460 RETURN
500 C=0:IF PS=71 THEN C=1:PL=1:REM FIND O
UT WHICH POST IT'S OVER
510 IF PS=127 THEN C=2:PL=8
520 IF PS=183 THEN C=3:PL=15
530 IF C=0 THEN RETURN
540 IF R=6 THEN 600:REM HOLDING A DISK
550 FOR X=1 TO 9:IF P(X,C)=0 THEN NEXT X:
RETURN :REM FIND THE DISK
560 S=P(X,C):P=(S-1)*5+1:P$=A$(P,P+4):R=X
+13:P(X,C)=0
570 FOR X=R TO 7 STEP -1:POSITION PL,X:?
#6;BL$:POSITION PL,X-1:? #6;P$:NEXT X:R=X
:SOUND 0,10,10,10
580 RETURN
600 FOR X=1 TO 9:IF P(X,C)<S AND P(X,C)<>
0 THEN RETURN :REM DON'T DROP ON SMALLER
DISK
610 IF P(X,C)<>0 THEN P=X-1:GOTO 630
```

Listing 20-2. Towers Puzzle. (Continued from page 237.)

```
620 NEXT X:P=X-1
630 FOR X=R TO R+6+P:POSITION PL,X:? #6;B
L$:POSITION PL,X+1:? #6;P$:NEXT X:R=0:P$=
BL$:SOUND 0,250,14,8:M=M+1
640 P(P,C)=S:RETURN
```

you want to place the disk on and press the red button again. If that pole does not contain a smaller disk than the one you are transferring, the disk will drop onto the pole. Try to transfer all nine disks from pole one to pole three.

Line 40 sets aside the memory needed for the strings and array.

Line 50 changes the mode to mode 1 without a text window. The graphics mode should be set before the display list is changed or the character set replaced. Every change in the graphics mode resets the display list and the character set. The variable A contains the high-order address of the amount of memory available less 8 (2K or 2048 bytes). This is the area of memory used for the new character set and the player/missile graphics.

Line 60 opens the file saved on disk as CHARS. The variable B contains the first byte that will be POKEd with the new character set. This is the character set created with the last program.

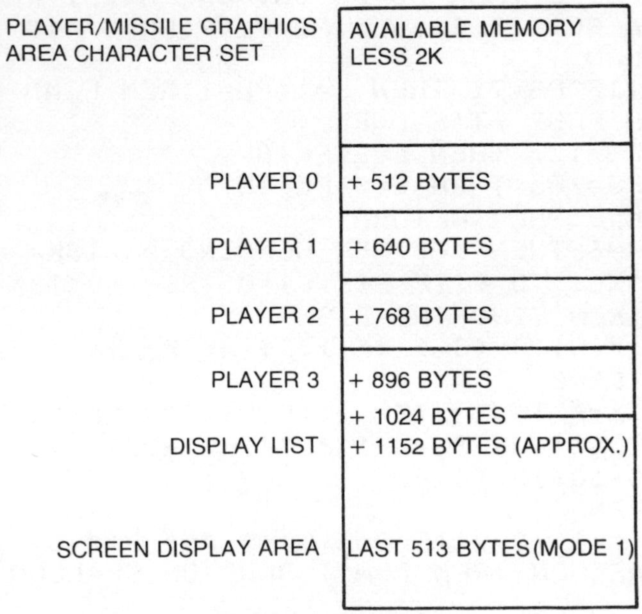

PLAYER/MISSILE GRAPHICS AREA CHARACTER SET	AVAILABLE MEMORY LESS 2K
PLAYER 0	+ 512 BYTES
PLAYER 1	+ 640 BYTES
PLAYER 2	+ 768 BYTES
PLAYER 3	+ 896 BYTES
	+ 1024 BYTES ———
DISPLAY LIST	+ 1152 BYTES (APPROX.)
SCREEN DISPLAY AREA	LAST 513 BYTES (MODE 1)

Fig. 20-2. Memory map for player/missile graphics and character set.

Lines 70-90 read the bytes from the disk and POKE them into the area of memory set aside for the character set. Location 756 is POKEd with the high-order address of the character set. The computer will now use these characters when printing on the screen.

Line 100 contains the elements of A$. This string is the nine disks used in the program. Each disk is given a field of five bytes. The smallest disk uses only one byte. The next four disks use three bytes in their fields and the last four disks use all five bytes.

Be sure the string format is exact:
space space reverse ! space space
space % ! & space
space reverse control D reverse control A   reversecontrol G
space
space reverse # reverse ! reverse (space
space ! ! ! space
reverse control E   reverse control A   reverse control A
reverse control A   reverse control F
reverse $ reverse ! reverse ! reverse ! reverse !
! ! ! (
reverse control A   reverse control A   reverse control A
reverse control A   reverse control A

This will generate disks in three different colors.

Line 110 calculates the beginning of the display list. We need this information to change one of the lines from mode 1 to mode 2.

Line 120 POKEs the seventh byte of the display list with a 7 (DL is the first byte of the display list). This changes the second line of the screen to graphics mode 2.

Line 130 changes the colors in two of the color registers and prints the title of the program on the screen. Be sure to include the parentheses on both sides of the wordtower. This symbol has been changed to a character in the new character set.

Line 140 POKEs location 559 with 46. This sets the player/missile graphics for two-line resolution.

Line 150 clears any characters that may be in the player/missile graphics area.

Line 160 POKEs location 53277 with 3. This enables the player/missile graphics. POKEing location 623 with 4 sets the priority of the players. Any character that is printed in the same area as a player will cover the player. If this priority location was not set, the player would appear to be over the characters printed on the screen. Leave the POKE out and run the program to see the difference in priorities.

Line 170 POKEs location 54279 with the high-order address of the memory set aside for player/missile graphics. This is the same address used for the character set.

Line 180 draws the posts in the player area of memory. The posts will start 60 bytes from the beginning of each player's area and be drawn in the following 53 bytes. Since each player is given 128 bytes of memory, we can use a For . . . Next loop and step it by 128. 30 is POKEd into the player/missile area. The posts will only be 4 bits wide.

Line 190 POKEs a 12 in each byte just above the posts. This will give the posts a tapered look at the top.

Lines 192-195 draw the magnet into the fourth player's area. The data for the magnet is in line 195.

Line 200 draws the base for the posts. Since we want the base to be orange, we will use   **control A**   as the character to be printed.

Line 210 POKEs a color into the four color registers for the players.

Line 220 positions the three posts and the magnet on the screen. The PS variable will indicate the position of the magnet.

Line 230 uses the array to keep track of which post has which disks. Each disk is assigned a value. The smallest disk is a one, the largest a nine. All the disks start on one post. Each element of the array that represents this post is set to the proper value. The rest of the array is set to zeroes.

Line 250 prints the disks on the post. Each disk has a field of five, so the column used to print the disks does not change. The disks are printed from the bottom to the top. PL stores the print position for the disks. R stores the set to 0 because no disk is being held by the magnet.

Line 260 prints the number of moves the player has taken.

Line 280 checks the joystick to see if it is moved to the right. If so, it goes to the subroutine that moves the magnet to the right, then resets the attract mode so the screen will not start changing colors.

Line 290 checks the joystick to see if it has been moved to the left. If it has, the program directs the computer to the line that moves the magnet to the left.

Line 300 checks the fire button on the joystick. If it has been pressed the computer is directed to the subroutine that drops or picks up a disk.

Line 310 contains a timing loop to make it easier to move the magnet across the screen. Without the timing loop, it would be very difficult to get the magnet to stop over the center post. The sound is also turned off if it was on and the program goes back to line 260 to update the number of moves and check the joystick again.

Lines 400-420 move the magnet to the right. If PS is less than 183, the magnet can be moved. 56 is added to the value of PS since the posts are 56 positions apart. The new value of PS is POKEd into location 53251. The disk in the position below the magnet is erased and seven is added to its old position value. The disk is reprinted in the new position just below the magnet. The program returns to the main routine.

Lines 450-460 move the magnet to the left if it is not in the leftmost position on the screen. Again, the new position of the magnet is POKEd into location 52351. The disk is erased from the old position and reprinted in the new position under the magnet.

Lines 500-640 raise or lower the disk. C is used to store the number of the post the magnet is over. The position of the magnet is checked, and the position of the disk (PL) is set accordingly.

Line 540 checks the R variable. If it is a 6, we know the disk is under the magnet and it should be dropped. The computer is directed to line 600 to drop the disk.

Line 550 looks for a disk. The elements of the array in column C are checked for a value. If all the values are 0, there are no disks on that post and the program returns.

Line 560 saves the value of the first disk found on that pole in S. P is the first position of the disk stored in A$. The disk is stored in P$. Since X is the number of the row that has a disk, 13 is added to it. The tallest any column can be is nine disks high. The ninth or top-most disk is on the fourteenth row of the screen. The disk is removed from the array by storing a 0 in that element.

Line 570 lifts the disk off the pole by erasing the disk and printing it one row higher on the screen. Once the disk is under the magnet the value of X is stored in R and a sound is made. The routine returns.

Line 600 checks the elements of the array that represent the pole the disk is dropped on to make sure the disks are not dropped on a smaller disk. If the disks on the pole are smaller than the disk held by the magnet, the routine will return.

Line 610 checks to see if there is something in that element. If there is the disk will fall on top of it. The position the program is looking at less one is stored.

Line 630 drops the disk onto the pole. R is reset to 0 to indicate it is not holding a disk, the disk in P$ is erased, and a sound is made. The number of moves is increased by one.

Line 640 stores the disk value in the element representing its position in the array and the program returns.

As you can see, by combining player/missile graphics with the different modes and character sets, your ATARI can generate colorful games or simulations. You are limited only by your imagination.

Index

55 SIMPLE ATARI PROGRAMS

If you're intrigued with the possibilities of the programs included in this volume, you should definitely consider having the ready-to-run disks containing each of these software applications. This software is guaranteed free from manufacturing defects. (If you have any problems, return the disks within 30 days and we'll send you new ones.) Not only will you save the time and effort of typing the programs, these disks eliminate the possibility of errors that can prevent the programs from functioning properly. Interested?

Available on two 5¼" disks for the 16K ATARI 400 and the 16K ATARI 800 at $24.95, plus $1.00 shipping and handling.

_____ I'm interested. Send me the disks containing *55 Simple ATARI Programs*.

_____ Check/Money Order enclosed for $_____
_____ Visa   _____ Mastercharge
Acct. No. _____ Expires_____

Name _____

Address _____

City _____ State _____ Zip_____

Signature _____

Mail to: Windcrest Software Inc.
          P.O. Box 423
          Waynesboro, PA 17268